OF MINNIE THE MOOCHER & ME

OF MINNIE THE MOOCHER & ME

CAB CALLOWAY
and Bryant Rollins

with illustrations selected and edited
by John Shearer

THOMAS Y. CROWELL COMPANY *ESTABLISHED 1834* NEW YORK

Designed by Judith Woracek

Manufactured in the United States of America

Library of Congress Cataloging in Publication Data
Calloway, Cab, 1907–
  Of Minnie the Moocher and me.

  1. Calloway, Cab, 1907–   2. Jazz musicians—
Reminiscences, etc.   I. Rollins, Bryant, joint author.   II. Title.
ML410.C265A3   780'.92'4 [B]   75-45160
ISBN 0-690-01032-X

10 9 8 7 6 5 4 3 2 1

To my sister Blanche
who introduced me to the
wonderful world of entertainment
      and
To my wife and family
who have given me happiness
and love
and peace

INTRODUCTION

"Now here's a story 'bout Minnie the Moocher
She was a low-down hoochy coocher
She was the roughest, toughest frail
But Minnie had a heart as big as a whale."

That's how I'd start out; then somewhere in the middle of it, when the band was swinging and the feeling got right, I'd start to hi-de-ho. You know, singing:
"Hi-de-hi-de-hi-de-ho."
Then the band would answer:
"Hi-de-hi-de-hi-de-ho."
Then I'd sing back again:
"Wah-de-doo-de-way-de-ho."
And the band would swing, and sing:
"Wah-de-doo-de-way-de-ho."
When it really got to feeling good, I'd holler for the audience to join in.
"Wah-de-wah-de-wah-de-doo," I'd sing.
"Wah-de-wah-de-wah-de-doo," the band and the audience would holler back.

1

By now, the place is jumping. I'm dancing and leading the band. The horn section is hitting it. The drummer is driving us. The piano player is vamping. And the place is really rocking.

"Bee-de-doo-de-dee-de-dow," I holler.

"Bee-de-doo-de-dee-de-dow," everybody shouts back.

"Teedle-do-de-dee rah-de-dah-de-dah.
Teedle-do-de-dee rah-de-dah-de-dah."

Then I'd bring it back home, with everybody stomping and clapping and singing:

"Hi-de-hi-de-hi-de-ho.
Hi-de-hi-de-hi-de-ho.
Now here's a story 'bout Minnie the Moocher
She was a low-down hoochy coocher
She was the roughest, toughest frail
But Minnie had a heart as big as a whale."

I don't know how it got started, really, the scat singing. I think one night in the Cotton Club I just forgot the words to a song and started to scat to keep the song going. It was in 1931. And it went over so big that I kept right on doing it. It became a style that people began to identify me with. I did it because the people responded. And the people responded because it looked to them, I guess, like I was having such a good time just scatting it. It made them feel good. And it made me feel good 'cause that's all I've ever wanted, when you come right down to it—to have a house jumping like that, to see people really enjoying themselves, to entertain. Those are the things that have always made me happiest and given me the most satisfaction.

I've been all over the world, giving people pleasure and getting it back. It never mattered to me whether I was playing the Cotton Club in Harlem, the Palladium in London, the Sands in Las Vegas, or the little Sunset Cafe in South Side Chicago. To me, the satisfaction I get from making people feel good is always the same.

I'm sixty-nine years old now and in semi-retirement. I still go out on the road, occasionally singing at hotels and resorts and nightclubs. I don't do it much, but I have to do it sometimes. It's been my life, and I can't stop entertaining, just like that. I've slowed down, but I can't come to a full stop.

"I'm sixty-nine years old now and in semi-retirement."

This book is a kind of culmination of my career. A lot of funny, sad, and interesting things have happened to me in my life and I want to share them. I also want to set the record straight on a few things—both public and private. I don't intend to hurt anyone, but I do intend to tell the truth. I've made a fortune and I've had fame. I'd estimate that I've grossed over $9 million in my career. I live in a large house in White Plains, twenty miles north of New York City, with lots of land around. I have enough money to do pretty much what I want to do, and enough to take care of all the needs of my family. The hi-de-ho man had made it, but who is the hi-de-ho man? How many people really know me? Now that I have all this leisure time I sit, sometimes, and wonder about that. How many people really know me? Not many. People see me as Sportin' Life in *Porgy and Bess* or as Horace Vandergelder in *Hello, Dolly!* or as Heinzie in *Pajama Game*. Or if they're not afraid of showing their age they see me as Dr. Calloway from the "Quizzicale" radio shows in the forties, or as the fly bandleader and singer, dressed in a canary yellow zoot suit, talking that jive talk, dancing and laughing. I've played a lot of roles, and now in this book I'd like to play the real one— Cab Calloway.

What am I like off the stage? I'm a loner, and sometimes even shy. That's one of the reasons I think I can express certain personal things about myself better in a book than on the stage. And that's why this book is important to me. I want people who have seen me and been my fans to get to know me better, to find out who the hi-de-ho man really is.

Another reason I want to write this book is that, like any man, I've hurt some people in my life, and I want to set the record straight. Take my first manager, Moe Gale. Moe was the one who booked me into the new Plantation Club in 1930. Later I went over to the Cotton Club— about the biggest place to be in Harlem or all New York in those days— and the mob muscled Moe out. You read it right. I was managed by the mob for a number of years. In those days, that was about the only way a black entertainer could make it. More about all that later, but I just wanted to say that one reason for this book is to set the record straight on some parts of my life. You may have heard stories, but I'm going to tell you the truth. About the good parts, too. Like the fact that I was the first black to play in certain places. Or like some stories about the guys I worked with—the greats of the jazz and entertainment world. People like Ben Webster, Dizzy Gillespie, Chu Berry, Tyree Glenn, Quentin Jackson, Hilton Jefferson, J. C. Heard, Illinois Jacquet, Milt Hinton, Sam Taylor, Buster Hardy, Dave Rivera, Panama Francis, Pops Smith, Ike Quebec, Jonah Jones, Shad Collins, Doc Cheatham, and Benny Payne. The vocalists who sang with my band in the thirties included Lena Horne, June Richmond, Dottie Salters, and Mae Johnson, and I discovered Pearl Bailey in the forties. I don't mean to boast, but I'm extremely proud that the musicians and the vocalists who worked as part of my band were some of the finest people in the business.

My main purpose through it all has always been to entertain, and I guess that's what I want this book to do as well—to entertain you. Some artists make you think, others make you dream, and still others, like me, want to entertain—and to give you a picture of the world of entertainment in which I've lived and worked for nearly fifty years. But I want you to know that after you've seen the whole picture, after you've gotten to know lots of things about me, what still remains the most basic part of me is the entertainer. Scat singing, all that hi-de-hoing, those zoot suits and wide-brimmed hats, they were all a way of communicating joy to people. They were a way of telling people, "Listen, I know it's rough out there, but drop that heavy load for a while. Laugh and enjoy yourself. Life is too short for anything else."

And in the end, maybe you'll think about me—Cab Calloway, the hi-de-ho man—and think about my trials and tribulations and the fact that in the midst of all my problems, I've always been able to come out on the stage singing about one of my favorite ladies, old

> *"Minnie the Moocher. . . .*
> *Who was a low-down hoochy coocher*
> *She was the roughest, toughest frail*
> *But Minnie had a heart as big as a whale."*

HUSTLING

When I think about my life, when I look back over it, I sometimes wonder how the hell I made it. Then I say to myself, "Dammit, you made it because you are and always were one unrelenting, stubborn black son of a bitch." No doubt about it. I always was. When I was about fourteen or fifteen years old I was such a roustabout that my mother and my stepfather sent me off to an industrial school in Pennsylvania because in Baltimore, where we were living, I just wouldn't behave. I played hooky, hung out in the streets, hustled to make money, and was always in and out of trouble. So they sent me off to the Downingtown Industrial and Agricultural School in Downingtown, Pennsylvania. It was a church-run boarding school managed by my granduncle, a pastor in a Philadelphia church. I think it was a Baptist church, and they ran this school for black kids. They called it an industrial school, but it was really a reform school.

Mama was a teacher in the public schools in Baltimore and it was very embarrassing for her to have such a hell-raising son. I spent more days hanging out with the guys around Pimlico racetrack outside Baltimore than I did in school. I guess the two strongest memories I have of my youth are the great times we had cutting school to spend the day at the track and the lonely feeling I had when my mother and stepfather put me on a train and shipped me off all alone to Pennsylvania. It was the first time I had ever been away from home and I felt awful, like the world had come to an end.

I was born on Christmas Day, 1907. People have always tried to make something out of the fact that I was born on Christmas. Every year my wife, Nuffie, and the kids and friends have a big combination birthday party and Christmas party. And there are certain friends, like my buddy Moe Robinson in Boston and Benny Payne, the pianist who worked with the Cab Calloway bands for thirteen years, and Dizzy Gillespie—they call me every damn Christmas, never miss a year as long as they know where I am. Moe talks, Benny plays the piano, and Dizzy plays the trumpet—right there over the phone. That kind of thing does make it special that I was born on Christmas, but otherwise, it's never meant very much to me. Except that as a kid I only got presents once a year and other kids got them twice.

I was born in our house at 18 Cypress Street in Rochester, New York. I remember very little about the house or the neighborhood, or even about our family during those days. About three years ago, while I was playing a gig in upstate New York, I went back to Rochester and stopped at 18 Cypress Street. I wanted to see what the house looked like. It turned out to be a pleasant two-story wood frame house in a nice neighborhood. I understand that since I was there, the house has been torn down by urban renewal.

My family lived in Rochester for about ten years. My mother and father had moved there in 1906, and left around 1918.

As I said, I don't remember much about my early years, but when I decided to write this book and started thinking about my life, I went back to look at some old issues of the *New York Times.* This is what the world was like on Christmas Day, 1907: B. Altman's was selling women's suits and dresses for $12.50 and tailored broadcloth suits for $25, and Franklin Simon had long "chinchilla" coats for $8.50. Some man had just invented a new kind of false teeth. Jack Johnson was the underdog in his fight with the Canadian Tommy Burns in Australia, and Columbia University's basketball team had beaten City College 13 to 12. Nowadays you would find a lot of vacation advertisements by the airlines; on Christmas Day, 1907, there were travel ads too. The Chicago, Milwaukee & St. Paul Railway was advertising the Overland Limited from Chicago to California. A double berth went for $7. But

"I was born on Christmas Day, 1907. People have always tried to make something out of the fact that I was born on Christmas."

the big news in New York City on the day I was born was that the mayor had revoked the license of every moving picture theater in the city, all 550 of them, because people were protesting that they were open on Sundays. It was a different—and more puritanical—world.

On Christmas Day a year later, in 1908, there was another article in the *Times* that was of special interest to me. It had to do with Prohibition. A federal district court judge in Atlanta dismissed a case brought by some people who wanted to overthrow Georgia's Prohibition laws. This of course was before Congress had even thought of the Eighteenth Amendment, but there were still enough organizations like the Women's Christian Temperance Union and the Anti-Saloon League and enough nice ladies who didn't like the idea of their husbands staying out drinking or coming home plastered to ensure Prohibition in several states. In fact, by 1919, thirty-one states had Prohibition laws. And then in 1919 the Eighteenth Amendment to the Constitution was passed along with the Volstead Act to enforce that law. Prohibition remained the law, if not the rule, in America for thirteen years. As I look back, the item about Prohibition in Georgia is interesting to me because, indirectly, Prohibition was responsible for my first big break as a star. Nobody paid much attention to the Volstead Act. Booze was sold all over the place—in speakeasies, under the table, behind the counter—everywhere. The federal agents who were sent around to enforce the act were, in my experience, mostly out for bribes. Once they got their money they would turn their backs. What Prohibition did do was place liquor under the control of the underworld gangs. And as long as the underworld controlled liquor, they controlled a number of clubs in Harlem as well. The cops knew damned well what was going on, but they were on the tab, from the precinct captain to the flatfoot on the beat.

The underworld saw to it that there was booze all over the country in those days, but there was more of it in Harlem. Just like there was more and better music in Harlem in those days. The Jazz Age in Harlem. Hell, jazz grew up in Harlem after it left New Orleans and Chicago. When you hear about places like the Cotton Club, where I got my first real break in 1930, and where Duke Ellington had got his a few years earlier, or when you hear about places like Connie's Inn, where Fletcher Henderson's band was knocking them out, or the Savoy, where Joe Oliver and then Luis Russell were swinging, or Small's Paradise, where Sam Wooding was doing his thing, you know that Harlem was swinging. Those were the places where high-society white people came to hear jazz, and where, during most of those years, Negroes weren't allowed in the audience. They were okay on the stage or in the kitchen, but not in the audience. Well, those white people came uptown to hear the music but they also came to drink. They sold that *baaad* bourbon called chicken cock in tin cans for a dollar and a setup for fifty cents. All under the table, of course, but all out in the open, if you know what I mean. But I'm getting ahead of myself. In 1907, Prohibition was still a state, not a federal, matter.

I really don't remember Rochester very well. Our family has always been a little vague about the reasons my mother and father left for Baltimore. As I understand it, my father had some problems in his real estate business. No one was more explicit than that. Baltimore was a logical move for us because our family had been there for quite a while and they were pretty well known in the Negro community.

My mother had gone to Morgan State College and she was a teacher in the public schools. My father was a lawyer. He had gone to Lincoln University in Lincoln, Pennsylvania, then clerked in a Baltimore law firm. So our family had status in the Negro community. But that didn't mean we had money. Negro professionals were paid a hell of a lot less than white professionals with the same jobs.

My earliest memories are of the years after we moved back to Baltimore. I was about eleven years old then and we lived with my grandmother Calloway, my father's mother. My father's name was Cabell Calloway, like mine, and so was his father's. I'm not sure where either of those names comes from, but there was a Cabell family in Danville, Virginia, where my father's parents are from. It's possible that my grandfather got his name from them. As far as the Calloway part is concerned, during the early days of slavery we were probably originally from Calloway, Georgia. It was the practice then for slaves to be given the last names of the plantation owners. It's possible that the town of Calloway was named after a plantation owner too. It's been impossible for me to trace this any closer; records of the comings and goings of Negroes are very spotty for the years after Emancipation. It seems the whites only kept accurate records on us as long as we were their property.

My father's parents, Cabell Calloway and Elizabeth Johnson Calloway, moved from Danville, Virginia, to Baltimore at some point in mid-1800s. They may have been slaves. I really don't know. They could have left Virginia after Emancipation, but on the other hand, there were a lot of free Negroes in Virginia even before the Proclamation. My grandfather Calloway owned a pool hall in Baltimore and was a some-time croupier at the New York Athletic Club as well. When I was a kid, he'd be gone for long stretches of time off to New York City. My mother later told me he was a hustler, a kind of Sportin' Life, if you know what I mean. Maybe some of it rubbed off on me, but what I seem to remember best about him was his long absences. Even when he was at home in Baltimore, I didn't get to see much of him. The pool hall was off limits. We were a religious family, and my mother and grandmother didn't think a pool hall was the best place to bring up a boy. Instead I went to Grace Presbyterian Church. I'd be in church every damned Sunday, rain or shine, from early in the morning till late afternoon. My mother and father and all the sisters and brothers would get dressed up and walk nicely to church together. My mother was the church organist and so we all had to be there. And then, of course, after the regular service there'd be Bible school. I'm an Episcopalian now—I converted in the 1930s—and I'm still a firm believer in church and in God. I don't think of myself as a religious person. I love to live. I like the good life. I enjoy entertaining and I get as much satisfaction out of giving people pleasure as I do out of going to church. Maybe entertaining is my way of expressing godliness. Lord knows, there are worse ways.

Even though we were strong churchgoing people, the family was always very open about my grandfather's owning the pool hall and about his life in New York. In fact, we were all proud of it. No one else in our neighborhood had a grandfather who went off to New York City for months at a time and owned a pool hall as well.

I know even less about my maternal grandparents. Mama's parents were Andrew and Anna Credit Reed. As far as I can learn, my mother's family was always from Baltimore.

When we came to Baltimore from Rochester, there were four children in the family. My sister Blanche was six years older than me, around seventeen or eighteen at the time. Blanche preceded me into show business and had her own very good band act for a long time. It was Blanche who actually helped me to get into show business when I was around eighteen. Then came Bernice, who is now a retired chiropodist and still lives in Baltimore. She was two years older than me. And my brother Elmer, nine years younger than me, was only one or two years old when we moved. Elmer is a high school teacher in Atlanta now.

Mama later had two other children by my stepfather, John Nelson Fortune, who we all called—and still call—Papa Jack. John was twelve years younger than I was, and Camilla fourteen years younger. John is in the maintenance business in Philadelphia now and Camilla is in the real estate business there.

When we arrived in Baltimore, we moved in with my father's mother. We called her Grandma Calloway. She was a very rigid woman—too rigid for my taste. Man, we couldn't do anything in that house, especially not the things that kids just naturally want to do. Her strictness was the cause of a lot of my problems later on. After I was out of her house, I sort of went wild.

The house in Baltimore was lovely but that's all that was lovely about life with Grandma Calloway—the way the house looked. It was a nice old three-story wood frame building at 1017 Druid Hill Avenue in a section of Baltimore that was entirely Negro. I have a lot of bad memories about those years on Druid Hill Avenue. We weren't allowed to play in the streets after school or on weekends. All our friends on the block would be outside playing, but we would have to stay inside. We'd spend the afternoons with our noses pressed up against the windowpane looking at the other kids having a ball. And we weren't allowed to run around in the house either.

We were inside just about all the damned time except when we went to church or school or the store with an adult. At dinner we had to fold our hands on the table until grace was said. And we never dared talk back or sass anybody or we'd get our damned necks broken.

About two years after we moved to Baltimore, my father died. To this day I don't know what he died of. Everybody was very mysterious at the time, and for years afterwards my mother wouldn't talk about it. I'm the spitting image of my father. When I look at pictures of him today, I think I'm looking at myself. And I hope it doesn't sound immodest if I say that he was a damned handsome man. That year he died, in any case, we didn't see much of him. He was having a lot of problems, and he finally had a nervous breakdown. He was institutionalized and I never saw him again. Mama simply came to us one day and said,

"Your father has passed." I don't remember mourning. I don't remember feeling sadness or remorse. I don't remember feeling anything.
He and I had never had much of a father-son relationship. He was busy
and troubled all the time about one thing or the other. Soon after he
died, his own father died. It was pretty bad around the house those
days. Mama and Grandma Calloway argued a lot and finally there was a
blowup and mama packed us up and left. We went to live with her
mother, my grandmother Reed.

The first few years in Baltimore had been a rough time for my
mother, but I don't remember her ever showing sadness or anger or
frustration in front of us kids. We knew she was having a bad time with
her mother-in-law, especially after my father died. Perhaps Grandma
Calloway blamed my mother for my father's death. I wouldn't be surprised. Anyhow, when we moved to my grandmother Reed's house, everything changed. The atmosphere there was loose and open and free.
All of a sudden mama, who I believe had been hemmed in as much as
we kids in my grandmother Calloway's house, came alive. We would
spend the evenings sitting and talking and reading and eating. There was
laughter and the house was filled with noises and good smells. Mama
usually got home in time to cook our dinner, but when she had a church
meeting or a meeting at school, one of my sisters or I used to cook dinner. We took good care of each other.

One of the nice things about my grandmother Reed's house was that
there were other young people there. My mother's two brothers, Uncle
Andrew and Uncle Milton, were still living at home, and it was lots of
fun for us kids. They would joke and play with us, and often they took
us places. Grandma Reed's house was not far from Grandma Calloway's, but it was a world apart in spirit. It even looked like Grandma
Calloway's house—a three-story wood frame middle-class home—but if
you had lived in both houses, you knew they were very different.

As dissimilar as life with those two women was, it was always a
clean, secure, middle-class environment. Not all blacks in Baltimore
had that kind of life in 1920. When I was twelve years old, Negroes
made up about 15 per cent of the total population of the city. Slavery
had been an accepted part of the Maryland colony when it was founded
in 1632, so there had always been Negroes in Baltimore. By 1920, most
of the Negroes in the city who had good jobs were teaching in colored
schools, preaching, or working as domestics. In the 1920s and 1930s,

the servant industry in Baltimore earned around $19 million annually—
and the servant industry was entirely Negro.

When I say that not all of the Negroes in Baltimore lived in the kind
of middle-class world that we did, I mean it. In the 1920s, there was an
area in northwest Baltimore known as Lung Block. It was bounded by
Pennsylvania Avenue, Druid Hill Avenue, below where I lived, and
Biddle and Preston streets. The area was called Lung Block because so
many Negroes down there had tuberculosis. The death rate for TB in the
area was 958 per 100,000 people compared with a rate of 131.9 for the
city as a whole. Around 1924, the Baltimore Urban League was formed
and it raised so much hell about Lung Block that the city finally had to
do something about it. I was seventeen years old, and Lung Block
seemed worlds away.

At Grandmother Reed's I began to break out of the restrictions of
Grandma Calloway's house. To begin with I stopped going to church,
although my mother was always on me about it. But now there were
more important things to do on Sunday morning, like selling newspapers. I guess I went from one extreme to the other. One year I was
spending three or four hours in church every Sunday plus Bible classes
during the week, Bible school every day during the summer, and singing in the junior choir, and the next I was a part of a gang of guys who
were basically young hustlers. We had two interests—making money
and having a good time. I got back into church and the choir for a while
when I was in high school, but that was because I had eyes for the
daughter of the minister at the Bethel African Methodist Episcopal
Church.

Those years between eleven and fifteen when I was wild and independent and wouldn't listen to anyone were fine for me and frustrating for
the people who loved and worried about me. During those years I began
to appreciate the value of making money, because money meant in-
dependence. No matter how upset my mother got when I hooked school
and hustled in the streets all day and half the night, she always welcomed the $20 or $25 I brought home at the end of every week. We
needed the money I made. We may not have had much money, but we
always had food on the table, though it was poor folks' food—lima
beans and navy beans. We never had much beef, and when we did, it
was what you call chipped beef. Occasionally there'd be pork chops,
and potatoes and ground beef cooked up loose in a frying pan with

tomatoes and liver and sausage and eggs. And sometimes we'd splurge on bologna sandwiches from the delicatessen on the corner for ten cents and a bag of potato chips and a soda for a nickel. That was the best fifteen-cent meal around.

Those years when I said to hell with school and began to concentrate on making money weren't easy—for any of us. People would tell mama they saw me here and there when I was supposed to be in school, and then she would sit down with me and try to convince me how important school was. Mama wanted me to be a lawyer. School was necessary, she would say, and I'd listen and promise to do better. For a few days I *would* do better. Then the next thing you know, I'd be back on the streets again, making that money.

That paper-selling was something. Boy, did I hustle. People working downtown would have to come through our area in north Baltimore on the streetcars to get to and from their jobs. In the mornings I'd sell the Baltimore *Sun* for three cents. I got a penny a paper. I'd start out at around eight o'clock each morning and hustle those streetcars. I'd ride all the way up Madison Avenue to the car barn on one car, then I'd hop a car coming downtown and sell papers all the way back. I'd also leave a stack by the Grace Presbyterian Church at the corner of Madison and North avenues, and people coming past in the morning would take a paper and leave three cents. I guess if I did that today, somebody would come past and steal both the papers and the change. Anyhow, that was how it was in those days in Baltimore. I'd ride up and down selling the *Sun* on the streetcars until around ten o'clock every morning. Then, when I felt like it, I would go to school. Of course I was late by then, and I'd get scolded by the teacher, but I didn't much care. I was going just to please my mother. I really didn't dig school until later, in high school.

On the days that I did go to school, it was only for a couple of hours. I'd leave and dash downtown around noontime to get the afternoon papers, the Baltimore *News* and the *Star*. I'd hustle the afternoon papers on the streetcars just like the morning papers. And during the racing season, I'd sell the racing form to people going out to Pimlico. Sometimes I'd go back to school after I sold the afternoon papers, but whenever Pimlico was open I'd head straight for the track. I'd sell papers and then catch the last streetcar that would get me to Pimlico in time for the first race. The races were my real love, and still are to this day. Next to entertainment, thoroughbred racing is where my heart is.

It was a fifteen-minute ride on the trolley car from my house out to Pimlico, and I'd stay out there in the barns and stables for the rest of the day. When the horses would finish a race, I'd bring them out and cool them down by walking them around and help wash them. It was called walking the hots, to cool off a horse that's just finished a race. I loved the horses and the jockeys and the trainers and the rest of the stable-boys. I guess it seemed romantic. Those guys traveled all over the country and saw a lot of excitement. And the horses were just beautiful. They were huge animals, but so gentle and graceful. And the jockeys were always laughing and joking and playing cards or shooting craps between races. They were all loud, vulgar, regular guys. It was a great world. I loved to hear the crowd cheering during a race. I loved every-thing about the track. That's where my love for horses and racing began, there at Pimlico.

After the races were over, and I'd finished with my last horse at around 6:30 or so, I'd hustle shoes. There was a stand near the track where I'd shine shoes until around eight or nine o'clock. That was my daily schedule from the time I was eleven until I was fifteen, when they sent me off to reform school. I don't know where I got the energy, but once I started making it like that, I never stopped. I'd wind up with three or three and a half dollars a day, and I'd go home and give it all to my mother.

I wasn't alone while I was doing all this hustling. There was a gang of guys on our street that hung out together. It was a nice block, but there were a few rough cats. A lot of the guys were around my age and we hung out together all the time, as boys that age do. We sold papers together, went to Pimlico together, and got into trouble together.

We were hustlers, but we were kids too and we had our games. We used to play baby in the hat, where guys would put their hats on the ground and one guy would throw a ball into the hat. If he made it, he'd have the right to punch whoever owned the hat. We played baseball too, up in Druid Hill Park, and basketball some, but basketball wasn't very popular then. I didn't get into basketball until I was in high school, and then I got damned good at it.

During those years I was hanging out, I remember one Sunday morn-ing when I was supposed to be in church and we were waiting for the Sunday papers to come. We had a crap game going on the steps, those big marble steps right up on the corner at the trolley-car stop. It was the best place to sell papers on Sunday. It was also only half a block from my house. I was holding the dice, and I was just shaking them and getting ready to roll when a hand grabbed me. At first, I thought it was some guy joking, but when I looked around I saw it was mama on her way home from church. "Boy, what are you doing here, shooting dice on the Lord's Day! I thought you went to Sunday school this morning. Get yourself up and get on home." Lord, was she mad! I didn't sell any papers that day.

I was around fourteen when that happened, and it may have been the thing that convinced her and Papa Jack that they had to get me off the streets. There probably was nothing worse to my mama than shooting craps on the corner on a Sunday morning.

MAMA, AND PAPA JACK

My mother's name was Martha Eulalia Reed and she was a truly wonderful woman, though I guess most men think that about their mothers. She was very gentle and loving, and though she wasn't strict she had her rules. She would scold us for not going to school or coming home late for dinner, but most of the time Papa Jack was the one who did the scolding.

Mama was something to look at, too. I've always thought she was as nice-looking outside as she was good inside.

I was quite a disappointment to Mama, until I started making it in the entertainment business. She wanted an A student on his way to being a lawyer and all she had until I broke into show business was a hustler on his way to nowhere. At least in her terms.

She was a steady, hardworking woman. She may have missed some school days, but I don't remember many. She had started teaching in the public schools in Baltimore as soon as she graduated from college and she went on teaching for most of her life.

Her work wasn't the only thing she was conscientious about. She may not have seen much of us during the week when she was working, but she spent all her time with us on weekends. Or at least all the time she wasn't busy playing the organ for the church choir. She did that every Sunday, regular and steady.

"My mother's name was Martha Eulalia Reed and she was a truly wonderful woman, though I guess most men think that about their mothers. She was very gentle and loving, and though she wasn't strict she had her rules."

Mama was very conscious of what other people thought. I've never given a damn about that. Of course, I care about the people I love and I've always felt close to the bands I've put together, but I never cared what other people said about me. As far as social restraints are concerned, I've lived my life as I damned well pleased. Not my mother, though. She cared a lot what other people thought.

I guess I wasn't the only one in the family who disappointed her. Blanche left home when she was around fifteen. She went straight to New York, and then to Philadelphia. Blanche was determined to get into show business. Mama was trying to hold things together, to influence us to go in one direction, and we, at least Blanche and I, wanted to go in another. Mama didn't like the idea of our going into show business. She was heartbroken when I dropped out of college in Chicago. By that time, so was Blanche. Blanche had seen enough of show business to know how rough it was.

To get back to our life in Baltimore: Not long after we moved into Grandma Reed's house, mother began to bring home a new man. His name was John Nelson Fortune. He was a tall, handsome, light-skinned man with large teeth and wavy hair. At the time he was working in a department store and moonlighting as a chauffeur. I don't suppose Blanche, Bernice, Elmer, and I gave poor Jack much of a welcome. We had hardly gotten over moving and we didn't like the idea of Mama remarrying. We gave both of them a rough time, but it changed everything for us kids too. Whenever Jack tried to tell us to do something, we'd tell him where to go. You have to understand that we were street kids—just naturally loose-mouthed and aggressive. We always respected our mother, but Papa Jack was an outsider. So he would tell us to go to the store or to take the garbage downstairs and we'd tell him, "Shoot, man, you're not our father. You can't tell us what to do." At first, he would just back off and call my mother. And she would shout at us and plead with us to treat him right. But later on, when they'd been married awhile, Papa Jack became the one to give the spankings.

Mama and Papa Jack tried their best to control me, but I had broken out and was feeling my oats. In some ways, though, Papa Jack and I were like buddies. He had a job in a department store and still worked as a chauffeur for some white family in Baltimore. He'd bring home that big car at lunchtime sometimes. Papa Jack would drive it up the street, proud as he could be in his chauffeur's uniform and cap. He had big white teeth in front and a huge smile, especially when he drove up in that car. We kids would be all around it. It was a beautiful light grey Winton Six, and the tires had sidewalls the same color as the car. He wouldn't let us get into it, of course, or even touch it—we might spoil the shine—but it was beautiful just to look at.

In those days most of what I was learning came from the streets. Papa Jack told me recently that he always felt that I had passed the point where he could teach me much about life, even though I was only twelve or thirteen at the time. He thought that I knew just about all a kid my age needed to know—and maybe more.

Around this time Papa Jack opened a little grocery store down on Pennsylvania Avenue. It was one of those places you had to walk downstairs to get into. Papa Jack sold "pigs' feet and cheap talk," as he used to say. I liked to hang out in there talking with him and the customers and helping him run the place. A lot of the money in that little place came from the bootleg gin Papa Jack made and sold. Anybody who had a bootleg setup was doing all right. I never will forget, one day Papa Jack told me to take this bottle of gin over to some guy down the street. I went down there with the gin, and the guy says to sit down while he checks the gin to see if it's all right. So I sat down, and the guy starts to sip the gin. Then he starts to put his hand on my leg and rub it. I said to myself, "Oh, oh, let me get the hell out of here." I ran like hell. And that was from the third floor of an old warehouse. I never told Papa Jack about that until a couple of months ago. He laughed like hell. "Dammit, Cab," he said, "I wish you'd told me that story when it happened. I know just who that guy was. A short stocky dark guy, and a rough rascal, too. I sold to a lot of the guys in that warehouse, but a few years later, when I was working for the insurance company, I went into that very same warehouse to settle a claim and the claim turned out to be by this same guy you had a run-in with. After I'd finished and was about to go, the guy said to me: 'I'm sorry, all I have to offer you is a little wine, but sit down and have some with me.' Well, I told him that I don't drink and started to leave and that guy grabbed my arm and I was damned surprised. He was pretty strong, but I got into a position where I could protect myself, and I gave him quite a whirl, and he hit the door so hard that his jaw broke the damned doorknob. I told the guy, 'Listen, I'm going on out of here and I ain't coming back because I don't want to have to kill nobody.' I was ignorant about that kind of stuff but I knew enough to get on out of there.''

"Not long after we moved into Grandma Reed's house, my mother began to bring home a new man. His name was John Nelson Fortune."

Papa Jack was some guy. He and I didn't get along that well when I was young—we had all sorts of disagreements—but there was one thing he always insisted on: He wouldn't put up with any of that stepfather business. He would say that we were either his children or not, but none of the "step" business. And I know now that he really loved us and cared for us, even though we gave him plenty of trouble. And he did provide for the family. He was always working two or three jobs to keep things together. After he and Mama had two children of their own that was no easy job. Papa Jack still talks about the shoe shop down the street. He'd be in there every week with another pair of shoes; that's how fast we'd run through them. Every week was a different child. This week was Blanche's week for shoes to be fixed; the next week was Bernice's; the next week it was my turn, and on and on. And when he'd run through all of us, over five weeks, then the first one's shoes would be run down again and he'd have to start all over.

In April of 1919, Papa Jack got a new job. Until then he had been chauffeuring, waiting on tables in several restaurants around town, running the little store—and the booze—anything he could find to keep us in clothes and food with a roof over our heads. Then in 1919 a white man told him about an opportunity down at the Commercial Casualty Insurance Company. "Listen," he told Papa Jack, "this is a real opportunity for you. The company has never had a colored man working for it, not as a porter or anything else, but you have a chance to work there now." Commercial Casualty was one of the biggest insurance companies on the East Coast at the time. So Papa Jack of course said yes. And he got hired. Only he couldn't work in the office downtown; that was all white. He had to work out of our house. Papa Jack says he thought about that for a while—the discrimination, I mean—but he didn't think too long. He'd been struggling all his life and he recognized a real opportunity when it came along. So Papa Jack became the first black insurance salesman to work for a major white company. He worked for Commercial Casualty for fifteen years. He was very proud of the whole thing and he took his responsibilities seriously. Papa Jack said when he first got the job his boss had sat him down and said, "Jack, the population of this town is now 125,000 people. And instead of one man giving you orders, you're going to have 125,000 people telling you 'Come and see me tonight. I've got a problem.' And if it's raining, you go, and if it's snowing, you go, and if it's hot or cold, you got to go when they tell you to. They'll be giving you orders. They want to be served, and you have to go when they want to be served. It's up to you.''

But proud of his job as he was, Papa Jack felt peculiar about not being able to work out of the downtown office. He used to say, "Just shows you how prejudiced Baltimore is. It's worse than Florida.'' And then, after a year with the company, Papa Jack had done so well they brought him into the office downtown and gave him a desk next to a guy named Proctor who was his competitor in the district where we lived. Proctor was a white man, naturally, and Papa Jack would come home at night talking about Proctor did this and Proctor did that. Papa Jack did not like Proctor, and Proctor did not like Papa Jack. And best of all, Papa Jack was outselling Proctor in the district. Proctor had to take a lot of heat because of it. The other guys would kid the hell out of him, asking how the hell this rookie Fortune had outsold him in his own district. Proctor was getting more and more angry. The way Papa Jack told it, one day Proctor leaned back in his chair and said, "I don't see why we need a nigger here anyway.'' Proctor weighed 220 pounds and was about 6'4", but Papa Jack grabbed him off his chair and said "Take that back, you son of a bitch" and slammed Proctor back into the chair. The chair broke up into splinters and Proctor was sprawled all over the damned floor. The next morning, the supervisor came over to Papa Jack and to Proctor and said: "This office ain't big enough for the both of you, and Fortune's staying.'' Papa Jack loved to tell that story.

Papa Jack built up the insurance business in the black community. He was probably the first insurance broker to really educate black schoolteachers, doctors, dentists, and other professionals in Baltimore about life insurance. He says that within a couple of years he had over 80 per cent of the Negro teachers in Baltimore.

Papa Jack was an easygoing kind of guy most of the time. I didn't really appreciate him then the way I do now, but I was a rebellious kid and there was nothing that anybody could tell me. My mother used to raise hell when I skipped school, but Papa Jack took a different approach. He would say to me, "Cab, you know what your mother wants. She wants you to prepare yourself so you can study law. But you've got to decide for yourself what you want to do. If you decide you want to go in another direction, then you try it your way, and if you don't find things going the way they ought to, you know the door will always be open if you want to come back and try it her way.''

I guess Papa Jack was a kind of philosopher. He would tell me stories about parents who forced their children to go into this or that field. Then, if the children failed or were unhappy, Papa Jack said, they would always blame their parents.

After Papa Jack and Mama broke up in 1926, all the negative things I'd felt about him when he originally intruded into our family resurfaced, and for a long time he and I didn't communicate at all. I felt he had let my mama down. Papa Jack is now eighty-seven years old, and he and I are good friends. Maybe we both still miss Mama a little. She died in 1943.

When I was around thirteen or fourteen years old, I was left on my own a lot of the time. We had left Grandma Reed's and were living in the house Mama and Papa Jack had rented. Mama was working most of the time or playing organ for the church choir and teaching Bible school. Papa Jack was working, too, either in the department store, chauffeuring, in his little store, or later on, for the insurance company. That left us kids alone a lot. We didn't hang out together much because of the difference in our ages. Blanche had already left home to go into show business. Bernice was only two years older than me, but at that age the girls go in one direction and the boys in another. And my direction was hustling in the streets. One day Mama and Papa Jack sat down with me and told me how they were concerned about what was happening to me. They said they had arranged for me to go to a school in Downingtown where I could get out of the city for a while to get trained in some skills and have a chance to develop in a better way. The streets, they said, were having a bad influence on me. And the next thing I knew, I was on a train from Baltimore to Pennsylvania. That was one long, lonesome ride. I was leaving Mama for the first time, and heading for some unknown place. It was pretty gruesome. On the train I began to think about the guys on the streets and all the good times we'd had together. Before I was halfway there I was homesick as hell. I did have something going for me because the school was run by my grandma Reed's brother, Rev. William Credit of Philadelphia, and a couple of my cousins from Philadelphia were enrolled. But before the train had even reached Downingtown I decided that I just had to get back home.

Actually, once there, I adjusted pretty well. My cousins met me and they made me feel pretty comfortable. The school was really a big farm of about 200 acres with the school buildings and the dormitories right in the middle. We were supposed to cultivate the farm, learn a trade, and take regular academic courses like reading and math and history. There were about 200 students there, or what they called students. Actually we were a mixture of students and truants. Like I said, it was more a reform school than an agricultural and industrial school.

We did classwork one or two days a week and the rest of the time we were outside working on the farm or in the shops doing manual training. Manual training was mostly woodworking, which I enjoyed. In fact, once I got into it, the school wasn't as bad as I had expected.

One thing I never will forget about Downingtown was the scarcities. Even water was a problem. We had to go to the top of a hill, a good long walk, to get it. The boys' dormitory was a new building, but it didn't have any water in it. After a while we dug a trench to lay a pipe from a tank they were going to put on the top of the hill. It took us nearly three weeks to dig that trench. I never worked so hard in my life.

The big scarcity, of course, was food. Man, sometimes we didn't have any food at all, but nobody could complain. They were very strict about that. So the boys would get together and parch corn. We'd take the yellow corn, put it in a little pan, let it cook till it popped, and then eat it. It didn't taste like popped corn. It tasted like dried, fried kernels. We also used to go out in the fields and steal kale and take that up into the dorm and cook it. The people who ran the school always got angry when we stole food like that, but we were pretty rough—especially when we were hungry. There was very little meat to eat, and it was mostly scrapple. Like at home, the main food up there was beans— beans and corn bread. And I mean real corn bread, too, man, nothing but cornmeal and water. It was something. Sometimes we would go to bed very, very hungry, dreaming about food. Some of the mothers used to send boxes of stuff. When somebody got a box from home, man, he was the most popular kid in the school. Frankly, I very seldom got one. The other guys would get boxes from home with chicken and cake and all kinds of stuff in there, but I almost never did. I guess Mama and Papa Jack just couldn't afford it. I did get letters from home, but not many. I guess Mama and Papa Jack really didn't like the idea that they had sent me up there, especially Mama. How could a schoolteacher explain that her own son was having trouble making it in school? So maybe they just put me out of their minds for a while.

At Downingtown I hustled just the same as I had on the street, but I didn't make any lasting friends, and in the spring of 1922 after a year up there, I had had enough. I felt I was ready to return to Baltimore, and get down to work. If getting out of Downingtown meant going to school and studying, then I was ready to do just that.

Of course I didn't have any money at Downingtown, except what I earned by hauling trunks of other students from the school to the train station. One day I took the little money I had, packed my stuff into a suitcase, and went to the train station. The ticket from Downingtown to Baltimore cost $15, which was more than I had so I asked the man for a half-fare ticket. He said, "Son, you're too old for half fare. You have to buy full fare." Well, I wasn't about to let the fact that I didn't have enough money keep me from going home, so I picked up my suitcase and walked from Downingtown to West Chester, Pennsylvania, about twenty miles. There I got a commuter train into Philadelphia. I still had enough money for a ticket from Philly to Baltimore.

Jesus, did I feel great on that train! I knew I was going home. My family didn't know it, though. Nobody knew I had left Downingtown. I never will forget walking down the street that spring with my suitcase under my arm. It was just about dusk. People were out on the sidewalk and sitting on the stoops. Mama was outside with a neighbor, and when she saw me she looked like she was going to faint. She jumped up and ran over to me, hollering, "Here's Cab!! Where you come from, Cab? What you doing home? Why didn't you write you were coming?" And I just said to her, "It don't matter, Ma, I'm home now." And she said, "Well, come on in here, boy, and sit down." And we went inside and couldn't stop laughing and talking. Bernice came in later in the afternoon with Elmer and we had a hell of a reunion. By the time that Papa Jack got home from work later that night, we were in quite a state, and exhausted from reminiscing.

That year in Downingtown made a big difference. I walked into Downingtown a little boy, and I came out a man. What made the difference was being away from home and having to make it on my own. In Downingtown, if I made a mistake, there was no one to look after me but myself. It was me who would miss out on supper. It was me who would have to work after everybody else was finished. Suddenly there was nobody to bail me out. Downingtown was the turning point for me. I knew, from then on, I had to make it on my own.

At first when I returned to Baltimore, I went back out onto the streets, looked up the old gang, and began hanging out. But about six months afterward, Mama and Papa Jack moved the whole family out to a small suburban development seven or eight miles outside Baltimore called Wilson Park. Suddenly I was in a whole different environment. I never saw the guys any more. I entered Laureville School and for the first time I really applied myself to the books. I don't mean to say that I was a scholar—because I wasn't. But I was working and my grades went up. I found out for the first time that if I really went at it, I was pretty sharp in school. I was still hustling, too, and after school I had a job. I was a bus boy for about two years with Bernard Taylor, who had a catering company in Baltimore. Then when Bernard got the food concession at the Century Roof, one of Baltimore's finest and largest supper clubs, I went with him part-time as a bus boy and later as a checker. A checker is a guy who stands out in the kitchen checking each dish against the order as it goes out. I did that for two years while we were living in Wilson Park.

I liked living out there. The development was owned by Harry O. Wilson, a black insurance man. He had bought a couple hundred acres with some houses on it and named it Wilson Park after himself. He lived out there, too, and his children were about my age. We rented a great big house on a corner. It had four bedrooms, a garage, a big lawn, and hedges all around. But it was the Wilsons who had the nicest house in the park. It was at the end of a long drive, up on a hill, with a swimming pool.

I think one of the reasons I began going to school out there was because everyone did. The guys never played hookey.

It was a four-mile walk to the school and back. The school was just a little two-room building, and of course all the students were black. All the schools I ever went to were all-black until I went to Crane College in Chicago. Most of my friends in Wilson Park were black, too, but there were a few white boys around there that we played baseball with.

In Wilson Park two important things happened to me. First, I really began to study, and second, for the first time I got into organized athletics. We didn't really have a team, but the Wilson kids did have baseballs and bats and stuff. I enjoyed playing with them, but my real ambition was to work myself up to the point where I was good enough to play with some of the better sandlot teams around there. I was a pretty good shortstop and I batted second or third. My hitting was only fair, but at shortstop I could gobble up the ball pretty good—moving to the left or to the right. Anything down my territory and you were in trouble. I was very sure-handed, first in baseball and later on in high school when I started playing basketball.

Since Mama and Papa Jack were both off working in town, after school I would take Bernice and Elmer over to the ball field while I played. After a couple of hours, I'd take them home and Bernice and I would fix dinner. During this time out in Wilson Park, I became a damned good cook. I didn't particularly enjoy it; I would have preferred to be playing ball with the other kids, but I knew it was my responsibility.

So for a couple of years there I was playing baseball hard and studying even harder. I even wound up as junior high valedictorian—of course, there were only four kids in my class.

I'm very proud of coming out of a school like that and going on to do the things I've done in life. The conditions for learning weren't very good—we had few books or supplies—but the teachers gave us attention and love and understanding. They were stern, too. They pushed us to learn, but they were sensitive to each child so that nobody ever felt left out or uncared for. The quality of education at that school was less important to me than the feeling of confidence and security that I got from it. I don't really understand what's going on in the schools with colored kids these days, but it seems to me that perhaps a fundamental thing that's missing is the closeness and understanding that we had in that little two-room schoolhouse in the country. Basic things like that. How the hell can a kid be expected to learn when he's not only catching hell at home from parents who either don't care or are too busy, and then he goes to school and gets the same kind of indifference from teachers.

I may have been studying hard, but I was no goody-goody. I was still getting into fights. I used to fight with the Wilson kids because, frankly, I was jealous as hell that they always had nicer shoes and clothes than the rest of us and more money and their house was nicer. Harry Wilson, Jr., would get to teasing me that his house was bigger and he had more baseball bats and gloves and his clothes were nicer and newer, and I'd get angry as hell and go after him and we'd be at it. Then, the next minute, we'd be the best of friends.

The social life for adults was very active. We always had old friends of Mama and Papa Jack coming out to the house to play bridge or just to drink and talk. Mama was a very social woman. She belonged to several clubs in Baltimore, and the meetings would rotate from one member's house to another's. I never will forget, the first time that I got drunk was during one of Mama's meetings. I was around sixteen, and she had a group of women out to play bridge. I was helping Mama serve, and every time I went into the kitchen to fix a plate or fill somebody's glass I'd have a sip of the wine. I just kept serving and sipping and serving and sipping. The ladies were in the living room, talking and playing cards, when all of sudden, dammit, my head started to spin and my stomach turned over. I got sick as a dog and that was the way my mama and the ladies found me when they came into the kitchen. They thought it was funny as hell. Of course Mama didn't think it was funny. She was mad. But that was nothing to the way I felt. It was some time before I tried that again.

Papa Jack didn't have much time for social life. For him it was mainly work, work, work. Mama and Papa Jack were like my wife, Nuffie, and me; Nuffie's the social person, involved in clubs and parties and benefits for this and for that. I dislike formal affairs or big parties. Give me my work and the racetrack, and I'm happy.

While we were living in Wilson Park, I started going to church again. Going to church was like going to school—there was nothing else to do. Everybody went to church out there, so I'd get myself all dressed up and we'd walk down to the little church. Then, after church, the men would go out into the woods to shoot craps. We'd have a hell of a crap game every Sunday. Papa Jack was one of the few men who wouldn't go. He didn't believe in gambling, but I took his place and shot craps right along with the men.

The year and a half we spent in Wilson Park was like an interlude. It was good for me because it got me out of the city into an environment where there were very few temptations. Then when I was about sixteen and a half, we moved back to Baltimore. I'm not sure why; we didn't have the kind of family where Mama and Papa Jack would sit down with us and explain things or say, "This is what we expect of you." While we were in Wilson Park they never actually said to me, "Listen, Cabell, you're going to have to take care of Bernice and Elmer now because we're going to be late coming home because of the distance we have to travel." It just fell on me and I took care of it. So when it came time to move back into Baltimore from Wilson Park, they just said it was time to move back into Baltimore, and we packed up and moved.

We rented a house at 1306 Madison Avenue, not far from where we used to live on Druid Hill Avenue. We moved in the summer of 1924, and in the fall of that year I entered Frederick Douglass High School. Papa Jack changed jobs about that time, too. He left the insurance business and went to work selling ads for the Baltimore *Afro-American*. At that time, "the Afro," as everybody called it, was the largest Negro newspaper in the country.

I guess you could say that by the time we moved back to Baltimore, I had grown up. I was a combination of that old wildness that had gotten me into so much trouble and of the industrious, hustling moneymaker who helped to support the family. I've been a combination of those two qualities ever since. I've always worked hard and hustled to make money to take care of the people I love; and I've always been somewhat wild and independent. But underneath those characteristics, although I don't think about it very much—and probably wouldn't ever put it on paper except for this book—underneath those qualities is a man who is a loner. I have friends, bunches of friends, but I enjoy being alone and very few people know me well. Maybe there is nobody who really knows me well, inside and outside. I enjoy driving, for example, by myself, late at night after a gig, to the next gig. I was at the Concord Hotel in the Catskill Mountains in upstate New York recently and I finished a gig around 1:00 A.M., and I packed my bags and checked out and drove straight down to Baltimore, where I had another gig a couple of nights later. Maybe the fact that I'm a loner explains why I love entertaining people. On the stage I'm all alone, but among people at the same time.

I had a ball at Frederick Douglass High School. I was into everything you can think of. When I realized that I was a damned good athlete and could possibly go professional, I started to take basketball seriously. I also realized that I had the ability to make money, so I was working and hustling and I made a hell of a lot of money. And I also realized for the first time that I could entertain people. In high school I began to play drums and to sing with a small group and even do vaudeville with some kids from school. And best of all, I found out that I could get paid for entertaining. I could do two of the things most important to me at the same time—make people happy and make money.

"I had a ball at Frederick Douglass High School. I was into everything you can think of. When I realized that I was a damned good athlete and could possibly go professional, I started to take basketball seriously."

When I say I was hustling and making money in high school, I mean it. I was still working for Bernard Taylor, and in a given week, between catering and working the nightclubs nights and weekends, I'd earn about $35. I bought a car, and it was unusual in those days for a nigger in high school to own a car. It was a 1923 Oldsmobile. I bought it for $275 from a used-car showroom on North Avenue. Man, that car made me so baaad. I was the baddest cat in the whole school. On the day we moved into a new school building—it was my sophomore year—they had a big inauguration ceremony. Everybody was there. City officials, school department officials, parents, leaders in the community, ministers, everybody. The auditorium was packed. Negroes were proud as hell of having this new school. Suddenly, about halfway through the ceremonies, they had to stop everything to make an announcement. The school superintendent said that some teacher had parked a car out in front of the school in a no-parking zone, and would the teacher please move it. Well, you know damn well whose car it was. I jumped up and hollered so everybody in the place could hear: "Oh, yeah. I guess that must be my car. I'll move it." And people's heads turned as I strutted out. Man, I felt so big you couldn't even talk to me.

I should add that I bought that car with $75 down and the rest to be paid in notes. I never will forget when the man came and took the car away because I couldn't pay the damned notes. It taught me a lesson: Don't let your ego go where you head—and your wallet—can't follow. I've made other mistakes with money in my life—some damned big ones, too—but every time that I do, I remember that first one.

SINGING—A NEW KIND OF HUSTLE

As I said, I really began to get it together with music and entertainment during these years. When I was fourteen, I had begun taking voice lessons and singing with the choir in the church where Mama played the organ. One day Tom Moore and Robert Briscoe, a couple of boys from the old gang, and I were walking down the street harmonizing. We used to do that all the time. My mother was two blocks away, but we were singing so loud—my voice had always been loud—she could hear us coming, and she said to me, "Cabell, you have such a nice strong voice. You're going to take voice lessons." So she signed me up with Ruth Macabee, an ex-concert singer who was a good friend of the family's. Ruth, who taught music in the grammar school, gave me private lessons on the outside. She did a wonderful job; she really brought me out.

Ruth was a very exact person. She was erect and distinguished-looking and demanding as a teacher. She taught me the fundamentals; like how to breathe, place my tones, and use my diaphram to get the sound that I wanted. I would spend hours holding my tongue with a handkerchief and singing the scale, up and down, up and down, until I could sing a scale with a handkerchief around my tongue as well as most people without one. She also taught me elocution. She was always saying,

"Cabell, it is not enough to be able to sing and hold a key, people also have to understand your lyrics." So I would spend hours with her counting: one, two, three, four, five, up to ten and over and over to get the execution of the sounds precise and correct. Practice, practice, practice, with her during lessons and then all week at home. I took lessons from her every Wednesday evening.

I liked Ruth as a person, and I liked her warm and comfortable house. It was very much like ours, with a small piano in the living room, lace curtains on the windows, doilies on the coffee tables, and Tiffany lamps all around.

Later on, in high school, I took more voice lessons and basic musical theory from Llewelyn Wilson. He taught music at the high school and gave me private lessons at his home. I took from Ruth Macabee and Llewelyn Wilson for about two years each. The foundation for my technique comes from them, though I had a certain amount of natural ability. I had a lovely robust tenor voice—with a range from around C to B above C—but their teaching developed the natural voice that I started out with.

In high school I sang every damned chance I got, sometimes in the church choir but mostly in the clubs around town. From my days on the streets I knew some of the guys in those clubs. There was a place in Baltimore called the Gaiety, a little speakeasy next to a burlesque house. I walked in one night and got to the piano player and said I wanted to sing with him. We both knew the same pop tunes, like "Bye, Bye, Blackbird" and "Muddy Waters," so I started in and he followed and people dug it a lot. "Muddy Waters" became one of my favorite tunes. In fact, after I had been singing in the clubs a while, people nicknamed me Muddy Waters. Whenever I would walk into one of those clubs, people would say, "Here comes old Muddy Waters, gonna sing his song." I would walk up beside the piano and start to sing: "Muddy waters, say you see those muddy waters 'round my feet; I'm walking 'bout the Delta, muddy waters at my feet."

Now, I was still in high school at this time, and it wasn't unusual at the Gaiety, or at Bailey's Club, or at the Arabian Tent Club, for me to go in there at night for a gig and to find my high school teachers in the audience. I'd look down and there they'd be. And of course these places were all bootlegging liquor, so I wasn't supposed to be in there, but neither were they; so we had a kind of truce. I'd see them in school the next day and nobody would say anything to anybody about the night before, just like we had never seen each other.

Baltimore at that time was one of the centers of jazz. Some great musicians came out of there. Johnny Jones and his Arabian Tent Orchestra was one of the best in the city. Johnny was a six-fingered piano player; he had a spur finger on each hand, and God, could he play that instrument! And Chick Webb was from Baltimore, and he had a little band around there. In fact, Johnny Jones and Chick Webb were my inspirations. Later I developed into a singing drummer—that became my thing—and the idea for drumming came directly from Chick. He was a hunchbacked guy who would sit over those drums and pound your heart out. Everything was a straight two-four at that time, and dammit, you could sit with Chick for weeks and he'd never miss a lick. So I began to like the idea of drumming.

One day I was standing on a corner talking with some cats—you know, just rapping—and some guy comes up to the corner and joins the discussion. Soon it comes out, he's got this little four-piece band. And he says, "Man, we got a problem in the group, our drummer got in trouble and I need a drummer right away." So I said, "You need a drummer, man? I can drum. I'll play the drums for your group." And of course at this time I hadn't been anywhere near no drums in my life. So the guy said, "Well, I hope you've got your own drums, man, because the cat took his with him." To make it short, I didn't have any drums, but the guy and I went downtown to Conn Instruments, Ziggie Conn's place on Howard Street, and we had a little money and we talked Ziggie out of a set of drums. He rented them to us for just about nothing. So we went back to this guy's house and had a rehearsal, and I just played the rhythms the way I had seen old Chick Webb sitting up there slinging those sticks, and I got over. The next night we had a rehearsal again and went right on the job. The band was playing in a roadhouse out on the Washington Pike. Of course I wasn't the greatest drummer in the world and they were a little worried whether we'd make it, so I told the guys, "Listen, don't worry so much about the drums. I'll get up and sing and people won't notice my playing." Damned if it didn't work. I took it from there. We stayed there for a couple of months. Then we went down to another club in Baltimore, I think it was Bailey's Club, and one day when we finished rehearsing I told the guys, "Listen, I can get us more money and some regular gigs, but if I do, you gotta let me lead the band.'' They agreed. I guess they figured they had nothing to lose. I went around to some of the clubs and talked to guys that I knew and lined up some gigs. The first one was in the Dandy Restaurant downtown at Gay and Baltimore streets. We played dixieland and straight jazz. Hot music, they called it. And we stayed in there keeping things jumping all the time. People really liked it.

Later we played in the Gaiety. There I was, sitting behind those drums, man, keeping time and singing my music with this little four-piece band. We were so small and so raw that we didn't even have a name. But that was the beginning. I knew from then on I would always be with bands.

Later the same year I went with Johnny Jones's ten-piece band. Man, what a thrill that was—Johnny Jones's Arabian Ten Orchestra. We were still playing that straight-up turn-of-the-century jazz, a Baltimore version of New Orleans dixieland with a heavy two-four rhythm, pounding bass drum, banjo, piano, and jumping, syncopated cornets, and trumpets. That first little band I played in only had a piano, drums, bass, and sax. Johnny's group had five horns, two banjos, piano, drums, and bass.

There were other fine musicians around Baltimore at that time, too. Eubie Blake had been playing all around there; he eventually left and went to New York, where he became famous in *Shuffle Along,* the same revue that my sister Blanche started in when she went to New York. The pianist Ulysses Chambers was around Baltimore in those years and so was Harold Steptoe, another great pianist. I used to sing with all those guys in the Baltimore nightclubs. And at the same time, I was doing revues and vaudeville shows with a little group in the high school, and occasionally at the Regent Theatre.

Mama and Papa Jack and my voice teachers used to call the speakeasies ''low life'' nightclubs. Goodlow's, the Arabian Tent, the Gaiety and Bailey's were not clubs in the way we think of a club today. These were three-story houses with the living room converted into space for tables and chairs. There'd be someone cooking ribs and barbecue and pigs' feet in the kitchen. Everybody would be laughing and dancing and hollering behind the music, which was always loud. We drank gin, wine, and whiskey, mostly old, hard bootleg rye. Mama and Papa Jack and my music teachers didn't know I was performing in these places. Jesus, they would have been mad as hell. They forbade me to go near

Johnny Jones
and his
ARABIAN TENT ORCHESTRA.

"Baltimore at that time was one of the centers of jazz. Some great musicians came out of there. Johnny Jones and his Arabian Tent Orchestra was one of the best in the city."

them, but since they never went into them themselves, I was pretty safe. In fact, Ruth Macabee forbade me even to sing jazz. She always taught opera and classical music. Jazz was below her, she said. She thought she was training me for concerts, and there I was blowing jazz every night. Later on, my folks found out what was happening. They began to wonder where I was all the time. I had given up selling newspapers then, and I wasn't going to the track much either, so it didn't take them long to figure out that my sudden interest in music and my disappearance every night meant I was performing down at the clubs. We just didn't discuss it. They pretended that they didn't know, and I pretended that it wasn't happening.

The revues at the Regent Theatre usually consisted of various bands that would play instrumentals or accompany singers like me doing pop tunes like "Bye, Bye, Blackbird." Then the chorus line would come on and the girls would dance up a storm: tap dance, soft shoe, and some jazzed-up ballet numbers. The costumes were always out of sight, colorful and flamboyant, and the guys in the bands always dressed formally, in black tuxedos with white shirts and bow ties. It was something to see.

Between playing in the clubs and the revues at the Regent, I was making pretty good money. I'd take home $30 or $35 a week and that was damned big money then, especially for someone seventeen years old. I took just about every penny home to Mama. Money was still tight in the family, especially with two new kids, and she was grateful for what I brought, but she was worried too. She would corner me every now and then and remind me, "Law is the thing for you. You go on to college; never forget that's your ultimate objective." I would listen to her and say, "Okay, okay," but in my heart I was beginning to think that entertainment was my world.

But I was studying pretty hard, too, and turning into a darn good athlete. At this point I wasn't certain whether I would go into entertainment or professional athletics. At night I was hustling the nightclubs and during the day I was deeply involved in school athletics. My basketball career was going strong, but my football career was shortlived.

We had some damned good football players at Douglass. Our nickname was the Ducks, after our coach, Duck Gibson. I was so good in athletics generally, I figured, hell, I can make the football team, so in my freshman year I went out. I started playing halfback with the junior varsity, working my way up through team scrimmages to the varsity. I was pretty cocky and a lot of the varsity players didn't like me or the idea that a freshman might bump one of the upperclassmen off the varsity. They didn't want it to happen, and they made sure it didn't.

One day Coach Duck Gibson called me out to practice with the varsity. The varsity quarterback called the play and I was supposed to go through a hole at right tackle. I grabbed the ball and started for the right side, but when I looked around for my interference I saw it had gone the other way. That was the last thing I saw before the whole defensive line hit me. With everything they had. They piled on, and I wound up out cold with a couple of cracked ribs. I was in the hospital for three days. That was the beginning and the end of my football career.

After that I went back to basketball full-time. I was a guard, the best on the team. I averaged around 10 or 12 points a game, and in those days 35 points would win a game. In one game I scored 22. That was the night I had a little gin before the game, and every damned thing I threw at the basket went in. Douglass High School played against the other Negro schools in the Baltimore area, and in 1927 and 1928 we had just about the best team in the Baltimore-Washington region.

In my senior year I started playing professional basketball with the Baltimore Athenians. Those guys were tough. We played in West Virginia, Ohio, New York, and all around the Chesapeake Bay area in a Negro professional league. I was a star guard, hitting about 12 points a game. They paid us $10 a game. In Baltimore, and sometimes on the road, there would be a dance afterward. First I would play in the game, and then I'd be up there singing and drumming with Ike Dixon's band.

Unlike the high school league, we played some white professional teams as well as black. There were Negro basketball leagues all over the country in those days, but colored guys couldn't get into the major leagues, and professional sports lost some of its best players because of discrimination. It was a damned shame then, and it's a damned shame now that baseball has just within the last year or so gotten its first Negro manager in Frank Robinson. Professional basketball has just begun to open up, and there isn't a black head coach to be seen in professional football.

I say a "black" coach now, but I wouldn't have used the word in those days. Our people were colored or Negro, never black. To call somebody black was an insult; and, of course, to call me black, light-skinned as I was, was a triple insult. Whenever people ask me where the white blood in my family is, I tell them, "Hell, there was a nigger somewhere back there who jumped over the fence—and, man, something happened." Somewhere down the line, somebody jumped a fence, and something happened; otherwise I wouldn't be the color that I am.

People talk so much these days about integration; well, personally I am fully integrated. Some of us call it "nighttime integration." Blacks and whites have always been integrated in this country but it's been kept quiet. God knows how many black people or colored people there are walking around who think they're white and don't know that somewhere in their background somebody jumped a fence and integrated them the quick way, without any busing or anything. As far as I know, on my mother's side, there was an Irish family named O'Neil somewhere around Baltimore and at some point one of them married somebody black and that started it. I've never gone into it any further.

I've always accepted the fact that I'm Negro. I don't know anything else. I've been kicked in my ass all my life because of it, and, hell, I've come through it and become a star. Everybody has got to endure a certain amount of ass kicking to make it. People will step on you as you move along and there's no way to avoid it. The only difference between a black and a white entertainer is that my ass has been kicked a little more and a lot harder because it's black.

Even black people have given me a hard way to go sometimes. They've called me dirty yeller and poor white. That went on for years in the thirties and forties. Some people were bothered because they couldn't classify me easily; they thought I was Cuban or Puerto Rican. It's a horrible thing when people want to classify you or resort to name calling, but I've come through it because I've always known, from the days when I was a nigger kid selling papers and hustling shoeshines and walking hots out at Pimlico—hell, I'm a nigger and proud of it.

White people have given me hell over the years. It wasn't so bad when we were kids. All of us black kids went to all-black schools and we lived in streets that were black. When we played with white boys it was because we wanted to, not because we had to. And there was very little social mixing in Baltimore. But when I got older and began to move around, began to move out, white folks sometimes made it rough. I grew up on the streets, so I don't take crap from anyone. I'll fight as soon as look at a man who insults me.

"The only difference between a black and a white entertainer is that my ass has been kicked a little more and a lot harder because it's black."

One time in the forties I had my band in Kansas City playing a theater. Whenever I was in Kansas City I would stay with a friend, Felix Payne, a Negro politician. Well, on this trip, Felix's son, Felix, Jr., was home on vacation from Lincoln University in Jefferson, Missouri. I had run into my friend Lionel Hampton in the street one day and he invited me over to the Playmore Ballroom there in K.C. to hear his show. So Felix, Jr., and I went over one night to see the show. I walked up to the box office and bought two tickets. But when I got to the turnstile the usher wouldn't let us in. This was an all-white audience. Well, I started to argue with this usher, next thing we were fighting. Come to find out, this guy was an off-duty cop; he pulled out his revolver and busted me in the head. Felix jumped in and the place was in pandemonium. I was bleeding like a stuck pig, so they took me to the hospital, bandaged my head, and then Felix and I wound up in jail. We were bailed out in a few hours—Felix, Sr., was quite a well-known politician—but the wire services carried this story and it made headlines all over the country. Felix and I sued the city and the Ballroom, but it was one of those courtroom situations where the judge is looking out the window and an all-white jury is sitting up there knitting. It cost me personally about $15,000 in lawyers' fees, but nothing ever came of it. The point is that I wouldn't stand for that kind of treatment. Hamp was a friend of mine and he had invited me to see his show and there was no way that usher was going to keep me out of there without a fight.

Another time, around 1943, I was playing with a sixteen-piece band at the Zanzibar Club at Forty-ninth Street and Broadway in Manhattan and living at the Lincoln Hotel, which became the Manhattan Hotel, on Forty-fourth Street and Eighth Avenue. I was separated from my wife, Wenonah, by then and living with Nuffie at the hotel. A friend of mine, a song plugger named Nat Debin, dropped in one night. Song pluggers would come into the Zanzibar every night with songs some guy had written that they wanted me to sing, and Nat Debin had become a close friend. I told Nat I'd been living in hotels long enough. I wanted a home. "Listen, man, here you guys come around here to hear the great Cab Calloway and to beg me to plug one of your songs. Sometimes I do, and sometimes I don't. But when you're finished, you all go back to your lovely little homes and I go back to the Lincoln Hotel. Shit, I want you guys to help find me a place to live."

I didn't have any money at the time; my first wife, Wenonah, had everything tied up. So I knew damned well that I couldn't afford a house.

I was barely paying the rent at the Lincoln. But Nat Debin, for some reason, had fallen in love with me, the way men can sometimes. We had a warm, loving, manly relationship. We used to hang out and get drunk together. Nat contacted some guy he knew—I think it was a guy in the rackets—and arranged for me to meet him. I met him a few times, and he was a really sweet guy. He had a beautiful summer house out in Lido Beach. The guy said, "Listen, Cab, if you want to use my place, you can use it, and don't worry about the rent." Well, by the forties I was quite a big star. I was known all over the world. It was still the era of the big bands, and my sixteen pieces were one of the best in the country, probably second as a jazz band only to Duke Ellington. That forties band was probably the best I've ever had. Don't take my word for it. Barry Ulanov, one of the great jazz critics, wrote in 1943: "How many people realize what a great band Cabell is leading right now, a band extraordinary in every aspect, in its clean musicianship, its jazz kicks and its brilliant showmanship." Buster Harding was my writer and arranger; Chu Berry was there on sax, along with Ben Webster and Hilton Jefferson. Dizzy Gillespie was playing trumpet with Jonah Jones. Milt Hinton was on bass, Cozy Cole was the drummer, and Benny Payne was the pianist. That was one hell of a band. We were doing radio shows weekly and national tours twice a year. So when this guy was asked by Nat Debin if I could use his summer house, I guess he figured, "This is one hell of an honor to have Cab Calloway staying out at my house."

Nuffie and I moved from the Lincoln Hotel out to Lido Beach, and we hadn't been out there a day before the signs started to appear. We'd come home at night from doing a show and there would be signs stuck into the grass: "Nigger, go home." "Nigger, leave here." "We don't want niggers in Lido Beach." It was a hell of a thing and it hurt us. I tried not to pay any attention to it, and I've never blamed anyone for it. It was a Jewish community and they had never had a Negro out around there. I just told myself, "There's bad in every group. You can't blame the whole group for what one or two people do; that's a shitty way to treat people." I lived out there in this guy's house for about twelve years. Can you believe that? Nuffie brought her mother and father and sister and brother out, and we all lived together. We were quite a family. And we soon found out that in spite of the way we had been welcomed, there were some damned nice people out there.

All that's a long time away from those basketball teams back in the twenties, though I guess the prejudice didn't change much. But although we were restricted to playing mainly in Negro leagues, we were able to make pretty good money. As I said, we made $10 a game playing basketball, and then I'd make another $10 or so for the after-game show. And I was making $24 or $30 singing in the evenings and week-ends in the clubs and theaters around Baltimore. At the age of seventeen or eighteen I was making about $50 a week. That was a bundle of money then. Almost all of it went to Mama and the kids. They always came first.

I guess that I grew up quickly and somewhat disjointedly during those high school years. On the one hand, my family and my music teachers, whom I loved and respected, were rather puritanical people: churchgo-ing, middle class, strivers. On the other hand, I spent a lot of my time in that rough and raucous Baltimore Negro night life with loud music, heavy drinking, and the kind of moral standards or lack of them that my parents looked down on. I managed pretty well in both of these worlds, I suppose, because I was accustomed to thinking for myself. I didn't get taken in entirely by the night life, but I didn't get taken in entirely by the middle-class values either. I've been like that ever since. I can manage well in almost any kind of environment because I say, "To hell with it, I'm me and I'm always going to be me. I live my life the way that I want and nothing is going to prevent me from doing what I want to do and going where I want to go."

There's one event of my high school years that I haven't mentioned. There was quite a debate in my family as to whether I should go into this subject, but in the end the decision was mine, and I decided to talk about it. I've always tried to be honest. Hell, that's one of the reasons I'm writing this book. So, against the advice of some members of my family, I have decided to share a difficult, but beautiful and important, event in my life with the public.

When I was seventeen years old, I was going around with a girl of about the same age named Zarita Steptoe. Her father was pastor of the Bethel African Methodist Episcopal Church in Baltimore. In fact, the main reason that I was going to church at all those days was to be near Zarita. But like most boys that age, I had a wandering eye. In my senior year I discovered Zelma Proctor and she was real fine. Zelma had a lot of boyfriends and every one of them was my competition. But I was a big basketball star, a handsome, successful singer and drummer, and a guy with quite an ego. I just had to be her boyfriend, or at least one of her boyfriends. I began to take her out and in no time at all became her favorite. One of the reasons was that her aunt, whom she was living with then, liked me better for some reason than all the other guys Zelma was going around with. So whenever I called on Zelma, I would get a royal welcome, while other guys got the cold shoulder.

One day Zelma and her aunt and I went out to the races at Pimlico, and when we got back in the evening Zelma's aunt said she was going out to a movie and I could stay until she got back. Now, this was very unusual. Those were the days when a boy very rarely got a chance to be alone with a girl except in public places. I never figured out why her aunt left us there like that. So we started petting, and before we knew it we had made it together. That was my first time. Hers too.

We were in love. There was no one else in sight for either of us. We were inseparable. It was the kind of romance that only young people that age can feel—all that innocence and rashness and total love. Well, you can probably guess what happened. Zelma became pregnant. We were still in high school and we had this tremendous decision to make. I was uncertain what we should do, but not Zelma. She wanted to have the baby. I said, "Okay, if you want to have it, then I want to marry you." But Zelma wouldn't have that. She said, "No, I'm too young and you're too fly-by-night to be getting married."

My mother and Zelma's aunt were horrified. They both thought the whole thing was terrible. My mother's first response was, "Well, Zelma's had a lot of boyfriends, and no one would blame you if you didn't marry her." I told Mama, "Listen, that doesn't matter. That's neither here nor there. I want to marry her." But Zelma would have none of it.

When she was about seven months pregnant, Zelma and I left Baltimore. I had no money, but she didn't want to have the baby there. It was embarrassing for her and for her aunt. She wanted to go to New York, where her Aunt Jennie lived. We left in my old car, without a penny. We stopped off in Atlantic City, a big, fancy resort with a lot of jumping nightclubs. I figured I could hustle up some money there. We checked into an inexpensive hotel and I went out into the streets with my fingers crossed. I walked into the first honky-tonk nightclub I saw and went over to the piano player. "Listen," I said, "I'm a singer just come up from Baltimore. How about letting me sing a few songs and hustle up some money." So the guy said okay, and we hooked up a few popular tunes that we both knew, the same old standards I had been singing in Baltimore. And it went over. Then I passed the hat and that got me and Zelma started. For the next two weeks in Atlantic City I sang in every joint on the beach—speakeasies, clubs, restaurants, wherever there was a piano or a little combo. When I walked in I said, "Say, man, let me sing a few tunes," and afterwards I'd pass the hat and collect a few bucks and move on to the next joint. We were doing all right. I was able to make some good money there. But after about two weeks, Zelma said, "Cab, I'm going to New York—and I've been thinking about it. I want to go alone." We talked about it and we agreed that if that was what she wanted to do, she should go ahead. So we split up. I went back to Baltimore and Zelma went on to New York.

The child, Camay Proctor, was born in Harlem Hospital on January 15, 1927. From the moment that Zelma left me in Atlantic City, I began to send her money in New York. Throughout the years, I've sent her money regularly. I helped to see Camay through school and through college. When she needed more, I sent her more. Money doesn't buy love; I know that. Only a fool would ever believe that. Anyhow, my career was developing, and I was anxious to live my own life—there was only so much I could do. But whenever I could, I called and sent money to help support them, and tried to show them I cared. When I finally got to New York, after two years in Chicago, Camay was three or four years old. Since then Zelma and I have both married and remarried. But all of us love and respect each other as adults to this day: Zelma and her husband, Bunny, and Camay's husband, Booker Brooks. They live in Washington, and we're like a family when we're together. Whenever I do a television show, they are the first ones to call to say how great it was. And whenever I have a gig in Washington, or Baltimore, the whole crowd troops over. They're always right there in the front row.

Camay is quite a success in her own right. She is a supervisor in the Arlington, Virginia, public schools and an educational consultant. Only her close friends have known until now that Camay Brooks is my daughter. It's no secret to anyone in the family that she is the apple of my eye. She can do no wrong as far as I'm concerned. I'm as proud of her as any father could be, and she loves me as if we'd spent all these years together. I guess, in a way, we have. She's gone through the good times and the bad with me. Zelma has, too. And they've managed to bring into the relationship all the people who have come into their lives: husbands, friends, and children.

Camay and Booker have a son, my oldest grandson, Christopher Brooks, who is in his third year at Duke University. Damn, was I proud when he was born! And I'm still proud. He's so smart it makes your head swim. In addition to Christopher, Camay and Booker have a second son, Peter. He's fourteen now. I have five grandsons, not a single granddaughter among them, but I guess it works out, because I have five daughters and not a single son among them.

Camay is now a successful woman established in educational circles in Virginia. It's hard to know whether people will look at her differently because her mother and I were not married. I've talked to her about it and she has told me, "Listen, Daddy, it's your book. Do it your way." That's Camay. And I suppose that's the attitude I've tried to instill in all my children. People are people. Accept them for what they are and how they treat you, not for their pasts, not for their race or religion or class in life. Hell, everybody's made mistakes and gone through changes. Accept people for the way they treat you and the lives they live. When Camay said, "Go ahead, Daddy, do it your way," I felt so damned proud again that I could have cried.

FROM BALTIMORE TO
JAZZ CITY: CHICAGO

After I left Zelma, I returned to Baltimore to finish my senior year. It was a hell of a year—singing in the clubs, going to school, playing ball, and still working with Bernard Taylor on weekends and evenings whenever I had time. I saw Mama and Papa Jack from time to time, coming and going. They were hustling to feed those two additional mouths and I was hustling to do my thing, and try to help out with the money at the same time. I didn't graduate with my class, because I failed a chemistry course. Mama was very disappointed. So was I. I tried to be blasé about it, but it hurt my pride to see those kids I had gone through three years of high school with all dressed up for graduation while I was left behind. When I finished that chemistry course the next year, I was really proud, though; so was Mama. That was 1927, and in the summer of that year Blanche came back to town.

I hadn't seen her for five years, and we had a hell of a reunion. To me she was a big star. She came to town with the musical *Plantation Days,* a revue with an Old South theme and great music and dancing. Blanche had one of the leads and she was staying downtown at one of the hotels with the cast. The show was at the Royal Theatre for two or three weeks, and I was at that theater every damned day. I had been around shows before, but they were mainly high school revues and vaudeville things. This was a professional cast of about twenty-five, with a sixteen-piece orchestra and costumes and fine music, and there was my sister Blanche in the middle of it, singing and dancing. Blanche was vivacious, lovely, personality-plus, and a hell of a singer and dancer, as well.

Plantation Days was one of the biggest hits of the twenties. It was one of the first major black revues, and everywhere it went Negro audiences packed the theaters. I hung around the show and talked to people and got tips from them and got to know everybody. By this time I had just about decided that one way or another I wanted to go into show business. It seems to me that Blanche and I had the same conversation every night. She would say, "Cab, you don't want this business. It stinks, its no way to live, and Mama's heart is set on you going into law and you ought to. You're smart; you can make it." And I would say, "No, Blanche, I know what I want to do. Maybe I'll go to college, maybe I'll go for law, but I want to try show business, too." We would talk back and forth like that, and for two solid weeks she tried to convince me to stay away from show business and for two solid weeks I fought her.

There was a quartet in the show that sang pop tunes and some blues. They were pretty damned good, and during the second week one of the singers got sick. When I heard they were looking for a replacement I told Blanche she just had to help me. I wanted that part and I wanted to get to Chicago. I guess I had worn her down by that time. She just smiled at me—I'll never forget it—and sighed and said, "Okay, Cab. I think it's a dumb thing for a kid as smart as you to go into this lousy business, but I'll get you an audition if you promise that when we get to Chicago you'll enroll in college." Man, I would have promised anything at that point. The idea of going on the road with a hit show like *Plantation Days* just blew my mind. Blanche got the audition for me and I got the part. I began singing tenor with the group, high tenor, what they used to call the juvenile part.

Then Blanche and I had the problem of telling Mama. We went up to the house on Madison Avenue one evening when the show was near the end of its run in Baltimore, and I just told her straight out. Mama was terribly upset. "Cab," she said, "I don't want you to do it. If you go and get into that show, that will be the end of college. I know you."

"No, Mama," I said. "I want to work my way to Chicago with this

"Blanche was vivacious, lovely, personality-plus, and a hell of a singer and dancer, as well."

show. Then Blanche promises to enroll me in Crane College.'' Eventually we convinced my mother that it would work out, but first I had to swear on a stack of Bibles that I would enroll at Crane and study seriously. I think she was also convinced because Crane College was a public school, and using Blanche's residence I could go for free. Mama knew she didn't have the money to send me to college.

Plantation Days, which was a Chicago show originally, had been on the road for about a year. It was scheduled to close in Chicago in September, which would work out perfectly. I could enter college then.

So we went out on the road. The company, as I said, was about twenty-five singers and dancers. The main musician was Harry Swanigan, who was the pianist for the famous pop and blues singer Ada Brown. She was the lead in the show. Twenty years later, Ada and I met up again in the movie *Stormy Weather,* the classic Negro film of the forties, starring Lena Horne, Bill Robinson, Fats Waller, and me. Harry Swanigan was the only musician who traveled with the show. We used sixteen-piece house orchestras everywhere we played.

I'll never forget the way that I left Baltimore. I still had my drums, and I pawned them to buy a suitcase to carry my one suit, three shirts, and a suit of underwear. It cost $10, and I gave all the rest of my money to Mama. The show was only paying around $30 and I was used to making more than that. I was still sending it all back to Mama. Those were lean times, but I dug the show and being on the road so much that it didn't matter.

It was my first time on the road as a professional, and I went as wild as a March hare. I chased all the broads in the show and caught one finally, a Japanese-looking colored gal, light-skinned and big and fine. I went for her and she went for me, and we made it together the whole trip. We traveled for about eight weeks, from Baltimore, to Pittsburgh, then Detroit, and on to Columbus, Ohio. In those days we used to call it the T.O.B.A. Circuit. It stood for Theatrical Organization and Benevolent Association, but it was the circuit all the Negro bands and shows followed and we used to call T.O.B.A. (Tough on Black Asses). We moved from town to town by bus across those bumpy roads and usually in the dead of the night, sleepy as hell after a show in one town, rushing to get into the next town in time to rehearse the new band and open the following night. Negroes weren't allowed to stay in any of the main hotels in the places we played, so everywhere we went the company had a list of Negro families that would rent us rooms. The twenty-five of us would be spread out all around town, and these beautiful folks would rent a room and feed us some of the best damned cooking around for $10 a week. They'd always say it was a pleasure, even an honor, for them to be housing members of such a famous company. They were mainly middle-class, working, churchgoing people who had small, wood-frame, two-story houses with comfortable sofas in the living room and lace curtains. I've always appreciated the kind of treatment black people gave Negro musicians and entertainers who were on the road. Thousands of people in the Midwest and South opened their homes to hundreds of musicians, singers, dancers, and comedians. We couldn't have done those road shows if it hadn't been for such people, warm, loving, gentle folk who treated us like family for the week or two we were in their town. That practice existed until the forties, when some of the lily-white hotels began to admit Negro entertainers.

Mama later told me that she missed me an awful lot when I left Baltimore. The house seemed empty, she said, because I was always the liveliest of the children. Even though I caused problems, I took on a lot of responsibility and made things happen. I guess it was a lonesome time for her. She and Papa Jack had broken up the year before. She knew I would always send her money, but she was still reluctant to see me go.

After Pittsburgh, Detroit, and Columbus, we hit Chicago. What a city! What a world I had been missing. There were so many people and so many buildings, and so many things to do. And the music. Chicago was just full of music.

In those days the South Side in Chicago was to jazz what Harlem came to be a few years later. There were basically two groups of musicians there, the white and the colored, and I was fascinated by both. Two of the best white ones were Eddie Condon and Red McKenzie. By the time I got to Chicago, they had combined bands into the McKenzie-Condon Chicagoans. Bix Beiderbecke and Pee Wee Russell were around Chicago then, and Bud Freeman, Mezz Mezzrow, Muggsy Spanier, Benny Goodman, Art Hodes, Harvey Brown, Wild Bill Davidson, Rosey McHargue—and I think Gene Krupa might have been out there then too. The colored bands were led, of course, by Louis Armstrong. King Oliver and his band had just left Chicago when I got there, so I had to wait until I got to New York to hear his music, and by then he was on the way down. Jimmy Noone was over at a club called The Nest with his group. In 1929 Earl Hines moved his new band into the Grand Terrace, a beautiful new club on the South Side and one of the few places in the city where both black and white patrons were served.

I moved in with Blanche at first. She had an apartment on South Parkway on the South Side. She was making it pretty well and we had six or seven rooms. Blanche was living with a guy named Watty. I never even knew his last name. I just called him Watty. Watty was a hustler. He played the horses and gambled and seemed to make a hell of a lot of money. He ran games, too—crap games and card games—all around Chicago. And from time to time he'd go out to Fort Wayne or Gary, Indiana, places like that, and stay for four or five days gambling and running games. He was always hustling and he always had a lot of money. Later on he wound up with a stable of horses. I never did know how many he had. He raced them on tracks in the Midwest. Watty was quite a character. A solid dresser, very sharp all the time, and slick to talk to. He could talk a cat into buying air. He had a beautiful car, a 1925 Lincoln. He and the other hustlers would park these big old cars on Thirty-fifth Street in front of the barbershop and spend the afternoon shooting craps or just talking. Then they'd go out in the evenings to the gambling rooms around town and drink and gamble.

I admired Watty because he was living exactly the kind of life he wanted to and was successful at it. But I never got into that life. Watty always saw me as a kid and maybe something of a square from Baltimore, although in those days, in my own eyes, I was just as sophisticated as I could be. Anyhow, he took a liking to me, and eventually helped me to get some gigs. He knew just about all the club owners on the South Side.

We had arrived in Chicago at the end of the summer. *Plantation Days* played at the Grand Theatre on State Street for a couple of weeks, and the crowds were incredible. I had never seen crowds like that before. The people jumped up and down in the theater and had a hell of a time. Then, after two weeks, the show closed, and Blanche took me down to Crane College and helped me enroll. I started classes right away. The studying was pretty heavy, and I was determined to make it in college so for a while I buried myself in my books and forgot everything else. But after about four months, around January of 1928 when I had just turned twenty, I asked Blanche and Watty if they knew somewhere that I could do some part-time singing. I was sure I could handle both studying and singing. Watty took me to a place called the Dreamland Cafe down on State Street. That was my first nightclub gig in Chicago. It was a corny club, but it was crowded every night. The people came in to drink and talk, not to listen to the music, and it was always noisy. It was also small and a little shabby, but I didn't care. I was singing in Chicago. I was making it. They had a little trio in there, and we would do popular tunes and jazz. It was nothing special, but it was special to me.

I began to make some friends around that time, too. Blanche and Watty belonged to a pretty fast group of show people and hustlers, and I was the student who had to be up every morning to get to school, but I had a cousin, William Credit, who was in Crane College and who I had known in Dowingtown. Through him I met a number of students who lived in Chicago. We used to hang out together, and have a ball partying on the weekends.

By this time I was playing basketball at the college too. My best friend was Toots Wright, a star athlete. Crane's basketball team wasn't really very good, so when Toots and I heard that the Harlem Globetrotters were in town we went over to a gym on the South Side to try out. A lot of damned good players were there, but Toots and I did pretty well and afterwards Abe Saperstein offered us both positions. I went home and talked about it with Blanche, and she brought up the old college argument again. I knew I couldn't travel with the Trotters and go to college, so I gave the idea up, but it was exciting just to have had the chance.

It was a different kind of life when I started to sing again. I didn't really have the time to study, so I started to cheat a bit. I had a little girl who used to do my work. She would write my papers and help me to get ready for tests. Thelma Eubanks was her name. I needed her help because I was beginning to get into everything again, just like I had in high school. I was playing basketball with the Crane team, lousy as it was, going to classes days, and singing nights and on weekends. On a typical day, I usually had to make class around ten. No breakfast, just get up and go. Blanche and Watty were night people, and the house was dead when I got up. After I got to know Watty he let me take his car to school. I'd finish classes around three or so and bring the car back and then go out and hang out on the corner with the kids or go on to basket-ball. I'd be home around five in the evening and have dinner with Blanche—Blanche was a damned good cook—and then I'd go on and make the gig.

We had shows every night. They'd start at 8:30 or 9:00 and the last show would be around midnight. I'd get home at 3:30 or 4:00 in the morning, sleep a few hours, and then off to school again. Some days, of course, I didn't make it to class, though God knows I tried. Weekends were tougher than weekdays. We had three shows on Saturdays and Sundays at the Dreamland Cafe. They worked my ass off and paid me as little as they could. I guess I made around $50 a week, and sent most of it home to Mama. That didn't leave me much to live on, and I didn't like the idea of Blanche and Watty carrying my load, so I pitched in with them to help keep up the apartment. As soon as I could, I wanted to get my own place. I couldn't wait to be on my own.

After a few months in the Dreamland, Watty told me he could get me into the Sunset Cafe. Now, that was class. The Sunset was the most popular club on the South Side, farther down on the Thirty-fifth Street strip where most of the good jazz was being played in those days. Right across the street was the Plantation Club, and next to that was The Nest. The Sunset was a real swinger, like the Cotton Club in New York, with beautiful chorus girls, a ten-piece band, comedians, and solo tap danc-ers. Carroll Dickerson had the band in there at first, and then Louis Armstrong joined Dickerson. I was the house singer. That was the first time I met Louis, although I had admired him for years. His singing and playing have always got to me. I could never understand how a man had so many talents. And in addition, he was a person you could talk to. We became friendly the six months we were together in the Sunset. Two years later, Louis got me my first real big job in New York City. Louis was not as well known around Chicago at that time as guys like Dicker-son, the violinist who led his own band and later helped to put together Louis' famous New York City band. That band was breaking it up at Connie's Inn in Harlem in 1929 when I finally got to New York City.

Most of the colored bands around Chicago at that time were playing what they called "Chicago jazz," a mixture of dixieland and swing, with a lot of solos thrown in. Louis's favorite songs at that time were things like "Muskrat Ramble," "Gut-Bucket Blues," "You're Next," and "Oriental Strut." All of the songs he did were full of fire and rhythm, and he was scat singing even then. I suppose that Louis was one of the main influences in my career. Later on I began to scat sing in the Cotton Club with all of that hi-de-hoing. Louis first got me freed up from straight lyrics to try scatting.

Besides Louis there were some other great entertainers and musicians at the Sunset on and off. Mae Alix was probably the best dancer. She had an act where she would tap and ballet and sing for half an hour. At the end of her act, she would dash across the stage and slide into a full split, skidding right up to a ringside table, and the guy would put some money down her dress, and she'd do it again and again, until she had about $20 or $25 per show. She was cleaning up.

It was a treat working with such talent. After a few weeks in the Sunset, I stopped playing drums and just sang. I was doing one of the leading numbers with the great Adelaide Hall. She was a year older than me and could sing her tail off. Later on, in New York, she starred in the Cotton Club's fabulous *Blackbirds* revues of the late twenties and early thirties. Then she joined Duke Ellington's band and went with him to England in 1935. She loved London so much that she settled there, singing in the music halls, and eventually established a nightclub of her own. Adelaide had one of these funky low voices and she used to just growl into the mike sometimes, sexy and bluesy as all get out. She and Ada Brown were the two female leads in the show; the male leads were Jazz Lips Richardson, who got top billing, and Walter Richardson. From time to time, there was also a great team in the show named Brown and McGraw. They were from the old tap-dancing, soft-shoe tradition.

The Sunset Cafe was a fairly large room; it could seat around 250 people and had a large dance floor in the middle. There were murals of dancers and jazz players on the walls and the lights were always down low.

As soon as Watty got me this gig in the Sunset Cafe, things began to happen. For one thing my salary shot up to $65 a week, and within a year I was on the way. Things developed so fast that by the spring of 1929 I was married, I had lots of real money for the first time, and I was leading my own band, The Alabamians, as the house band at the Sunset. What had seemed like a dream when I left Baltimore with *Plantation Days* had suddenly become a reality. I was only twenty-one years old, and I was making it. A combination of talent and good luck put me there.

I got a big break about two months after I went into the Sunset Cafe as part of the revue. Right away I became friendly with Ralph Cooper of the dance team of Rector and Cooper. Ralph was also the master of ceremonies for the show. He was doing a hell of a good job, but he was sometimes a little unreliable. Ralph would just take off for a couple of days and nobody would know where the hell he was. One week, when he missed a few shows, the club's owner, Joe Glaser, asked me to take over as M.C. I jumped at the chance, and Glaser thought I was something else. When my buddy Ralph Cooper came back, he was out of a job. We remained friends, and to this day Ralph and I joke over that. Ralph went on to New York eventually, and became a star in Negro theater of the thirties and forties. He played in most of the great Negro musicals and shows before and after World War II, but at that point, he was out of a job. So there I was, in the spring of 1928, suddenly the master of ceremonies at one of the nicest clubs on the South Side. I stayed in the Sunset Cafe, with that revue, through the rest of 1928. The money was pretty good and I was having a good time. I was also still at Crane College, but just barely.

Ralph Cooper was instrumental in my life in another way: He introduced me to my first wife, Wenonah Conacher. Everybody called her Betty.

Ralph and I were hanging out one night after a show—he was still in the revue at the Sunset from time to time—and he told me he had this fine chick he wanted me to meet. So we went over to this house and he introduced me to Betty. She was about my age, tall and light-skinned and beautiful. She had light hair and light blue eyes and a lovely smile and she was full of fun, always laughing, always happy. Betty and I were alike in a lot of ways. We rarely worried and were always up. Neither of us cared very much about social conventions. She lived her life the way she wanted to and so did I. We both enjoyed having money and living the good life. We had one other thing in common. We immediately had eyes for each other. The three of us went out together that evening and had a good time. Later the same week, I went back to see Betty without Ralph; we started to talk and within a few dates we were real thick together. Before long, I moved in with her. Betty had an apartment on the third floor of a three-story brick frame house on Forrestville Avenue that was owned by a family named Jones. The husband was a taxi driver, but Betty was making enough money to take care of the whole family. She did all the work. The husband drove the cab and the rest of the family worked from time to time, but mainly they lived off what Betty made. When I met her, she was making around $50 a day, or $350 a week. That was a hell of a lot of money in those days. I was making around $125 a week myself in those days, working in the Sunset Cafe, and at various theaters on weekends. That, along with another $200 or so that Betty gave me, made me one rich nigger. I had a new car and clothes and lived the high life of a hustler. Betty didn't have any family in Chicago except her sister and an uncle.

My relationship with Betty was very simple. She enjoyed being with me, she loved the low life, the bars, the cafes, having high times, drinking and hanging out. She loved music and musicians and entertainers. That fast life really turned her on. I was a dashing, handsome, popular, talented M.C. at one of the hippest clubs on the South Side. I took care of her and protected her and made her feel good. And I was attracted to her. Besides that, she had a lot of money and didn't interfere with my career. In fact, her money gave me more leeway to do things. I was able, for example, to continue to support my mother and to pay for saxophone lessons. I began to take sax lessons from one of the famous Brown Brothers. They had a studio in downtown Chicago where they gave lessons during the day; in the evening they played in Chicago nightclubs. There were five of them in a saxophone quintet, and they made some very unusual melodic music—a totally original kind of jazz and blues. I could never have afforded sax lessons if it hadn't been for Betty's money. Or the other things—the car, the clothes, the high life, the gambling. I was having a ball without a worry in the world.

Well, almost without a worry. There was still my family. First of all, when I decided to move in with Betty, Blanche nearly had a fit. She didn't want me to be living there and taking money, even if it did help to take care of Mama. But Blanche couldn't say too much because she and Watty were doing the same thing. I mean, they were living together without being married, and she was living, in part, on the money he made by hustling. So I just reminded her of that, and there wasn't much she could say.

My mother was a different story. Earlier that year, Blanche and I had sent for Mama to bring John and Camilla to live with us in Chicago. Mama was having a rough time with the kids. She never had enough money. She and Papa Jack were divorced and he was having trouble making it. He couldn't give her much support, and it was hard for Mama to work and care for John and Camilla at the same time. So Blanche and I convinced her to come and live with us in Chicago. She moved into the apartment and it was a great reunion, but not long after she arrived I moved in with Betty, and two months later we decided to get married. Mama had been angry when I moved out of Blanche's to live with Betty but she was absolutely furious when we decided to marry. But as usual, she knew that there was nothing she could do. She hadn't been able to control me when I was twelve and there was no way in the world she could control me at the age of twenty-one.

There were other reasons—not Mama's—that I shouldn't have married Betty, but I couldn't see them at the time. I was too young to marry, and I married her for the wrong reasons. I didn't marry Betty for love but for the money and security she brought me. Betty and I divorced twenty years later, after many stormy, unhappy, bitter times. I finally realized that marrying her had been a mistake when I met Nuffie in the 1940s and fell head over heels in love for the first time. It was then I realized what I had been missing all those years I was with Betty.

I suppose that I had to learn about life the hard way—most impetuous, hardheaded people do. On July 26, 1928, we were married. By that time we had moved out of the Joneses' house to live with a woman named Mae Singleton in another house on the South Side. Mae had one fine house, and she did a beautiful business. She had two or three prostitutes living in there. You might think it would bother me to be living in a house run by a madam, but it didn't. It was a damned comfortable life.

In any case, Betty and I were living high and fast. We had lots of money and I figured, "Hell, the sky's the limit for me." And then it seemed that there was no limit at all when I got my big break at the Sunset.

Around the spring of 1929, Marion Hardy brought his band, The Alabamians, into the Sunset Cafe. The Alabamians were a fine, hot, jazzy 11-piece band of Chicago boys. Hardy's group replaced Louis Armstrong when Louis and Carroll Dickerson and their band left Chicago for Connie's Inn in Harlem. Louis and Dickerson had been breaking things up at the Sunset and all over Chicago for several years. Their band had included, at various times, Earl "Father" Hines, Jimmy Noone, Erskine Tate, clarinetist Johnny Dodds and drummer Baby Dodds, trombonist Kid Ory, Louis's wife, Lil Hardin, and a bunch of other great musicians.

When the Alabamians came into the Sunset they were being led by Lawrence Harrison, whose father, Richard B. Harrison, played the role of "De Lawd" in *Green Pastures* on Broadway. Young Harrison led the group and played violin, but he didn't have the drive to really develop the band, or the looseness to make music sound the way it should. They were playing both pop and jazz and some novelty numbers where the leader would sing a lyric and the band would respond, but Harrison just didn't have the fire that the band needed to reach its potential.

During rehearsals, every time Harrison would turn his back I'd jump up on the stage under the pretense of rehearsing as M.C. for a number and I'd make the band move. The sound was so different when I directed the band that it was almost embarrassing. I could bring out the various sections, highlight the soloists, and make the band lively and vital. Even Harrison knew how much better the band sounded, and after a while wouldn't even bother to come up on the stage during rehearsals. He just let me put the group through its paces, and the next thing he knew, he was out of a job. Like a lot of Negro bands during that time, the Alabamians were a cooperative. The band was owned and run by its members, democratically. They split the fees and the income evenly among themselves, and they made decisions about gigs and management jointly. So when these guys saw what a difference it made to have me conducting, they said, "Hell, this guy should be leading the band," and they voted Harrison out and me in. Just like that.

All of a sudden I had a band of my own, and I went stone crazy. I worked with these guys day and night. We rehearsed every day and played every night. I forgot all about school. To hell with school, I said. I had a chance to make it with a band of my own. And I was still emceeing the revue as well. It was a lot of work, but it was easy because it seemed so natural. It was exactly what I wanted to be doing.

I stayed with the Alabamians for a year. We really developed there, at the Sunset Cafe. We had three saxophones, three trumpets, a trombone, a bass fiddle, drums, a guitar, and a piano. The main writer, arranger, and composer was a sax player named Warren Hardy. He was a bitch. We were playing all the old 1920s jazz and pop tunes—"Tiger Rag," "Jazz Me Blues," "Royal Garden Blues," W. C. Handy's "St. Louis Blues," his "Beale Street Blues," and Louis Armstrong's "Gut-Bucket Blues." In addition, we developed a style of novelty arrangement in which the band members all had megaphones, and I would sing a line and they would hold up their megaphones and respond. The crowds loved our jumping, jiving style, and the dance floor at the Sunset was always hopping.

A few months after I took over as leader, Harry Voiler, who had bought the Sunset Cafe from Joe Glaser, decided to change bands. It was the custom in those days in a club like the Sunset to rotate bands regularly for a change of pace. Voiler came over to me one day and told me he was going to make the change. "But, Cab," he said, "I want you to stay at the Sunset to emcee and help handle the new band that's coming in." I thought about it for a minute. I thought about the great time I was having with the Alabamians—the fact is, I had gone nuts behind conducting this band—and I told him, "No, Harry, I'm sorry. The Alabamians are my band. I'm staying with them."

We were about to leave the Sunset to play other clubs in Chicago when Warren Hardy called for a meeting of the band. He told us that the Music Corporation of America was interested in managing us. We were excited as all get out. The Music Corporation of America was the booking agent for many of the major bands at that time. Then Hardy gave us the real news. "And if we go with them, they'll book us on the road for a few months and in September we go to New York City." Man, the guys roared! That was beautiful. There wasn't a jazz musician in the country that didn't dig coming to New York. Everybody cheered and hugged old Hardy and we all went out and got drunk together. We were going to New York!

We'd been hearing for the last few months how Louis Armstrong and Carroll Dickerson were breaking things up at Connie's Inn, about Fletcher Henderson at the Roseland Ballroom, Duke Ellington at the Cotton Club, Charlie Johnson at Small's Paradise, King Oliver's Dixie Syncopators at the Savoy Ballroom, where Chick Webb's combo played during the intermissions, and about the Panamanian composer Luis Russell at the Club Harlem. We all knew about McKinney's Cotton Pickers and Cecil Scott's Bright Boys, and, of course, the fabled New York City music of individual jazzmen like W. C. Handy, Jelly Roll Morton, James P. Johnson, Willie "The Lion" Smith, and Fats Waller. All of these names were more familiar and more respected than white musicians like Paul Whiteman, the so-called King of Jazz. As far as most of us were concerned, he really didn't play jazz despite his famous performance of George Gershwin's *Rhapsody in Blue* in 1924 at Aeolian Hall.

In May of 1929, we left Chicago and went on the road for three months, but all we could think about was our ultimate destination—New York City.

NEW YORK AND
THE COTTON CLUB

Once we were out of Chicago and on the road, we found we had two things going for us. One was the band itself, a nice little jazz and novelty group that could play almost any kind of music the crowd wanted. The second was me. I know it sounds immodest, but that's the truth. I pulled the band together and developed its sound, and then I was so energetic on the stage that I really turned people on. I did a little singing—some blues, dixieland, and ballads—but the most important thing was the way I conducted the band. The Alabamians were modeled, in some ways, on Warren's Pennsylvanians, a major white band in those days.

There had been a guy in Chicago named Benny Meroff who had a heck of a presentation band, as we called novelty bands in those days. Benny would run back and forth across the stage with a megaphone and carry on a kind of call-and-response with the band, directing, singing, hollering, bringing the whole dixieland thing to life. He was something else. I used to say to myself, "Dammit, if I could ever get a decent band, I would out-Benny Benny Meroff." Paul Ash was another white bandleader who I dug. He was at the Oriental Theatre in Chicago. Both guys had something going with their bands; they would really turn the audiences on. Of course they were white pop and novelty bands, and I was oriented towards jazz, but they taught me how to get a band moving and how to stimulate an audience, not so much from a musical aspect as from an entertainment aspect.

Now that I had a band of my own, I took their ideas and began to work with some of them. Bandleading, of course, was to be my career for the next thirty years, until I got into *Porgy and Bess*. The Cab Calloway bands of the thirties and forties were comparable to the bands of Duke Ellington, Jimmie Lunceford, Fletcher Henderson, Earl Hines, or Count Basie in terms of musicianship and popularity, although Lunceford and Henderson were better composers, arrangers, and jazzmen than Doc Cheatham, Foots Thomas, or, finally, Buster Harding, who worked with me. The Cab Calloway bands were known around the country and the world. During the thirties and forties there wasn't a city or town where we played that we didn't break attendance records in nightclubs and theaters. Man, people would line up for blocks and blocks when we were in town. Radio helped, of course, but the Cab Calloway Cotton Club Orchestra, and later just the plain Cab Calloway Band ranked with the greatest in the history of jazz.

I understand kids today falling out behind the Rolling Stones and Stevie Wonder and Marvin Gay and Eric Clapton and Bette Midler. I understand it because in the thirties and forties my band received the same response. People loved us and I loved the response. It was beautiful.

Besides the pleasure of being in the spotlight and being admired, there was, for me, always the beautiful feeling of molding those musicians into a particular sound, a particular feeling.

As I said, we had a lot going for us on the road, but after we had been out for a while it became clear to me that if we were going to make it in New York we would have to change our style. The Alabamians were a fine novelty and dixieland band, and occasionally we would do a straight-up jazz number, but I knew from talking with Blanche and other people who had been to New York that folks in Harlem were the hippest people in the world. You couldn't come into Harlem playing no jive square music; you had to be playing up-to-date real-live jazz or swing, shooting from the hip. And our band wasn't playing like that. We were fine in Chicago and the Midwest, but New York was something else.

We were working our way to New York doing one-nighters around the Midwest, and all we talked about was making it to New York, where we were booked for November in the Savoy Ballroom, one of the

"The Cab Calloway bands were known around the country and the world."

hippest clubs in Harlem. Out of Chicago, we played first in Mendota, Illinois, in a small, dark club where the people jammed the dance floor and sang with the band during the novelty numbers. Next we headed for a little club in Springfield, Illinois, that had a gambling room in the back. At that time there was gambling run by the rackets all over the Midwest. We spent two months in Kansas City playing at El Tarion Ballroom—mainly white, but occasionally we'd play in a black club after hours. In September we played the Luna Pier in Toledo, did some one-nighters through Ohio, and then went into Pittsburgh for a few days. When we left Pittsburgh, we were headed for New York and the Savoy in Harlem.

During the summer we had traveled in cars, and some of the guys took their wives along. Betty, of course, was with me. We were an eleven-piece band and made quite a caravan, going from town to town like that.

I never will forget coming into New York City. I had never been there before, nor had Betty, though a few of the musicians had. On the road we had all listened to their stories about how hip New York was and how big and jazzed up the nightclubs were. By the time we got to New Jersey, I was a bundle of nerves. We drove up through New Jersey to Fort Lee, where we had to wait for the ferry to get across the Hudson River. The George Washington Bridge hadn't been built yet. I never will forget standing there in the late afternoon. We could see big, bad old New York across the river. Of course there wasn't as many skyscrapers as there are now, but we could see the enormity of the city. I was scared to death and excited as hell. We all stood there, five or six carloads of people, waiting for the ferry, with that wide, beautiful Hudson River all that separated us from New York. Finally the ferry came, and we got on and made that long, slow trip across the river to 125th Street. We drove around Harlem for a while, awestruck by the whole scene. I had never seen so many Negroes in one place before in my life. Finally we started to break up. Various guys in the band had made arrangements to rent rooms with families, and the guys went their separate ways. Betty and I dropped off the musicians who were traveling with us and then drove up Seventh Avenue, the glamour street of Harlem in those days. It was beautiful. Just beautiful. People out in the streets, and nightclubs all over, nightclubs whose names were legendary to me. Then we drove to 139th Street, where we had rented a room with Flet-

"*Besides the pleasure of being in the spotlight and being admired, there was, for me, always the beautiful feeling of molding those musicians into a particular sound, a particular feeling.*"

cher Henderson. One hundred and thirty-ninth Street running from Lenox Avenue across Seventh to Eighth Avenue was called Strivers' Row then because it was the most beautifully kept up block in Harlem. The people who lived there—maids and butlers and postal clerks and cab drivers and mechanics—had saved their pennies all their lives to buy a house. Fletcher's house, between Seventh and Eighth avenues, was three stories and nicely furnished with soft old couches and rocking chairs and lace doilies and fine, flowered wallpaper.

The place was so lovely Betty and I nearly flipped. We had a room on the third floor. Several other musicians and entertainers also rented rooms there. Usually Lee, Fletcher's wife, would cook dinner and the whole "family" would eat together before we went our separate ways to our gigs. That included Lee, because Mrs. Henderson was a fine trumpet player in the pit orchestra at the Lafayette Theatre.

I was damned impressed by Fletcher. He was around thirty years old, a handsome, thin, fair-skinned man with a mustache. He had been born in Georgia, attended Atlanta University, and then came to New York in the early 1920s. He said he had come to do graduate work, but some of us suspected he really came to play jazz. He joined up with W. C. Handy, and before anyone knew it he was leading his own band at the Club Alabam. By the time I came to New York, he was at the famous Roseland in midtown Manhattan, playing a style of music that was strictly his and that later came to be known as "swing." Years later, of course, Fletcher joined up with Benny Goodman and wrote and arranged many of Benny's hit tunes.

Fletcher's band at Roseland was something else. His lineup included himself on piano, Coleman Hawkins on clarinet and tenor sax, Bob Escudero on tuba, Buster Bailey on clarinet and alto, Benny Carter on alto and soprano sax and clarinet, Kaiser Marshall on drums, Russell Smith, Elmer Chambers, and Joe Smith on trumpet, and Charlie Dixon on banjo and guitar. It was a hell of an outfit. When I arrived in New York the first thing I did was go down to Roseland with Fletcher to hear what kind of music he was playing. Then I went over to Connie's Inn to see my old buddy Louis Armstrong, who was the star of Carroll Dickerson's big orchestra and was also featured with Leroy Smith's band in the revue *Connie's Hot Chocolates* playing down at the Hudson Theatre on Broadway. It was in that show that Satchmo introduced "Ain't Misbehavin' "—his first big hit. Thanks to Louis I later joined the show.

As I made the rounds of New York jazz clubs and variety shows, I began to realize that my little band was in for trouble. We had come out of the Midwest playing old-time, unhip, novelty tunes with a little weak dixieland jazz. Compared to the jumping jazz they were playing in New York, we were strictly from the sticks. I had seen the problem coming and I had argued with the guys all summer. I tried to get them to loosen up, to expand their repertoire, to include some straight-up jazz and swing numbers, but they fought me all the way. We had some pretty strong arguments about it, but it was a corporate band and I was outnumbered. We didn't change, and it was a disastrous mistake.

About a week after we hit New York, we opened at the Savoy Ballroom on Lenox Avenue near 140th Street in Harlem. Now, the Savoy Ballroom was strictly big-time. There were always two bands alternating sets of twenty minutes each, and the crowds were used to bands like King Oliver and Chick Webb, the drummer who had influenced me in Baltimore. It was in 1934 at the Savoy that Chick first played "Stomping at the Savoy," written for him by Edgar Sampson, and it was there that Chick created what came to be known as the "Savoy tempo," a semi-quick, two-four rhythm good for dancing. Dancing was the main activity at the Savoy. The place could hold hundreds of people and the dance floor was huge. The crowds were 90 per cent colored at the Savoy.

We opened at the Savoy in November 1929, barely a month after the crash. By the end of the year, investors had lost $40 billion and more than 6 million people were out of work, 5,000 banks had failed, and 32,000 businesses were bankrupt. There were breadlines everywhere and near-riots in New York. Everybody was angry with poor old Herbert Hoover. Everybody except people in the entertainment world, I guess. It's a funny thing, when things get really bad, when the bottom falls out of the economy, that's when people really need entertainment. It's just as true today as it was in 1929. During the great depression of 1974–1975, when 8 million people were out of work, the entertainment business was booming. The movie industry was making a mint, Broadway was having its best season in years, the record industry was cleaning up, and the number of concerts increased. I suppose that people figure, what the hell, let's go out and have a ball. It's one way to get away from the gloom.

That's the way it was in 1929. Jazz was swinging, the theaters on Broadway were cleaning up, and in Harlem the nightclubs, speakeasies, and jazz spots were packed every night. Everybody was making it. Everybody, that is, except the Alabamians.

We went into the Savoy opposite Cecil Scott and his band. Cecil, a saxophonist, and his brother Lloyd had brought their band to New York from Springfield, Ohio, in 1926. By 1929 Cecil had developed his own style and was running the band himself. He was a bitch; those guys played gut-bucket-stomping, gutsy New York jazz. Cecil was one of the most exciting and fiery horn blowers in Harlem.

I'll tell you the truth now. If you were to ask me to name the musicians I worked with in the Alabamians I would be hard-pressed to do it. It was a nice little band, but when I got to New York and dug what some of those bands were playing, well, there was no comparison. Compared to Cecil Scott's group, the Alabamians had no real musicians among them; they were amateurs. But the few that I remember are Eddie McKendrick on drums; Fats Turner on bass; Warner Seals and Marion Hardy on sax; and Eddie Mallory on trumpet. Playing with Cecil at that time were guys like Dicky Wells, the trombonist, who later played with Count Basie and Fletcher Henderson; trumpeters Frankie Newton and Bill Coleman; pianist Don Frye; saxophonists Harold McFerran and John Williams; and Lloyd, Cecil's older brother, who was still with the band. They were all top-caliber musicians.

In addition to playing up a storm, Cecil and his band would put on a hell of a show. Old Cecil would get to honking and march down off the bandstand and half the band would follow him, winding through the crowds on the dance floor just blowin' away. Man, the people would go crazy behind that, jumping and dancing and carrying on all over the place.

After Cecil and his band finished their first set, we came out. Man, we looked like a million dollars. The guys were eleven pieces of pure gold, dressed sharp as a tack—black Prince Albert coats and straight trousers, ascots, and black Oxford shoes spit-shined so you could see your reflection in them. Then I jumped out cool as an ice cube in a white tuxedo with a white baton. And of course the Savoy was such a pretty club, lights and colors all around. Man, we were beautiful—until we hit our first lick. Brother, when we started playing that dipsy-doodle music from the Midwest—"Come Up and See Me Sometime" or "Are You Home, Josephine," or "Bye, Bye, Blues"—the damned dance floor cleaned out. You could feel the place go cold. Cecil had damn near set it on fire and we just cooled it off. We were an absolute flop, bust, zero, nothing. Our music didn't suit those jazzed-up people worth a damn.

We got our notice that first night. Charlie Buchanan, one great tough guy who later became one of my best friends, was managing the place. He came up to us after the show, scowled, and said, "I'm sorry, fellas, but you had your chance. You've got to go." We had a two-week contract and on the first night we got our two-week notice.

I was furious with the guys in the band. "Dammit," I hollered, "I tried to tell you this jive music wouldn't make it in New York City. This ain't Toledo or Mendota, this is New York. You've got to come into New York swinging! I'll stay with you through the end of this gig, but after that, I'm splitting. You all can go back to Chicago or wherever you want, but that's it for me." They were all angry and upset, too, but there was nothing they could do. I wanted to make it in New York and I knew that those guys didn't have the stuff to get over. It was time for me to split.

The Savoy didn't know quite what to do. They had a two-week contract with a weak band and no way out. Then Charlie Buchanan whipped up a Battle of the Bands for our last performance and crowds started coming in, in anticipation of the great war that was to take place between the Alabamians and the Savoy's house band, the Missourians.

The Missourians had quite a band. They couldn't compare to Chick Webb or King Oliver, to Duke Ellington or Jimmie Lunceford, but they were a hell of a lot better than the Alabamians. And on our last night in the gig, the place was packed. The idea was that each band would play a couple of sets, trying to blow the other band away, and the audience would clap and cheer to decide which had won.

The Missourians ran us off the damned bandstand. We had tried during rehearsals to add a little swing to our sound, but it hadn't worked. We were blown away. The audience hollered for the Missourians. After we played, there wasn't a sound. Then the M.C. asked the audience which bandleader they preferred. I was holding my breath. I knew I had developed a style, and was known in the Savoy as quite a character. I would run across the stage, directing the band, singing along with it into my megaphone, leading the guys in call and response, and the audience loved it. Now, when the M.C. pointed to me, the audience stamped and screamed and whistled. I knew I had won and it felt great. But it didn't help my situation. The Alabamians left town and I was stuck without a job like millions of other guys across the country. I had enough money to get along—for a while—but I damned sure needed some work soon.

I was too young to know it at the time, but I learned an important lesson from that experience. Never make so many compromises that you end up doing somebody else's thing and not your own. I was too anxious to keep the band. I disagreed with the kind of music that the Alabamians went into New York with, but I said to myself, "Well, hell, they're not the best thing around, but they're the best I've got right now." I was young and looking for a start, so the only thing I could do at the time was swallow my pride—and my judgment—and stay with them. It may have been a mistake, but I learned from it. Since then I've rarely made compromises of that sort. When I've strongly disagreed with the format of a show, or the music a band was playing, or the way something was being handled, I've gotten out.

I've walked out of many a show because I didn't like the way things were being done. I walked out of *Pajama Game* when it was revived on Broadway a couple of years ago because the people who were producing it were stingy and shortsighted; I returned to the show only after some changes were made. In the spring of 1975, I was invited out to the West Coast to appear in a television special about the Cotton Club with Ray Charles and the Nicholas Brothers. I was pretty excited about doing it, but when I got out there I found that the whole thing was wrong. The people hadn't done their homework; they didn't know the first thing about jazz and swing of the twenties and thirties. They were trying to do a jazzed-up modern version of the old Cotton Club days. As I stood around waiting for my number to come up I watched how the show was put together, and I told them, "This is a phony, an insult to the Cotton Club and all the folks of the twenties and thirties who *knew* how to put on a revue." And I walked. To hell with that.

I've made compromises in my life, plenty of them. Any person who is successful makes compromises, but when I reach the point where the thing I'm doing has no integrity for me personally, then I say, "Screw it. Let someone else do it." The experience at the Savoy taught me that lesson.

When I realized that the Alabamians wouldn't make it, I began bugging Fletcher Henderson to let me do a few blues numbers with his band at Roseland, but he couldn't see it. A couple of weeks after we closed at the Savoy, I went to see Louis Armstrong. I wanted Louis to work out a spot for me at Connie's Inn, while he was making it back from *Connie's Hot Chocolates* at the Hudson Theatre. "Maybe I can do a little jazz, a little singing or something up here, to help warm up the crowd while you're on your way back from the Hudson," I told Louis.

"I don't think I can do that," Louis said. "The show at Connie's Inn is all set." I never will forget his words, because the next words out of his mouth were, "But, doggone, they need a singer for *Hot Chocolates*."

Now, when I say *Connie's Hot Chocolates* was a big hit, I mean it was the biggest, one of the biggest on Broadway that year. It had been running at the Hudson Theatre for nearly a year. Paul Bass, the juvenile lead that I was supposed to replace, was singing "Ain't Misbehavin'," "Sweet Savannah Sue," "Goddess of Rain," and "Rhythm Man"—all hit tunes. So Louis went down and talked to Connie Imerman and I got an audition—and the gig.

Jesus, was I happy! *Plantation Days* had been small potatoes compared with this. All of a sudden, I'm making $100 a week and hitting the Broadway boards. And I was a hit. Paul Bass had done a pretty good job with those numbers, but I really pulled the music out of them. Fats Waller was the pianist and songwriter for *Hot Chocolates,* so you know the caliber of music I'm talking about. The substitute pianist was a man who has since come to be one of my best friends. Benny Payne played with the Cab Calloway orchestras until 1948, and since that time he has been the pianist with singer Billy Daniels. The show needed a substitute pianist because Fats Waller was in his cups so often they were never sure he'd make it.

About a month after I joined *Hot Chocolates,* the show went on the road. Our first stop was Philadelphia, and then we went on to Boston, where we played the Tremont Theatre.

Hot Chocolates had one of the finest chorus lines you would ever want to see. Those girls were not only beautiful, but talented as well. The comedians Eddie Green and Johnny Hudgins were in the show, too. They had a famous courtroom scene invented years before; "Here comes the judge" was the famous line in it. People think that's a new line. It was being done by black comedians so many years ago that it isn't even funny. The singers in *Hot Chocolates* included Edith Wilson, Margaret Simms, and Jazz Lips Richardson, who I had known in Chicago. And the band was a hellfire one. Besides Louis and Fats Waller, there was Zutty Singleton on drums. Zutty was the best man after Chick Webb for getting the most rhythm and movement out of his bass drum. There was also Bubber Miley, who few people have ever heard of but who was undoubtedly one of the great jazz trumpeters—the way he could make that instrument growl on one end and handle a mute on the other. They used to say that Bubber was the first trumpeter to use the rubber plunger mute. He played at various times with King Oliver, Duke Ellington, and Noble Sissle. The *Hot Chocolates* band also featured Mancy Cara on banjo, a tight little player who stuck with Louis Armstrong and Carroll Dickerson while they were in New York, then sort of disappeared from the scene, and Jimmy Strong, a clarinetist and tenor-sax player who had played with Dickerson's band in Chicago. The show band was actually run by Russell Wooding, the arranger and bandleader. Since most of the guys were doubling in other gigs around town, a lot of them decided to stay in New York when we went on the road. Louis Armstrong and Fats Waller didn't travel with us.

In Boston, Benny Payne and I roomed together at Miss Hardy's house, where a lot of traveling musicians and entertainers stayed. Strange as it may seem, I was still a little disappointed about the Alabamians. *Hot Chocolates* was a big show, and I had the juvenile lead which was giving me lots of exposure, but I still wanted to have my own band. Benny and I became very close in Boston, and I used to say to him, "Listen, man. One of these days I'm going to have a band of my own again, and you're going to be my pianist. I promise you that right here and now." Benny thought I was kidding. A few years later, of course, Benny was my pianist in the Cotton Club; but I'm getting ahead of the story now.

Hot Chocolates was a big hit in Boston. Every night after the show, Benny and I would walk through those freezing Boston streets to the Railroad Club, an after-hours speakeasy where he would play piano and I would sing and we'd pick up a few more pennies jamming until around four in the morning. The Railroad Club was typical of a lot of the speakies around the country in those days. It was a dark little place in the basement of somebody's house, the kind of place where you had to know the secret knock to get in and that was always being raided by the feds.

While I was in Boston, Charlie Buchanan came up from New York

"Hot Chocolates *had one of the finest chorus lines you would ever want to see. Those girls were not only beautiful, but talented as well.*" Frank Driggs Collection.

and asked me to leave the show and come back to the Savoy to lead the Missourians. Charlie figured that since the Missourians, as a band, had won the Battle of the Bands, and since I, as the bandleader, had won against the Missourians' leader, Lockwood Lewis, the best combination would be me leading the Missourians. At first I said no. I was enjoying *Hot Chocolates*. I was playing the juvenile and I had learned all the other routines, including the comedy routines, so whenever someone was out sick, I played that part. It was really a gas. Also, I never liked the idea of breaking a commitment. I had made a commitment to the show, Louis Armstrong had put himself out to get me the audition, and I didn't think I should leave the troupe after such a short time.

Then we learned that *Connie's Hot Chocolates* would close soon. I was free to go back to New York, and I wrote Charlie Buchanan that I wanted to come into the Savoy with the Missourians. At this point I ran into my first agent. I'd had a little contact with the Music Corporation of America, but that was part of a package deal for the whole Alabamian band. When I returned to New York, I signed a contract with Moe Gale. Moe was a very bright little guy, and very knowledgeable about the music and entertainment business. We liked each other. Hell, I was just a kid, in my early twenties, what did I know. Somebody says he wants to sign a contract with me that will guarantee me a certain amount for the next ten years and I go for it. So I signed this great contract with Moe Gale. The contract was for $100 a week for ten years. Jesus, was I gullible! To me at that time that was all the money in the world. But Moe Gale knew exactly how much money it was—a lot less than I'd be worth in a couple of years. He knew I had talent and drive and that I'd make it. Hell, within a year after I signed, I was making $500 a week. If I had stuck with that lousy contract with Moe, I would have taken home $100 of that $500 and he would have taken home the rest. But that was all in the future. In the spring of 1930, with that contract in my pocket, I was set to go into the Savoy leading the Missourians.

The Missourians were a hell of a step up from the Alabamians. I never compared what I was doing with the great bands of the day, Duke or Jimmie Lunceford or Fletcher Henderson, but I knew that I was getting better all the time. I was on the way up and nothing was going to stop me.

Like the Alabamians, the Missourians were a corporate band. The guys all made decisions together. As with most bands of that time, the

"While I was in Boston, Charlie Buchanan came up from New York and asked me to leave the show and come back to the Savoy to lead the Missourians." Frank Driggs Collection.

personnel of the Missourians was constantly changing. The band was originally from Kansas City and they played a kind of smooth swing, with lots of high-register trumpets and a dixieland up-tempo rhythm. Kansas City was, of course, one of the main jazz cities. Coming up from New Orleans, the riverboats just as often turned west up the Missouri River to Kansas City as they went northeast up the Mississippi toward Chicago. A heavy black population in Kansas City supported several profitable, jumping jazz clubs. I had stopped in K.C. with the Alabamians before we came into New York, and I knew it was a good town for jazz.

In Kansas City, the Missourians had been heavily influenced by Bennie Moten. Bennie Moten was a native of Kansas City, and one of the best, and least recognized, pianists and composers of the 1920s and early thirties. To give you an idea of the kind of talent he attracted to his bands, dig this lineup from the band that Bennie had in K.C. In 1928 his brother, Buster, was playing accordion, Jimmy Rushing was his vocalist, Hot Lips Page and Joe Keyes were in the trumpet section, Ben Webster, Eddie Barefield, Jack Washington, and Harlan Leonard were playing the saxes, the bassist was Walter Page, and the trombonists were Dan Minor and Eddie Durham. And the second pianist was Count Basie. An offshoot of that band became Count's first big band in 1935 when Moten died. Bennie had an enormous effect on many, many fine musicians who came up through Kansas City, and you could hear old Bennie's trumpety, swinging sound in the Missourians.

One of the Kansas City bands heavily influenced by Bennie Moten's swinging style was formed in 1920 by a saxophonist named Dave Lewis. His band played for mainly white dances around the city. Two of the main people in that band were De Priest Wheeler, a trombonist, and a drummer named Leroy Maxey. They stayed together as the Missourians with different combinations of musicians through the midtwenties. They left Kansas City in 1926 with a ten-piece band and headed for New York. Within a short time, the Missourians had become the house band at the Savoy, where I ran into them in the Battle of the Bands. The principal personnel in 1929, in addition to bandleader Lockwood Lewis, were Wheeler and Maxey, Andy Brown on tenor sax, and R. Q. Dickerson and Lammar Wright on trumpet. Lammar had been playing with Bennie Moten's band back in 1925 before he joined up with the Missourians about the time they came to New York. Lammar stayed with me for seventeen years, and since he left my band in 1945 he has played with the bands of Don Redman, Louis Armstrong, Cootie Williams, Sy Oliver, and others. Finally, the guitar player for the Missourians at that time was Morris White, who in later years was replaced by Danny Barker.

These are not famous jazzmen. You won't find many of their names in any of the big glossaries on jazz or listed among the names of the great musicians. They were just good, solid players who carried early Kansas City Swing the way Bennie Moten used to play it to New York City and did well. Solid steady rhythms, good clear musicianship, clean lines and strong melodies. You hear about the Duke Ellingtons and the Louis Armstrongs, the Jimmie Luncefords and the Fletcher Hendersons, but people sometimes forget that jazz was built not only in the minds of the great ones but on the backs of the ordinary ones—ordinary musicians from down South who carried the music to the corners of the country, to little speakeasies in little towns where they played honkytonk music for $5 a night. Or less. Sometimes they played for drinks, and the sheer love of it.

That's the way a lot of us started out—including me. I was reading an issue of the *New Yorker* magazine recently which someone had given me because of an article on a white pianist named Jess Stacy. I remember Jess Stacy from Chicago. He played around there and he played well. He patterned his play after Teddy Wilson, the Negro jazz pianist. In this article Stacy was recalling the way he and Muggsy Spanier and other white musicians used to come into the Sunset Cafe on Chicago's South Side. Carroll Dickerson's band was in there at the time, and in this article Stacy said, "I'd go in there with Spanier and we'd stay until five or six in the morning, even though it would take us hours to get home. I was sitting there one night digging [Earl] Hines, who had an influence on me, when Jelly Roll Morton tapped me on the shoulder and looked over at Hines and said, 'That boy can't play piano.' Cab Calloway used to go around and sing at the tables, and we'd chase him away when he tried to drink our gin."

Stacy is right. Before I went into the Sunset as a regular, when I first got to Chicago, I used to hang out in the Sunset and in other clubs on the South Side, singing tunes between sets at the tables and hustling up coins and drinks. A lot of us lived that way. Singers, pianists, drummers, horn players, guitarists—we all hustled around the clubs for a drink when we were up against it. That was the way jazz spread in America, not through the big concert halls, not through the big fancy clubs like the Cotton Club and Connie's Inn, but through small cafes and gambling houses and speakeasies, where we could hustle up a drink in exchange for a little of our souls.

The Missourians were like that. Before they finally got themselves together in Kansas City, nearly all of them had hustled their way up through the speakeasies and clubs and gambling houses. That was the group I took over at the Savoy in March 1930.

When I returned to New York, I found that instead of going straight into the Savoy with the Missourians, we were scheduled to open up a beautiful, new club in Harlem called The Plantation Club. The Plantation was on 126th Street near Lenox Avenue. It was being set up to compete with the Cotton Club, which was located a little farther uptown at 142nd Street and Lenox.

The Plantation was a fine, fine place. It would hold about 500 people, the same as the Cotton Club. It was made up like an old southern plantation, with slaves' log cabins and so forth, just like the Cotton Club. The show was to be a big revue. Man, the Plantation Club was going to be something.

There was a tremendous amount of advertising and publicity, and if the place caught on the way it was expected to, it would mean real trouble for the Cotton Club, which was the most popular club in Harlem among whites. Except for celebrities, who could have their own table occasionally, blacks were not allowed as patrons in the Cotton Club.

The Plantation Club was ready. I was ready. And the band was ready. We had our last rehearsal in the club the afternoon before the show was to open. Then we left the music on the bandstands and all went our separate ways to get some rest for the evening.

That evening, Betty and I had supper at Fletcher's and I got dressed to come down to the Plantation Club. Betty rarely went to the shows with me. I got into my old Studebaker and drove down Lenox Avenue. As I approached the corner of 126th Street and Lenox, where the club was located, I noticed there was a lot of commotion out on the street. Firetrucks were there, and police cars and a huge crowd. I parked the car a couple of blocks away and pushed my way through the crowds. As I broke through, I saw strewn all over the sidewalk, cracked and broken and shattered, the Plantation Club's lovely bar. All the windows of the club had been broken, and pieces of half the tables and chairs were on the sidewalk and in the street. My heart sank, because as soon as I saw the wreckage I knew what had happened. I pushed my way inside and it was an absolute shambles. There had been mirrors on all the walls, but now they were smashed to smithereens. Somebody had taken an axe to the tables and chairs. The hanging chandeliers had been pulled down and smashed. The place, of course, like many of the Harlem clubs, was owned by one of the underworld gangs. Some of the men in the Missourians were there, and Jesus, were they disappointed. But I don't think anyone was more disappointed than me.

What had happened was simple. In typical gangland style, the owners of the Cotton Club had made sure that they wouldn't have the Plantation Club for competition after all. And they were successful. The club never opened.

Surprisingly our music was still intact beneath the rubble. Maybe the boys they sent in liked jazz; at least they hadn't torn up our music.

If there had been any doubt in the minds of the Harlemites as to who owned the Cotton Club, it was clear after the episode. There was only one man in all of New York who would dare pull something like that— Owney Madden, the kingpin of the New York City mobs. A couple of weeks later the cops found the body of Harry Block, one of Madden's close associates, riddled with bullets in the elevator of his apartment building in Manhattan. Just about everybody knew it was in retaliation for the job Owney and his boys had done on the Plantation Club.

We all figured that the other owners of the Cotton, along with Owney Madden and Harry Block, were bad old George DeMange, one of the toughest guys around, who everybody knew as "Big Frenchy," and a guy I knew as Little Angelo. Together they owned the Cereal Beverages Corporation, a beer-producing plant down on West Twenty-sixth Street in Manhattan, through which they supplied the nightclubs. It was also widely believed, but never proved, of course, that this group was responsible for the illegal booze that came into the United States from Canada, down the Hudson River to be dropped off at 142nd Street. But more about the gang and the Cotton Club later. That day, at the Plantation Club, I couldn't think about the mob. All I could think about was my big debut—which hadn't come off.

Moe Gale, Charlie Buchanan, and I sat down and talked it over, and they decided to put us back into the Savoy a couple of nights a week off and on. Then they started booking us around in little clubs. It was a bad time for me, worse than when the Alabamians flopped at the Savoy. That time the band had struck out, but I hadn't. This time I had been flying high with a good band behind me ready for the big break at the Plantation Club, and dammit, there I was back on the streets again. I began to wonder whether I'd ever make it. We were playing at small clubs, and I do mean small, tiny after-hours places, and then we finally got a regular gig at a little nightclub down on the Lower East Side of Manhattan, at the corner of Second Avenue and Second Street. I forget the name of the joint, or maybe it didn't have a name. It was a small neighborhood club with a small bandstand and bootleg liquor being sold under the table, over the table, and everywhere else. We were a big hit down there; the joint was packed every night and the guys in the band began to feel a little better.

We played there for about a month. The band was beginning to depend on me to make their contacts and handle their business. That was a change for those guys. As a cooperative band they had always made joint decisions. But I found that I enjoyed handling the responsibilities. And it put me in a position to influence the music and the style of the band more by working with the nightclub manager or with Gale to set the sequence of the numbers and get the music sounding the way I thought it should sound.

My idea about music is that it should always be exciting and stimulating. That doesn't mean it must always be hot or up-tempo. Blues should be real blues and a ballad should be a real ballad with all the feeling and mood possible. Music should also change with the times, though not with any fad that comes along but with taste. But it should keep up with the pace and feeling of life. The problem with the Alabamians was that they were playing music that was a generation too old and from the wrong part of the country. The Missourians were closer to what was going on in New York, but they still needed to work at keeping up with the times. That was exactly what I tried to get them to do: to know what was happening musically around New York and to stay hip with it.

It wasn't easy. Some of the guys in the band resented me, a newcomer, telling them what to do. They had been together, some of them, for nearly ten years, since their Kansas City days. They had gone through the hard times and good times together. Bit by bit I was taking things over, and every now and then I'd sense their resentment.

Through the spring of 1930, while we were playing on the Lower East Side and around at a few other clubs, I was still hustling on the side. That never changed, probably never will. I was only making around $125 a week with the Missourians. In Chicago Betty and I had lived on $325 a week and it was much cheaper to live there than in New York. When we got to New York she stopped working and I was the breadwinner. It was rough. We had some savings, but I had to hustle on the side to keep things together. Every night after we finished on the Lower East Side I made it back uptown and hustled around the Lafayette or the Rhythm Club to make some extra change, or sometimes some of the guys and I would go into the speakeasies and play and sing after hours to make extra bread.

After about two months, Moe Gale booked us into a club called the Crazy Cat at the corner of Forty-eighth Street and Broadway. Man, we were back in the mainstream again. It wasn't a big club, but it catered to the Broadway after-hours clientele, mainly white. We were the house band for dancing and a variety show. The place had a beautiful decor, and the bandstand was plenty large enough, quite a change from the tiny one on the Lower East Side. But most important, the Crazy Cat was a place where musicians and actors and actresses from the legitimate theater came after hours. And best of all, every night at eleven o'clock we broadcast a half-hour radio show live to the New York City area.

With celebrities coming in and our show going out live over radio, we began to attract a following. We weren't in there a week before the club was full every night and we were getting stacks of mail: People from all over the region were writing in, and we would sit around after the show or rehearsals and I would read the letters. The guys were astounded. A little band in a little club had become big overnight.

You have to understand the kind of band we were and the kind of show we were putting on. I had a pretty good tenor voice, so a lot of what we did was behind my singing. And I had a lot of energy: I was all over that stage, up and down, leading the band and creating excitement. The dance floor was jammed every night.

I was always a stern disciplinarian with my bands, and the Missourians were no exception. If our first set opened at 8:00, then by golly at 7:45 the band was there ready to play. Anyone who showed up late was fined. And since I'd been taking a stronger hand in planning the music and the show the Missourians had a pretty nice little repertoire worked up. We opened up swinging, right from the start, with a popular tune like "Struttin' with Some Barbecue" or "Carolina Shout" or "Muskrat Ramble." I'd be up front with a megaphone and a baton and I'd holler, "Are you all reet?" and the band would holler back, "Yes, we're all reet!" And I'd holler, "Are you all root?" And the band would holler, "Yes, we're all root!" Then I'd holler, "Well let's hit it and git it like we always do—one and two and three and four. . . ." And the band would swing into a number, and I'd be up front conducting and moving back and forth and the band would be swinging and the dance floor jumping and people jitterbugging and swinging. It was some show.

We weren't in there but a couple of weeks, though, when a peculiar thing happened. One night after our last show the headwaiter came over to me and said, "Cab, there's some guys here who want to talk to you."

"Who the hell are they?" I asked. "I'm beat, and I don't want to see no one."

"You better see them, Cab."

So I walked across the room to a table in the corner. The club was empty by then and four guys were sitting there with their coats and hats on. I could tell from the look of them that they were from the mob. Wide-brimmed hats, long cloth coats, one of them had on shades: They were all white guys. I tried to be cool, but inside I was scared to death. "What the hell do these guys want with me?" I wondered. "What have I done now?"

One of the guys said, "Sit down."

I sat down.

"Who's booking you?" one of them asked.

"Moe Gale."

"Yeah? Well you tell Moe Gale that we want you and your band to come into the Cotton Club."

"You gotta be kidding," I said. "Man, you must be joking." And I really did think it was some sort of a gag. The Cotton Club was *the* place to be in New York City.

"We ain't kidding, Calloway," one of them said. "We want you in the Cotton Club."

"But Duke's in there."

"He's going on the road to make a film and do a tour. We need a replacement and we want you. Be up at the club tomorrow afternoon to rehearse the show."

"But I can't leave this. I've got a contract. The whole band's under contract. You got to talk to Moe Gale about it. This is his operation. I can't. . . ."

The guys stood up. I stood up. Jesus, they were rough-looking dudes. The one who had done all the talking said, "We'll talk to Moe Gale. Just you and your band be up at the Cotton Club at two tomorrow afternoon to rehearse the show. That's all you got to worry about." Then they walked past me and left. So I went up to my dressing room to think it over. I didn't know what the hell to do, but I figured I'd better talk to Moe before I said anything to the guys in the band. Then the door opened and Moe came in. I knew from the look on his face that they had already talked to him. Moe had a very expressive face. Most of the time you could tell exactly what he was thinking before he'd even say a word.

"Cab," he said. "The Cotton Club boys talk to you?"

"Yeah."

"I guess you better tell the other men to be up at the Cotton Club tomorrow afternoon."

I'd never seen Moe Gale look so bad. And I'd never felt so good. I didn't ask him any questions. I knew better. The Cotton Club mob had just bought out my contract and the Missourians' contract the easy way. Pure muscle. I can imagine them telling him, "Don't give us any trouble about this, Moe." And coming from them that would mean, "If you give us any trouble you'll find yourself at the bottom of the East River with cement blocks tied to your ankles." And the mob didn't play games. They were for real. I later found out, however, that they hadn't cut Moe out entirely. Out of the goodness of their hearts, they had let him keep 10 per cent of the contract at the Cotton Club—until the following week, when they found out that Mole Gale had me under a personal contract for $100 a week for ten years. They said to hell with that, tore up the contract, and gave me a raise to $200.

I was nervous as hell that night. I went around and got word to the guys in the band. They were jubilant—laughing and shouting and clapping their hands. When I got home and told Betty she hollered too. We both knew what it could mean: record contracts, network radio, publicity, national tours. We were a couple of kids, a hustler from Baltimore who had struggled every day of his life, it seemed, and a once-poor girl from Chicago who had certainly gone through the hardest kind of times, and here we were, on the brink of something so big we could barely imagine what it might mean.

We told Fletcher and Lee, and they were so damned happy for us we had a big celebration at the house that night. It was beautiful.

The next day the band and I met at the Cotton Club. I'd been there a couple of times before, standing in the rear or in the wings watching Duke Ellington and his fabulous band and Leitha Hill and Aïda Ward and the chorus line and the Step Brothers make the place rock. The first show I saw there was *Blackbirds of 1929*. It was a great variety show and revue, which included singer Cora La Redd, a quartet called The Washboard Band, dancer Henri Wessels, Wills, Mordecai and Taylor, Ethel Waters, and George Dewey Washington.

I had seen some elaborate shows in Chicago, but nothing to compare with a Cotton Club revue. A large part of it was the club itself. It was a huge room. The bandstand was a replica of a southern mansion, with large white columns and a backdrop painted with weeping willows and slave quarters. The band played on the veranda of the mansion, and in front of the veranda, down a few steps, was the dance floor, which was also used for the shows. The waiters were dressed in red tuxedos, like butlers in a southern mansion, and the tables were covered with red-and-white-checked gingham tablecloths. There were huge cut-crystal chandeliers, and the whole set was like the sleepy-time-down-South during slavery. Even the name, Cotton Club, was supposed to convey the southern feeling. I suppose the idea was to make whites who came to the club feel like they were being catered to and entertained by black slaves.

The sets and costumes were stunning and elaborate, like operatic settings almost. The chorus girls changed costumes for every number, and the soloists, dancers, and singers were always dressed to the hilt—the women in long flowing gowns, if that was appropriate, or in the briefest of brief dance costumes. Talk about the String—these chicks wore less than that. Low cut and very, very risqué, if you know what I mean.

Sunday night was Celebrity Night at the Cotton Club, and everybody who was anybody in New York City came out, especially when Sunday

*"I had seen some elaborate shows in Chicago, but nothing to compare with a
Cotton Club revue."* Frank Driggs Collection.

was an opening night. The club ran two revues a year; one opened in September and the other in April. There was usually a month's break in March to prepare for the spring show and a month's break in August to prepare for the fall show. Opening night for either of the shows was bigger by far than a premiere on Broadway these days. Only the tops of the tops in terms of names or influence could get a reservation. But even on an ordinary Sunday night it was difficult to get in. Negroes from the Harlem community would line up outside to watch the limousines drive up—Cadillacs and Rolls Royces and Dusenbergs long enough to make you choke—and the celebrities come and go. Everybody was there, and the elite of society hobnobbed with the elite of the worlds of sports, literature, and the arts, and even mobsters and politicians. Lady Mountbatten visited the Cotton Club one night and nicknamed it "The Aristocrat of Harlem," a name that has stuck with it since.

Of course, ordinary folks in Harlem never did get to see the inside of the Cotton Club or the famous Cotton Club revues. In his book *Happy with the Blues,* the biography of songwriter Harold Arlen, who created many of the greatest Cotton Club shows, Edward Jablonski describes the Cotton Club's racial policy as it was stated by Carl Van Vechten: "There were brutes at the door to enforce the Cotton Club's policy, which was opposed to mixed parties. Although sometimes somebody like Bill Robinson or Ethel Waters herself could get a table for colored friends." That was the Cotton Club policy, all right, and the mobsters who ran the place had the muscle to enforce it.

Some of the proudest Negro musicians in the world played there and adhered to that policy of racial separation. The money was good, the shows were fine, and the audiences and the owners respected us and our music. What else can I say about it? I don't condone it, but it existed and was in keeping with the values of the day. It couldn't happen today. It shouldn't have happened then. It was wrong. But on the other hand, I doubt that jazz would have survived if musicians hadn't gone along with such racial practices there and elsewhere.

But that first afternoon I wasn't thinking about racial discrimination. My mind was on how impressive the place was. And it was even more impressive—and intimidating—when I arrived there for rehearsal than it had been when I was a spectator standing in the shadows in a corner.

When I got there Duke Ellington was waiting with Dan Healy, the master of ceremonies, and several of those tough-looking boys who had come into the Crazy Cat the night before were there. Everybody was very friendly and they all called me "kid." "How ya doin', kid?" "Glad you made it, kid."

I was twenty-two years old. Duke was about thirty. And I was so impressed by the man that I did feel like a kid beside him. I admired him so much. He had made it. He had the top band in the country. No competition.

He came over to me. "How you doin', man?" he asked. All I could say was, "Fine, man, fine."

"Glad you can make this change," he said. "You've got a nice little band there. Put on quite a show. If this works out, we may have to add some pieces, the Cotton Club needs about sixteen pieces. When I came in here the first time I only had a ten-piece band and we picked up six more. The room is so large the show demands it. You know what I mean?"

From there on it was strictly business. We went over the show music. He was taking his band out of town for a few days and the Missourians would replace him. If they liked us, we would become his regular replacement that summer. Duke was scheduled to spend the summer of 1930 in Hollywood doing the Amos 'n Andy film *Check and Double-check*.

He, Dan Healy, and I went over the show tunes and the pace and the sequence they wanted. I was listening, but I was mainly aware of Duke. I had always considered myself a pretty suave guy. But Duke was more than suave. He had something special and he carried it with him all the time. He was a handsome, almost shy-looking man, with his hair brushed straight back and a thin mustache. He wore loose-fitting comfortable clothes, and he was almost always smiling. But mostly it was that air of self-assurance that got to me.

Duke Ellington originally came into the Cotton Club in December 1927 as a replacement for King Oliver and his band. Before that, Duke and the Washingtonians, as they were called, had been playing at the Club Barron in Harlem and at the Kentucky Club in midtown. That band blew the Cotton Club away from the first night it was in there. Duke established a standard of music—musicianship and harmony and a beautiful jumping, swinging sound—that the club maintained until it closed about ten years later. Duke's Cotton Club Orchestra in 1929 included himself on the piano, Sonny Greer on drums, Charlie Irvis on

trombone, Elmer Snowden on banjo, Otto Hardwich and Johnny Hodges on saxes, Tricky Sam Nanton and Juan Tizol on trombones, Cootie Williams on trumpet, Fred Guy on guitar, and Wellman Braud on bass. That was one hell of a band.

Duke's reputation started to climb as soon as he came into the Cotton Club, and it kept going right on up when the two new radio networks, NBC and CBS, began to carry his shows live over their national hookups. People all over the country used to tune in almost nightly to listen to this hip, swinging band from New York City.

The original Cotton Club revues were produced by Lew Leslie, with the songs by Jimmy McHugh and Dorothy Fields, but Dorothy Fields wasn't really funky enough to write the kind of songs that would carry a Negro revue of that type. The real down-to-earth Cotton Club shows, with the double-entendre nasty songs and the hurly-burly and bump-and-grind mixed with high-class swinging jazz, were produced by Harold Arlen and Ted Koehler beginning in 1930. Clarence Robinson did the choreography. When I came into the club to replace Duke's band in the late spring of 1930, the club had just gone through a transition from the McHugh-Fields era to the Arlen-Koehler era. The revue that spring was called *Brown Sugar—Sweet but Unrefined.*

Those shows by Arlen and Koehler were a combination of vaudeville, burlesque, and great music and dancing. It's no accident that the name Cotton Club has come to be synonymous with the greatest Negro entertainment of the twenties and thirties. A lot of people worked hard as hell to pull those shows together. Ted Koehler was a maniac that way. He wrote the lyrics for Arlen's music, of course, but he was also a hell of a carpenter. He would be around the club all the time, day and night, when they were putting a show together. He wasn't just interested in how the songs were going to be staged, he was out there helping to construct the darned sets. Here is one of the most talented young lyricists in America at that time, walking around the Cotton Club with a hammer and nails and screwdriver. That was the Cotton Club spirit. Work, work, work. Rehearse, rehearse, rehearse. Get it down fine. Tops and professional in every sense of the word. The club was alive with music and dancing at night, but it was also alive all day long. If the chorus line wasn't rehearsing, then the band was. If the band wasn't rehearsing, then one of the acts was. We knew we were performing before some of the most critical audiences in the world. We knew we had a standard of

"Duke Ellington originally came into the Cotton Club in December 1927 as a replacement for King Oliver and his band." Frank Driggs Collection.

"It's no accident that the name Cotton Club has come to be synonymous with the greatest Negro entertainment of the twenties and thirties. A lot of people worked hard as hell to pull those shows together."

performance to match every night. We knew we couldn't miss a lick. And we rarely did.

One guy who knew the club inside out was Harry Sobol, jazz critic Louis Sobol's brother. He did public relations for the club and some of the performers and he was around all the time.

HARRY SOBOL REMEMBERS THE COTTON CLUB AND CAB

The Cotton Club occupied the second floor of a typical two-story taxpayer building in the heart of Harlem at 142nd Street and Lenox Avenue. (This area is now a huge, modern housing development.) It was opened, circa 1926, by Jack Johnson, the ex-heavyweight champion, as the Club De Luxe. It featured ordinary shows with minor acts and did less than ordinary business.

Johnson sold out to a syndicate in 1929. This syndicate could easily be spelled all in capital letters: BIG FRENCHY DeMANGE, bootlegger, a life parolee, small like Alan Ladd, china blue eyes, violent and fearless; MIKE BEST, big-time bookmaker, built like Walter Pidgeon, loudmouth; LITTLE FRENCHY, ex-welterweight fighter, as hot with a pistol as with his hands, also a life parolee; TERRY RILEY, built like boxer Billy Conn, Shylock and killer, also a life parolee. The club was fronted by Herman Stark, an ex-bookkeeper, personable, softspoken, handsome, family man of good reputation.

This was the Depression era, the Prohibition-speakeasy era, and the group owned, among other ventures, the Club Napoleon, the most glamorous speakeasy in New York, as well as midtown Manhattan's Club Argonaut, which starred the great Texas Guinan.

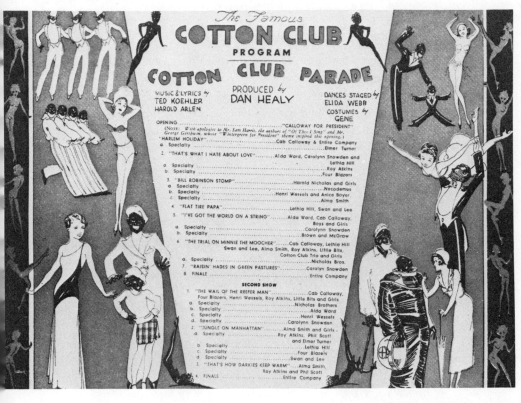

Frank Driggs Collection.

*Owney, Frenchy, Mike, and the boys were accepted. Sobol,
Sullivan, and Winchell sat at their tables. This was ages before
Tom Dewey and these men were considered high on any celebrity
list of the period.*

*They hired Jimmy McHugh and Dorothy Fields to write special
music for their first show, the great Duke Ellington, and Leitha
Hill as leading lady of the show. This was the period when chorus
girls received $35 a week, and waiters were paid $1 a night—and
often paid a go-between to get the job. The show was bawdy with
lyrics to match. On opening week the stock market crashed and
business crashed with it.*

*It was apple-selling days when the Cotton Club put on its next
show. They had hired a young man from Buffalo to write music,
Harold Arlen, and a little redheaded lad, Teddy Koehler, to write
the lyrics. The peripatetic Cab Calloway and his band headlined.
Again Leitha Hill and a new button-eyed shake dancer and singer,
Cora La Redd. A week before the opening, Big Frenchy was
kidnapped by the crazy killer "Mad Dog" Vincent Coll, out of a
pinball play palace at the corner of Fifty-second Street and
Broadway. He was paid the $10,000 ransom and machine-gunned
to death in a telephone booth at Twenty-third Street and Eighth
Avenue the night before the opening. That was our town in those
days. Winchell tipped off the killing at the bottom of his column
the night before, a tip given to him by Texas Guinan. A week later,
Texas went on a road tour and the "boys" never allowed her to
return to New York.*

*Kid Griffin, a white-haired little Negro, was the Cotton Club's
headwaiter. Ex-fighter, handler in later years of the great Joe
Gans, he wore his dinner jacket elegantly, spoke well, and was a
great favorite of the celebrities. The word was out that this was a
great job and Kid had his hands full this opening night.*

*Attending that Cotton Club show were our number one
celebrity, Major Jimmy Walker, and Betty Compton;* New Yorker

*cartoonist Peter Arno and actress Sally O'Neill; Harry Richman
and Clara Bow; Edmund Lowe and the beautiful Lylyan Tashman;
Dutch Schultz, the gangster, who put two bottles of Scotch on
Jimmy's table before he sat down at his own; Morton Downey,
Bea Lillie, Irving Berlin, George White, Earl Carroll, Fannie
Brice, Jack Donahue, James Barton, Jack Dempsey, Jock Whitney
and his Liz, Warden Lawes of Sing Sing, Will Rogers, Corinne
Griffith, and dozens out of the social register. And Bing Crosby.*

*Six songs were featured in that show; two became classics:
"Between the Devil and the Deep Blue Sea" and "Kickin' the
Gong Around." The youthful Cab Calloway stunned the audience.
In a dramatic white silk evening suit, his black hair streaming over
his forehead, he kicked the gong around in a fashion never seen on
a New York stage. At the end of the number even the quiet Earl
Carroll stood and applauded. It was through Bing's efforts that
Cab was booked into the Paramount to co-star with him two weeks
later, doubling from the club, and was hired by Lucky Strike to do
a nationwide radio show, the first Negro to break through the
network color barrier.*

*Newspapers in that day reviewed big nightclub shows as they do
the theater today. Ed Sullivan, Louis Sobol, and Winchell wrote
the reviews for their papers and raved, as did Abel Green for*
Variety. *Particular attention was paid to the young genius Harold
Arlen. What the scribes didn't know, and it would have made no
difference in that period of small salaries for big talents, was that
Harold's deal with the Cotton Club was $50 a week as long as the
show ran and all he could eat. Dan Healy, who staged the show,
was an ex-Ziegfeld dancing star, and with John Steele, the singer,
was glorified by Ziegfeld—the only two men who got that honor.
Glorification with Flo meant top billing and pictures in the
advertisements and programs. Clarence Robinson, the
choreographer, also got great notices, and he and Dan continued
in the same capacities until the last Cotton Club show in 1940.*

*Arlen and Koehler followed with other magnificent shows and
with such classics as "I've Got the World on a String" and the*

immortal "Stormy Weather." Ethel Waters really came into her own that night, and after the opening Irving Berlin signed her for his new show, Easter Parade. Remember Ethel in that one singing "Heat Wave"? Duke Ellington's music was sweeping the country and Sunday night became a must at the Cotton Club. After the show, Dan Healy would come on the floor as master of ceremonies and introduce the celebrities, and they loved it. Irene Berdoni sang Cole Porter's "Birds Do It"; Tony and Renee De Marco danced; Winchell did a buck and wing; George Raft danced to "Sweet Georgia Brown"; Harry Richman would break it up with "Puttin' on the Ritz." About four in the morning, Dave's Blue Room on Seventh Avenue and Reuben's on East Fifty-eighth Street would divide the last-cup-of-coffee crowd.

A new show every six months with new talent, new hot songs. This was making show business history and Variety duly noted that the Cotton Club shows were running longer and to more business than the Broadway theater. This was the day when a six-month run in the theater meant full return to the backers. (The Children's Hour was produced for $10,000. Once in a Lifetime was brought in for $18,000). A beautiful little girl out of the chorus got her chance and did a lovely song, "Waiting in the Garden." This was Lena Horne. But she meant nothing at the time. Nina Mae McKinney, Ethel Waters, Aïda Ward—those were the stars.

But it wasn't singing that got the crowds to the Cotton Club in the show that Lena worked in. It was a new dance—"Truckin'," to music by Rube Bloom and Ted Koehler. The Nicholas Brothers led the chorus girls in the number and that year the entire country trucked. Other great dances introduced at the club were the Suzy-Q and the Shorty George, and today you see traces of these dances in all musical shows.

A word about the chorus. They were not only the prettiest girls in the country, but each was a fine dancer. There were sixteen chorus girls and eight show gals. The chorus girls were billed as "Copper Colored Gals" and the show gals as "Tall, Tan and Terrific." The names were taken from song titles written for one of *the shows by Benny Davis and J. Fred Coots. Louis Armstrong, who starred in many of the shows in later years, found his wife, Lucille, in the front line of the chorus. Noble Sissle's wife came from the show gal group. Harold Nicholas married the beautiful Dorothy Dandridge when she worked there with her two aunts in a singing trio called "The Dandridge Sisters." Working in Cab's band at this time was a young trumpet player destined for big things—Jonah Jones.*

In 1936 the area was condemned for a building project and the boys decided to move to Broadway. They rented the famous old Palais Royale at Forty-eighth Street and Broadway, where Paul Whiteman had starred for many years and where the Latin Quarter now stands. The boys added a partner, Big Bill Duffy, who owned Primo Carnera. Maybe it was Bill's friendship with the sporting world, but scarcely a night passed that didn't find the greats of that world at ringside. Max Schmeling, Max Baer, all the Yankee ballplayers, Canzoneri, Don Budge, Jim Londos, etc. And the biggest favorite of all, Joe Louis.

The opening night program featured Bill Bojangles Robinson and Cab Calloway with twelve supporting acts: the Berry Brothers, Avis Andrews, Henri Wessels, Katherine Perry, Whyte's Lindy Hoppers, Tramp Band, Anne Lewis, Dynamite Hooker, the Bahama Dancers, Broadway Jones, Wan Talbert's Choir, Kaloch, Cab's orchestra, and fifty girls. Book, lyrics, and music by J. Fred Coots and Benny Davis. The demand for opening-night tables was so great that the boys shut off the phone three days before the opening and placed sorry-no-more-reservations ads in all the papers.

News columnists Dorothy Kilgallen and Leonard Lyons were at the opening. Winchell, Sullivan, Sobol, and Mark Hellinger, too, of course. Plus four one didn't see too often at nightclubs—Maury Paul, the famed Cholly Knickerbocker, cynical Damon Runyon, and Westbrook Pegler. Winchell's guests were Edgar Hoover and Clyde Tolson, the G-men. Sobol had Ethel Merman, and Sullivan had those intrepid aviators Dick Merrill and Harry Richman. Jesse Owens, the Olympic champ, was resplendent in tails and

To - my
Pal & Partner
Cab Calloway —
It has been a
real pleasure to
work with you —
Good luck always.
Bill Robinson
'B

"The opening night program featured Bill Bojangles Robinson and Cab Calloway with twelve supporting acts."

white tie. Marlene Dietrich with Eric Maria Remarque and Cole Porter. Franklin D. Roosevelt, Jr., with Ethel Du Pont. Cantor, Jolson, and Ed Wynn.

The reviews for that show read smash success, and it was mardi gras business every night. Dietrich, the Roosevelt boys, Toscanini, the columnists, the Hollywood producers, and the visiting stars. Bill Robinson was picked from that show to star in The Hot Mikado *and many Shirley Temple pictures. Rube Bloom's "Don't Worry About Me" is still tops with the album makers, and especially with Sinatra.*

Ponderous Tom Wolfe came in every other night with Leonard Lyons and Orson Welles, and visiting firemen asked for Tom's autograph, mistaking him for Heywood Broun. Sailors off the Bremen *Heil-Hitler'd at the bar and got the mickey treatment. Huey Long got bounced for trying to join the chorus line and it hit the front pages. Saroyan and young Gene Kelley came every Sunday night. The Dorseys, Glen Miller, Benny Goodman, Artie Shaw, all the bandleaders came. La Guardia, tough on nightclubs as a rule, had his aide escort visiting dignitaries to the club but wouldn't visit it himself.*

Doris Duke—and there's a story. Doris asked Bill Robinson to teach her to tap dance one night when she was in the Cotton Club. I don't know what the fee was, but Bill set the first lesson for the next afternoon. He insisted on absolute privacy, but the press agent for the club had a very deaf ear. While Bill was showing Doris a step or two the next afternoon, he heard a sneeze behind the stage curtain. Standing there, not a bit embarrassed, was John McClain, a reporter for the New York Journal. *Hello, Doris, he said. Hello, John, she said. The hell with these hellos, shouted Robinson, and he pulled out a pistol from his back pocket. Doris grabbed Bill's arm, and John ran. It was front-paged next day in the* Journal, *of course. Zanuck sent Bill a wire (tongue in cheek) telling him that under the terms of his contract with 20th Century Bill couldn't give anyone lessons except Shirley Temple. But he would rescind this order if Bill would get Doris Duke to sign with Fox.*

THE COTTON CLUB AND
THE WORLD

As you can see, at that time the Cotton Club was the place to be, and I was absolutely awed by it all—the people, the glitter, the fast life, the famous celebrities. The best singers, comedians, dancers, and musicians all seemed to have come together to one place at one time. I knew that the Missourians and I had some growing to do if we were going to make it in this world, so while all of this was going on around me my main concern was the Missourians. I wanted to make them into the best darned band that I possibly could.

There were a lot of other things going on in the twenties and thirties that helped to make Harlem a center of Negro culture. The Harlem Renaissance was a movement of writers and poets that included people like Langston Hughes, Claude McKay, Countee Cullen, James Weldon Johnson, and others. Those of us in the music and entertainment business were vaguely aware that something exciting was happening, but we weren't directly involved. I mean we had all heard about Langston Hughes and read his poetry, but his was a very different kind of world. But we'd be in an after-hours place sometime and somebody would say to me, "Say, there's Langston Hughes" or "There's Countee Cullen" and the names would ring a bell with me; I'd associate them with a particular poem I'd read, but the two worlds, literature and entertainment, rarely crossed. We were working hard on our thing and they were working hard on theirs.

We played in the Cotton Club whenever Duke had a gig somewhere else, but the first time we were in there for any length of time was the summer of 1930, when Duke took his band to Hollywood, where he became the first Negro to have an orchestra in a major film. That, by the way, was Irving Mills's doing. He broke down so many darned barriers for Negro musicians you couldn't count them. And if it wasn't Irving, it was Herman Stark, and if not Herman then the guys in the mob.

Beginning with that summer of 1930, Duke was on the road more and more. Things had really taken off for him, and maybe the Cotton Club had become too confining. The club wanted mainly show music, pretty straight stuff. Duke was beginning to experiment with longer musical suites and more inventive things. He could do those in theaters and in concerts, but when people get out on the dance floor expecting to jitterbug you really can't lay a "Mood Indigo" on them or some other piece of mood music.

We were a big hit that summer. Duke came back in September for a couple of months, and then around Thanksgiving we were back in there again. The Missourians had only ten pieces, and I immediately began to augment the band with the best musicians that I could find. I hired five or six guys right off to fill it out. And the new men began to change the nature of the band. The Missourians had been a cooperative, but the new guys in the band weren't into that. The cooperative idea had died out a decade ago and these guys just wanted to play music and be paid. In the past, the Missourians would come into a club and the manager would pay whoever had arranged for the gig and that person would pay the rest, but at the Cotton Club the mob handled the money and I paid the boys in the band. And when Duke or Healy wanted to talk about the show they would always talk directly to me, and I would pass on the information to the band. I was handling the money, taking care of the business arrangements, and making all the real decisions.

This new setup was formalized a few days before we were due to open at the Cotton Club for our second long run, in the fall of 1930. Benny Payne remembers it well. He was one of the first new musicians I brought into the band. I reminded him that I had told him when we were in Boston together in *Connie's Hot Chocolates* that one day I'd have my own band and he'd be the piano player. All he could say was,

"We played in the Cotton Club whenever Duke had a gig somewhere else."

"I guess you knew what you were talking about. And I'm damned glad you kept your promise."

Benny has always called his first encounter with the band a Thanksgiving Day present. On Thanksgiving Day of 1930 we got all the guys away from their turkey dinners for a two-hour meeting and rehearsal. After the rehearsal, which we held at the Audubon Theatre in Harlem because the chorus line was rehearsing in the club itself, Herman Stark told the band that though they had been a cooperative in the past, from now on I was the leader. Stark said, "I'll pay him and he'll pay you. He's responsible for making all the arrangements and for doing all the hiring and firing. On the road or in the club Cab is the guy you have to deal with. What he says goes." And that was it. There were no questions. There were not if's, and's, or but's. Then he added, "And anybody who doesn't want to go along with that can leave now." Nobody moved. It was tense as hell in there. Those guys were really over a barrel. They had no choice. They were making more money than ever and the band sounded better than ever, but that doesn't mean that they were happy about the change. There was a lot of grumbling from the original Missourians for some time to come. But that was about all they could do. Grumble. All of a sudden it was my band. Sometime during the next year, when it became clear that I was a hit and that Duke would be out on the road most of the time, we changed the name of the band from The Missourians to Cab Calloway's Cotton Club Orchestra.

In addition to Benny, I brought in Ruben Reeves, a trumpet player from Chicago who had been with Fess Williams' band at the Regal Theatre, and I hired Pike Davis on trumpet. Then Ed Swayzee, who had played trumpet with Sam Wooding, the first Negro jazzman to really make it in Europe, in 1931 with a big band, joined us. We all called Swayzee "Son." I never did know where the nickname came from. In 1932, around the same time that I hired Swayzee, I brought in Orville Harris on sax, then Lammar Wright and Doc Cheatham, the trumpeter who had played with McKinney's Cotton Pickers. Later in the thirties, of course, I had guys like Illinois Jacquet, Dizzy Gillespie, Jonah Jones, and Milton Hinton.

We went back into the Cotton Club for the second time in the fall of 1930, and again we were a smash. Suddenly I was one of those celebrities that I had been watching from a distance. Everywhere I went people knew Cab Calloway, and Jesus, what money I was making—more than I'd ever expected in my life.

"Benny has always called his first encounter with the band a Thanksgiving Day present."

We were on the radio almost every night when we were in the club and Ted Husing, the announcer, always gave us a big buildup. We would play live dance and show music, and I would sing a ballad or a blues or a hot show tune.

By the time I was twenty-two, my career was just about made. In the spring of 1931, we cut our first records. About that time I began to write songs, working with guys in the band or outsiders who were songwriters or composers. When we weren't in the Cotton Club we were out on the New York–New Jersey theater circuit. The big bands were top billing in theaters in those days.

In the spring of 1931 I began making plans to form a corporation with Irving Mills, our agent, called Cab Calloway, Incorporated. Until that time, I was just winging it. I was paying enormous taxes every year because the money would come to me, but I didn't know much about the business end of things. I was never good in handling money, probably because I had never had that much to handle. And I was afraid to let anybody know because I would look foolish and the guys in the band might take away my responsibility. When Irving Mills saw how little I knew, he and Herman Stark took me under their wing and showed me all the tricks of managing a big band. I hadn't even known enough to take the full expenses of the band as tax deductions, for example. Here I was taking all this money as personal income and not writing off any of it as expenses, and at the end of every year I was paying one hell of a tax. I began to keep books and get my accounting straightened out. Then we set up the corporation and it handled all of the money. I owned 50 per cent of the corporation and Irving Mills owned the other 50 per cent. I read recently in Duke Ellington's book, *Music Is My Mistress,* that he owned 50 per cent of Irving Mills's half of the corporation, so I guess that Irving actually owned 25 per cent, Duke owned 25 per cent, and I owned 50 per cent. All of the business that I did and that the band did went through the corporation. I had a contract with the corporation where I received $500 per week as a straight salary, the corporation paid the band and took care of all traveling and other expenses, and at the end of the year I received 50 per cent of the corporation's profits. By the end of 1931 I was making about $26,000 in salary and about an equal amount from the profits of the corporation—more than $50,000 a year in the middle of the Great Depression. God, what money. Betty and I had all the clothes and cars and fast living that you could want. I should say we could have had all that, but we really didn't spend a hell of a lot. I gave almost all my income to Betty. And she saved it. Betty had big plans for the future.

Even at that time Betty and I were going in different directions. She wanted to move up in the world and I liked hanging out in Harlem, traveling with my band, playing my music, and living the life of an entertainer. I didn't need much money because everywhere I went people paid for me—food, booze, clothes. I couldn't buy anything. But I'm getting a little ahead of myself. In 1931 I was making more money than I had ever dreamed about.

The second thing that happened to me during the spring of 1931 was that Irving Mills and I wrote "Minnie the Moocher," and whammo, I had my first big hit.

Every band in those days had a theme song. Duke's theme song that year was "Mood Indigo." Well, the Missourians became Cab Calloway's Cotton Club Orchestra but we still didn't have a real theme song. At the time, we were using "St. James Infirmary," a traditional blues that had been around for years. In the early twenties Louis Armstrong and Kid Ory made it famous, but nobody knows who wrote it. One day Irving Mills came to me and said, "Cab, it's about time you had a theme of your own. You're on national radio, you're doing national tours. The band needs a tune that it can be identified by."

The problem was that people were already identifying our band with "St. James Infirmary," so we figured that we ought to try to write something that would have the same feeling, and a melody that wasn't too different. We first wrote a tune that was very similar to "St. James Infirmary." If you listen closely to "Minnie," you'll hear some of the same changes and harmonies. In fact the melody itself is pretty close in some sections. Then Mills and I got together on the lyrics. There was a song going around at that time called "Willie the Weeper." I don't know who wrote it, but it was pretty popular. And there was another one called "Minnie the Mermaid." They were both torch songs. We combined our rendition of "Infirmary" with the basic concept of those two popular songs and called it "Minnie the Moocher." We created her as a rough, tough character, but with a heart as big as a whale. Walter Thomas—Foots, as we called him—who had joined the Missourians in 1929 just before I took over, and who had previously played for two years with Jelly Roll Morton, did the first arrangement on "Minnie." I hummed the tune we wanted and Foots put it down on paper with a little vamp before it; it became our first hit and the tune that I have become identified with personally.

The "hi-de-ho" part came later, and it was completely unexpected and unplanned. Scat singing was not new, of course. My favorite scat singer has always been Louis Armstrong, but there were many others. In fact, there was a tune called "Scat Song"—no lyrics, just straight improvisation—that a lot of us used to sing at the time.

During one show that was being broadcast over nationwide radio in the spring of 1931, not long after we started using "Minnie the Moocher" as our theme song, I was singing, and in the middle of a verse, as it happens sometimes, the damned lyrics went right out of my head. I forgot them completely. I couldn't leave a blank there as I might have done if we weren't on the air. I had to fill the space, so I just started to scat-sing the first thing that came into my mind.

"Hi-de-hi-de-hi-de-ho. Hi-de-hi-de-hi-de-ho. Ho-de-ho-de-ho-de-hee. Oodlee-odlyee-odlyee-oodlee-doo. Hi-de-ho-de-ho-de-hee." The crowd went crazy. And I went on with it—right over live radio—like it was written that way. Then I asked the band to follow it with me and I sang, "Hi-de-hi-de-hi-de-ho." And the band responded. And I sang, "Dwaa-de-dwaa-de-dwaa-de-doo." And the band responded. By this time, whenever the band responded some of the people in the audience were beginning to chime in as well. So I motioned for the band to hold up and I asked the audience to join in. And I sang and the audience responded; they hollered back and nearly brought the roof down. We went on and on for I don't know how long, and by the end the rafters were rocking and people were standing up and cheering. A day later we were flooded with letters from the radio listeners.

From that night on, "Minnie the Moocher" and "hi-de-ho" have been one and the same as far as most people are concerned. And Minnie, hi-de-ho, and Cab Calloway, too.

I've named this book *Of Minnie the Moocher and Me* in part because she helped me to make my fortune, but also because Minnie represents to me that moment, that special moment when so many things came together that went far beyond money. It was a combination of luck, talent, hard work, and the cooperation and assistance of a lot of friends and co-workers. And it was, especially, the role, the very important role of the audience. My main ambition has always been to please an audience, to know that the charisma that I have is reaching out across the footlights and touching people, the way Minnie the Moocher, that low-down hoochy coocher, has touched so many people and made them laugh and made them wonder. There must be something about Minnie that strikes people in some special place. I don't know what it is any more than I know what it is that gives me the talent to sing and dance and bring music to millions of people and perhaps relieve some of the uncertainty and misery in this life. In many ways the story of my life is the story of Minnie and me.

Since 1931, when we wrote "Minnie," I've written more than a hundred tunes, some of them alone, often out of my own loneliness, and a few of them with other people. Some of them have been completely original, others my co-writers and I have taken in part from other tunes. I don't need to add that none of them has ever been as important to me as "Minnie," though I have had a lot of fun with many of them. There was a song I wrote in 1933 called "Lady with the Fan." I wrote it for the finest fan dancer the Cotton Club had ever known, Amy Spencer. A fan dancer, for those of you who don't know, is a lady who comes out on the stage with her legs and arms and shoulders bare and only a fan in front of her. You're never sure whether she's wearing anything else, and the lighting is handled to enhance the effect—and the mystery. Amy Spencer was one hell of a fan dancer, and I wrote that to tell her so. Another song that had special meaning for me when I wrote it was called "That Man's Here Again." I wrote it in 1938 and the man I was talking about was the rent collector. I liked writing "Good Sauce from the Gravy Bowl," too. We used to call booze "sauce" and the gravy bowl was a cup. I have always enjoyed booze and will until the day that I die, and that song was dedicated to a good strong Scotch and soda, bourbon and water, rye and ginger, rum and coke, or whatever your poison is.

I wrote the song called "Are You in Love with Me Again?" in the wilds of Opelousas, Louisiana, around 1938. I was down there with the band playing in a gambling joint and the owner really loved our music. He took me out back into the kitchen to introduce me to his son, who was about seventeen or eighteen years old. They were white, and the owner was a humble, very decent man. I can't say the same for his son. When the owner introduced me to his son I stuck out my hand. The kid looked at me like I was crazy. "I don't shake hands with no niggers," he said. Normally I would have knocked him on his rear, but his father was such a sweet guy and I knew he was embarrassed. I let it go, but it obviously hurt me. I stayed up all night writing "Are You in Love with Me Again?" I must have had somebody in mind, but I don't remember who. Maybe the feeling just came from my anger and my hurt.

There were many other songs. Some had no meaning at all, just a feeling of joy or sadness. "Zaz Zu Zaz," for example, is just a scat expression we made into a tune. The same with "Boogit." There are also a number of songs that come from Negro slang. "Are You Hep to the Jive?" is an example, or "Jumpin' Jive." Negro slang became very popular in the late thirties and early forties. For a number of years, from 1938 to 1944, I published what was called *The Cab Calloway Hepster's Dictionary*. The last *Hepster's Dictionary*, for 1944, is attached as an appendix to this book, along with another publication I put out called *Professor Cab Calloway's Swingformation Bureau*. The *Swingformation Bureau* taught people how to apply the words in the dictionary. Jive had passed into everyday language. English had absorbed many quaint expressions that had their origin in Harlem. It was not uncommon to hear people in all walks of life say that a band sounded corny (from the brassy sound of a cornet) or that they were in the groove. It's gratifying to know that we musicians contributed some of the most colorful expressions that liven the tongue of a great people.

Irving Mills was mainly responsible for getting me into songwriting. He was a complete manager, and he knew the business up and down.

I had some guilty feelings about Moe Gale and the way he had been pushed out, but those feelings died one day in Philadelphia. We were booked into the Pearl Theatre as part of a tour we played when Duke went back into the Cotton Club in the spring of 1931. At this time Gale still had 10 per cent of the contract with Stark and Mills; they had worked him into it some way and as long as it didn't come out of my piece of the show it didn't matter to me. I felt bad about Moe being edged out, but not bad enough to give up some of my share to keep him in. On this trip he was still around helping me to manage the band on the road.

We did a tremendous business at the Pearl, and we were getting about $1,500 or $1,600 a week for the band. That was the ten-piece band. We only used the full sixteen pieces when we were in the Cotton Club. During the run I got friendly with Sam Steifel, the manager of the theater, and I used to go up to his office in the theater and chew the fat with him. We were in there for about a week that first time and we went around the area to other theaters and came back into the Pearl about a month later.

When we came back, Moe Gale said that he wanted me to go up to his summer home in Long Branch, New Jersey, and take a rest for a few days. He said that I looked tired, I had earned a short vacation, and nobody was using his house. I said all right. I could certainly use the rest. We were playing nightly gigs seven days a week and sometimes an afternoon show as well. Sometimes we'd end up playing three different gigs in the same area in one day—a matinee, an early evening show, and a late-night midnight show. I was beat, but I thought it was very strange just the same for Moe to suggest the vacation.

"Who's going to manage things while I'm gone?" I asked. "Who's going to pay the band and stuff?"

"Oh, I'll take care of that," he said. "Don't worry."

Well, it still sounded funny, but I went anyway and got a good rest. When I came back, Sam and Moe Gale and I were chatting in Sam's office and I said to Sam, "Well, we've raised hell in this town, breaking every damned record anybody ever made in this place. Why the hell are you guys so stingy? Why don't you give us a raise? Get up off some of that big money we're pulling in here."

Sam looked at me in surprise. "What do you mean, Cab? What more do you want? I gave you guys a raise from $1,600 to $2,500."

Moe hadn't paid the guys anything extra and he hadn't told me about the raise. Moe's eyes dropped to the floor and he started stammering and stuttering, "I was gonna get it straight with you, Cab. I was gonna tell you."

I can't write in this book what I told Moe Gale that day, but we got our money back from him and I paid the guys. Moe Gale and I had very little to do with each other from then on. I was always thankful to Sam Steifel, though. He knew exactly what he was doing when he told me about the raise in front of Moe.

Later on Moe Gale sued Irving Mills for some money he said Mills owed him. He was really just angry at being cut out of the contract, especially since I was making big bread now. Moe got a court in Pittsburgh to put a lien on our receipts after a concert there and it took some time for us to get paid. But it was too late. Moe was out of it. The mob and Herman Stark and Irving Mills had just run him out, and that crap he pulled in Philadelphia had lost him his last friend in the group—me.

Around this time, with things improving and the money coming in, Betty and I decided to move out of Fletcher's house and into the Dunbar Apartments over on Seventh Avenue. The Dunbar was the most glamorous apartment building Negroes had in New York. Betty and I still couldn't quite afford our own place, so we moved in with a family named Johnson. They had six or seven rooms, so we had more privacy. We paid around $5 a week, and then, about a year later, we moved again, to the Dorence Brooks Apartments in a very exclusive section of Harlem, St. Nicholas Avenue at the corner of 138th Street, right across from St. Nicholas Park. For the first time we had our own apartment.

We lived there for three years, from 1934 until 1937, when we moved into Betty's house in Riverdale. I say Betty's house because all this time, while I was climbing higher and higher, Betty and I were getting further and further apart. She didn't care much for my work, and she didn't like to come to the clubs. Other than our 1935 trip to Europe, which was a tremendous success for the band and me but a disaster for Betty and me, she never traveled with the band. Betty was very jealous. Of course, I was no angel. I liked women, and until I met and married my present wife, Nuffie, I was sowing my wild oats. And Betty knew it. It was no secret. I had quite a reputation as a lover. At times I went with some of the foxes in the chorus line at the Cotton Club, and man, they were some fine women. So Betty, in fact, had some reason to be jealous. I guess we ran each other ragged. I made the money, gave most of it to her, and she spent it, or saved it for the house she wanted to build.

Finally, around 1937, she got her damned house—in Fieldston, an all-white section of the north Bronx. Not a nigger in sight. The people planted "Nigger go home" signs on our lawn the day we moved in. I didn't want to be up there anyhow. I loved Harlem. I loved being with my people. Who the hell wanted to live in a section of the Bronx where, if I wanted to go out at night for a drink, there was no place to go. Hell, who needed any of it? That's why it was Betty's house. And she wound up with it when we finally got divorced, too. It cost around $60,000 to build back in 1935 and she got it. But she didn't get me.

I'll give you an example of what I mean when I say I loved Harlem. Harlem in the 1930s was the hottest place in the country. All the music and dancing you could want. And all the high-life people were there. It was *the* place for a Negro to be. God knows it wasn't such a ball for everyone. There were a hell of a lot of poor Negroes, too. But still, no matter how poor, you could walk down Seventh Avenue or across 125th Street on a Sunday afternoon after church and check out the women in their fine clothes and the young dudes all decked out in their spats and gloves and tweeds and Homburgs. People knew how to dress, the streets were clean and tree-lined, and there were so few cars that they were no problem.

Trolleys ran down Lenox Avenue to Central Park. People would go for picnics on a Sunday afternoon, and the young couples would head for the private places between the rocks to spoon and make eyes at each other. I'm not being romantic. Harlem was like that—a warm, clean, lovely place where thousands of black folks, poor and rich, lived together and enjoyed the life. Everybody was struggling. Even those who had made it were struggling to keep on making it.

The night life in Harlem was something. Probably no one knew it better than a guy I met at the Dunbar Apartments, a man who became my closest personal friend, E. Simms Campbell. Simms and I were the same age. He had been born in St. Louis but later went up to Chicago to study at the Art Institute. Then he came to New York, where he became the first Negro cartoonist to make it big. He free-lanced for a while and then went to work for *Esquire*. Not many people know, I suppose, that Simms Campbell created the *Esquire* magazine insignia, the Esky, and also the famous harem cartoon series that went on for years and years. By the time I met him, Campbell was a well-established cartoonist. He was also, like me, a hard worker, a hard drinker, and a high liver. I used to think that I worked hard. Cotton Club shows six or seven nights a week, matinees at the theaters a couple of afternoons, theater gigs sometimes in between the Cotton Club shows, and benefits on the weekends. But Campbell outdid me. He drew a cartoon a day, not little line drawings, but full watercolor cartoons.

But Elmer Campbell played as hard as he worked. He loved to drink. When we got to know each other, we would go out at night to the Harlem after-hours joints like the Rhythm Club and just drink and talk and laugh and raise hell until the sun came up. Somebody would get us home and pour us into bed, and we'd be back at it again the next night.

One of my favorite cartoons by Simms shows a boys' choir in a big

"... my closest personal friend, E. Simms Campbell. Simms and I were the same age ... he became the first Negro cartoonist to make it big. He free-lanced for a while, and then went to work for Esquire."

church. All the choirboys are white except for one big-eyed Negro. The choir master is getting ready for the Sunday service, and he's looking at this Negro kid with a reprimand in his eyes. The caption reads: "And none of that hi-de-ho stuff." Elmer Campbell did that cartoon in 1934, and it was published in *Esquire* in October of that year. He and I were tight friends by then. Jesus, I loved that man. He was one of the straightest, most natural men I'd ever met. Unaffected, you know, just honest and open; loud and noisy when he got drunk, and ornery as hell when anybody disturbed him while he was working. In 1936, Simms and his wife Constance, a beautiful, wild, graceful woman, moved up to Elmsford, New York, in Westchester County. They were the second Negro family to move into Westchester County and they built a beautiful flagstone house on a big piece of land. Years later, when Nuffie and I were looking for a home, Elmer Campbell convinced us that we should move to Westchester, and his wife Vivian, Constance's younger sister whom Simms married after Constance died in 1940, actually found us the house in White Plains that we've lived in for the last fifteen years.

Over the years we stayed close to each other. Many a night, when I was drunk and couldn't make it home, I would wind up at Elmer Campbell's place. Many a night he and I would hang out together screwing around, drinking bad gin straight in after-hours joints. I would complain to him about my wife, and he would complain to me about his. We were personal with each other, and we could holler at each other about our problems while we laughed at them. We complained about white folks not paying us enough money, and we complained about discrimination. "Hell," I would tell Simms, "if I was white I would be doing a hell of a lot more than Benny Goodman or Paul Whiteman or any of those guys." "Hell," Elmer would tell me, "if they didn't discriminate against Negro cartoonists, I would be making a lot more money than I am." We joked and laughed and shared things, man to man. There are few men I've had that kind of a friendship with.

In 1935 Elmer drew a map of Harlem. It's not an ordinary map, and it gave a better idea of what Harlem was like in those days than I can give you with all these words. I always loved that map and I still have the original of it in my office at home.

Elmer Campbell reached his peak in the thirties and forties. In the 1950s the *Esquire* format began to change, and he decided to move to

Switzerland. I was sorry as hell in 1957 when he left with Vivian and their daughter, Elizabeth. Except for a brief visit to Switzerland when I was in Europe with *Porgy and Bess,* I didn't see him again for about fourteen years, and when I did, he was dying of cancer.

Elmer died in January 1972, less than a year after Vivian. They had lived in Switzerland for fourteen years. After she died of cancer in the fall of 1971, he came back here. That winter he found that he had cancer, and by February he was dead. I have lost many relatives and friends in my years, but other than the death of my mother, none has struck me as Elmer Campbell's did. It was because the man was so full of life that his death hit me so hard. I was playing in a club in Miami when Nuffie called to tell me that he had passed. I flew back for his funeral. I was heartbroken. When I got to the funeral home, the casket was closed. There were other people there, but I didn't see them or care about them. I kept thinking about this man and his feeling for life and his hell-raising spirit. I walked up the aisle to his coffin. All of a sudden I felt more than sorrow. I was angry that he had left me. The feeling came upon me so suddenly that I had no control of myself. This goddamn man who I had known for so long and spent so many drunken and sober, joyful and serious hours with had left me. My fists seemed to lift themselves and I pounded on his casket and hollered, "Goddammit, Elmer, what the hell right you got to do this to me? You got no goddamn right to do this to me." I screamed like that until Nuffie and some others came and pulled me away.

I mention a lot of famous names in this book. I've known and worked with people like Duke Ellington, Pearl Bailey, Lena Horne, Dizzy Gillespie, Jonah Jones, and Bill Robinson, to name just a few. But if you want to know the name of a guy I loved, remember E. Simms Campbell. My friend.

But back in the thirties when I met Elmer, death was a lifetime away and we'd go out drinking and carrying on and no one could raise more hell than the two of us.

After Duke and his band had come back from Hollywood in September of 1930, the Missourians and I went out on tour around New York. The circuit had been worked up by Irving Mills. He had hustled his tail off to get first Duke into these places and then me. They were white clubs that had never had a black band before, and some of them were reluctant to let one in. But Irving Mills pounded their doors and paved the way. The tour included the Loews Valencia Theatre in Jamaica, Queens; the Roseland Theatre and the Paradise Loews in Brooklyn; the Jefferson Theatre on Fourteenth Street in Manhattan; and places in Harlem like the Lafayette Theatre on Seventh Avenue between 131st and 132nd streets. The Lafayette operation later moved to the Harlem Opera House around 1938 or 1939 and a few years later became the Apollo Theatre.

We also played over in Newark and Jersey City, New Jersey, at the Adams Theatre and the Jersey City Loews. The show was about five acts, some of which had been in the Cotton Club. The reception was fabulous everywhere we went in the New York area. You have to understand that in those days the big bands were hitting the theaters like dynamite. People would stand in line for hours and hours to get into a Cab Calloway concert or revue. There was, of course, no television, and people were regular theatergoers. In those days, you could count on several thousand regulars turning out for a concert or a revue. They had heard us on the radio or read about the Cab Calloway Cotton Club Orchestra in the newspapers. Many of these people in Brooklyn, Queens, and New Jersey didn't have the money to come into the Cotton Club to see a show, but they would turn out at the theaters. The audiences were mostly white, except around Harlem.

We went back into the Cotton Club for our third long stint in early 1931. My name became identified with the Cotton Club and Minnie the Moocher, we cut some records with the American Record Company, then the hi-de-ho thing came along, and all of a sudden Cab Calloway was famous. We were on the radio from the Cotton Club three nights a week, Monday, Wednesday, and Friday, with the new Columbia Broadcasting System, National Broadcasting, and Mutual Broadcasting. Each of them had us for thirty minutes one night a week. Years later, when I took the band to the Midwest, people came out in droves and they would tell us that the first time they ever encountered what they called New York City–style jazz was over the radio from the Cotton Club. We had built up a hell of a following around New York, and although I didn't know it then, across the country. Our announcer for those shows was Ted Husing, a celebrity in his own right, and one of the first announcers on live radio. Jimmie Wellington sometimes sat in when Husing wasn't available.

At the same time, I was working with Irving Mills and Herman Stark to improve the Missourians as a band. The second year in the Cotton Club, I brought in some fine musicians and we made our first trip to the deep South. Now, that was an experience.

I've always considered Baltimore a northern town. Negroes who had escaped from the deep South used to think of Baltimore as North, and whites, who liked to think of the good old days when Negroes knew their places, liked to think of Baltimore as South. My attitude was always that I was so free in Baltimore that it just couldn't be a southern city. As far as I was concerned, I had never been South. So when Irving Mills came to me in 1931 while we were touring the theaters around New York City and asked me if I would take the band into the South, well, I really had to think about that some. Mills had been approached by a woman from North Carolina named Knowles. I never did learn her first name. She was Mrs. Knowles to everyone—including Irving Mills. She made a deal with a bank in Raleigh to promote the Cotton Club band tour. It was to be the first tour of a big Negro band through the deep South.

That may seem strange; after all, jazz originated in the South. But it was always played there by the small combos hidden away in whore-houses and speakeasies or on the riverboats. This was to be a big public tour with all the publicity and fanfare. They couldn't get us into some of the concert halls; the South wasn't ready for that. After all, we had just broken through the color barrier in the white theater circuit around New York City. I thought about it for a while and finally decided, okay, we'll try it. Some of the guys in the band weren't too happy about it, but they all came along. You have to remember that at this period in the South the Klu Klux Klan was killing and maiming Negroes right and left. Between 1880 and 1920, 2,000 Negroes were lynched, burned, hacked to death, and shot by the Klan, the Knights of the White Came-lia, and other racist organizations that were doing everything they could to put the Negro back in "his place." We used to say that if a Negro in Georgia or Carolina or Alabama looked sidewise at a white man, his next move better be to head North, and fast!

It was no easy decision to make that trip. A lot of the guys in the band were from the South, and they had had it with that kind of crap. We were all nervous.

We played in all kinds of places. In Durham, North Carolina, we played in a tobacco warehouse that was as big as Madison Square Garden, and they put a rope down the middle of the warehouse and the whites danced on one side and the Negroes on the other. In Atlanta and a couple of other places, they had a white dance first, and all the Negroes sat upstairs in the balcony and watched; then they had a Negro dance, and all the whites sat upstairs in the balcony and watched. We played all the joints, too—little shacks, tiny clubs, barns, auditoriums, dance halls, whatever they had.

The trip was trouble from the beginning. Mrs. Knowles was from Raleigh, North Carolina, and owned her own buses. For her, I guess it was a way to save money hiring buses; for us, hell, we figured it was safer to be in a couple of rundown buses than to travel through the deep South in our fine New York City cars. State troopers in the South at that time could give a Negro hell—especially a Negro of any status. I've known colored physicians in the deep South who owned their own cars; in order to travel safely on state highways from one town to the next, they put on a chauffeur's cap so the troopers would figure the car was owned by a white man and not some uppity Negro.

We started out with some gigs in resort towns around the Maryland shore. While the rest of the band traveled in the old buses, my buddy Benny Payne, our pianist, and I went ahead in my car to make preparations in the next town. Benny used to tell me, "Hell, Cab, you may think Maryland is the North, but as far as I'm concerned, it might as well be Alabama. They've got us coming in and leaving from the backs of theaters, dressing in toilets, and eating while we sit on potato sacks in the kitchen. You know damned well they don't treat white bands like this."

The first problem came as soon as we crossed from Maryland into Virginia. Mrs. Knowles was riding in one of the buses, and as it went through a toll gate the collector saw a white woman in the bus with a bunch of Negroes. We hadn't gone two miles, man, before three cars full of Virginia state troopers pulled our buses off the road. The troopers wanted to know who owned the buses. Mrs. Knowles said she did. "I've hired these boys for a concert tour." The troopers got on the bus, and one of them said, "You got to get off this bus, lady. There's a law in Virginia that nigras cannot be on the same bus together like this with no white woman."

Nobody knew if there was a law that said that, but with those cops around, all the cats in the band could think was, "Lady, please, don't argue with the people. Get the hell off the bus like they say.'' Mrs. Knowles was a tough old lady, though. She argued with those cops for ten minutes, but they just wouldn't let the buses go with her aboard. We had to get to a dance so she finally got off the bus, angry as hell, and nearly in tears, and the cops took her on into Virginia.

We had one doozy of an opening in Virginia Beach. Now, you have to understand that this was our first trip of any distance together, and my first time on the road with the Missourians. The last time I was out on the road was when I brought the Alabamians through the Midwest from Chicago to our flop at the Savoy in New York.

Virginia Beach was a resort town for middle-class whites, and when I say middle-class I mean ordinary, ornery working people. The show was due to go on at 8:00 that evening, but at 7:30 Benny and I got a call telling us that one of the buses had broken down and the other one had stopped to wait for it. They would be at least an hour late. I said to Benny, "Jesus, man, how we gonna keep these people happy?"

Benny said, "I don't know, Cab, we can either let them sit there waiting, and hope they don't get too angry, or we can go out and entertain them the best we can until the band gets here."

We were already late at that point, and I could hear the people hollering for the show to start. So I looked at Benny and frowned and said, "Benny, I think we best go out there and see what we can do."

The M.C. announced that the band would be an hour late and there was lots of hooting and hollering. Then he announced that fortunately I was there and they would be entertained by me and my pianist until the band arrived. Well, half the damned people there thought it was a trick. They were sure that we were trying to cheat them out of their money, so they started hollering again, and raised a whole boatful of hell.

Benny and I went out there, and I started singing show tunes and pop tunes like "Ain't Misbehavin' " and "St. James Infirmary." People were hollering and stomping and somebody shouted, "Let's take this nigger out and lynch him." All of this was going on while I was trying to sing, and I could see Benny sweating and I was sweating like hell, too. I was just waiting for somebody to jump up on the stage and start something. Around 9:15 the band got there. Jesus, was I relieved! They set up and we played until 2:00 the next morning, packed up, got right back into the buses, and headed for the next town. I wasn't sorry to leave.

We weren't used to that kind of treatment. In the Cotton Club we were the cream of the crop, and we were used to being celebrities. In New York we were the toast of the town with big cars and sharp clothes and broads all over the place. Now, all of a sudden, we were forced into small broken-down buses and kept out of restrooms and restaurants. That hostile white audience was the last straw. Hell, a couple of the guys were ready to split the scene right then. But I said, "Listen, we made a commitment and the money's good. And besides, anybody who leaves is gone for good; you'll never get back with this band." So by hook or by crook, we kept the thing together.

From Virginia Beach, we went to Norfolk, about twenty miles to the north, and then to Wheeling. On this tour, we were a couple of days behind Ben Bernie's big band, which Mrs. Knowles had signed up on the same circuit. Maybe Mrs. Knowles figured that Ben's band would soften up the crowds for their first Negro big band.

We soon found that a lot of our fears about the South were unfounded. Oh, we had some bad times, but in Tybee Beach in Savannah, Georgia, for example, they had a police escort come out to meet our buses at the town line. Tybee Beach was one of the poshest resort areas in the state, and they gave us a royal welcome. We stayed in the resort area itself, and were the first Negroes to be out there as guests. Everybody else who wasn't white was a servant. We swam at the beach and stayed in guest cabins.

When we got to Raleigh we had quite a time. The city had just built a new auditorium, a beautiful place. Ben Bernie's band got there the night before we were due, and opened the place for the white folks. They had a big all-white dance until midnight. After midnight, Cab Calloway and the Cotton Club Orchestra were scheduled to play for the black folks. Ben christened the place for the whites, we were supposed to christen it for the Negroes. We were backstage while Bernie was playing, and after he was finished he came over to my dressing room and said, "Cab, you better get your money before you play because this Knowles woman has come up short with me." I was with a friend from Raleigh, an insurance broker named Ed Merrick, who had brought a gallon jug of corn whiskey. Ned Williams, a guy my own age, who was sort of valet and helper and road manager, was with us on this trip. So I sent Ned over to collect our money from Mrs. Knowles. Ned came back and said Mrs. Knowles wanted to talk to me. I went over to her office and she said go ahead and play, they're counting the receipts, and we'll pay you afterwards, but I told her no, we wanted to be paid out front. Then I went back to my dressing room and proceeded to get drunk with Ed Merrick and Ned Williams.

We could hear the crowd hollering. They came for a dance and they wanted to dance. They kept clapping and stomping, and we just sat there in the dressing room. We weren't coming out until we got our bread.

After about a half-hour, this Knowles woman comes into my dressing room with an enormous bag full of nickels and dimes and pennies and quarters. We were supposed to make $5,000 for that gig, but I was so blind from Ed Merrick's corn whiskey by that time that I knew I would never be able to count the money.

"Well, all right," I said. "We'll play now." We went out and played from around one in the morning until four. All the time Ned was in the back sitting on the sack of money, and I'm wondering how we're going to get it out of there.

Usually after a gig, the guys are so tired that they split to the houses where they're staying, but this time we waited until everybody was ready—and that meant until Leroy Maxey had packed up all his damned drums—and we walked out the stage door together, with Ned in the middle with the sack of money. We put it into my car and drove right on out of town and on to Durham.

It was Easter Sunday morning. Lord, I never will forget that morning. Here we are, on the highway between Raleigh and Durham with all this money. Nobody's slept for a couple of days, and since we left Raleigh in such a hurry, nobody's eaten. And of course it's hard to find a place that will serve Negroes on an ordinary day, but on Easter Sunday morning it was impossible. None of these little white roadside joints would serve us, and we were fit to be tied. Finally we sent one of the white bus drivers into a hamburger joint and he brought back a sack of them. We stood on the side of the road eating hamburgers and washing them down with Dr. Pepper. Then we got back into the buses to drive on to Durham—a bunch of guys, each with two or three hundred dollars in his pocket, who couldn't buy anything to eat or drink because we were Negroes. We were not what you would call docile Negroes; we were tough guys who had played the whorehouses and gambling houses, and it took something out of us to accept that kind of crap. A few of the guys found one way to get their own back. They picked up a couple of white chicks somewhere in Maryland and hid them in the bus, and those girls traveled with them all the way through Virginia and North and South Carolina.

The worst incident of the whole trip occurred in St. Petersburg, Florida. It involved our drummer, Leroy Maxey, who had been one of the original Kansas City Missourians. Maxey was quite a character. He was a sharp, dark-skinned young guy, handsome as hell, and he knew it. Leroy and I had more suits than anyone in the band. He liked to get dressed up and stand in front of the mirrors and check himself out. A real delightful, happy guy who loved to play drums and who loved life. He was a meticulous man. Leroy would spend hours cleaning his drums. When you're on the road, a set of drums can begin to look a little scruffy. I always told my band that we were going to be the cleanest, best dressed, sharpest band on the circuit, and Leroy took it to heart. He'd polish and shine his drums the way other men clean their cars. And because Leroy had been one of the old Missourians, he felt a special responsibility to set an example. He used to say to me, "Cab, we've got to keep these new guys in line." The new guys, of course, were some of the best musicians in the country.

Maxey was a short guy, who always wanted to look best and appear educated. He would study the dictionary, pick out the longest, most complicated words, and throw them into his conversation. In the dressing room, he would line up ten or twelve bottles of perfumes and lotions on the wash table; he could always tell if anyone touched them and he would raise holy hell. In the Cotton Club and other places where we had individual dressing tables, Leroy always set up special lighting in front of his mirror so he could see himself in the best light. He always wore lots of lotion and perfume and powdered his body and face heavily. One night, when we were playing in Louisville, he didn't have a mirror, and he put too much of the damned stuff on. He was late coming on stage, and since he was in the back and the lights were low, nobody noticed until the lights came up, in the second number, that he had put so much damned powder on he looked like a powder puff. We were in the middle of a tune, and a couple of the trumpet players in the back row started to laugh so hard they couldn't play. I was up front wondering what the hell was going on until I looked at Leroy. Then I cracked up, too. We got through the number as well as we could, and I took a short break and told Leroy to go get his face together.

In St. Petersburg, on this first trip south we were playing to an all-white audience in a tobacco warehouse. As the evening went on, the crowd got louder and drunker until at around one in the morning some drunk threw a coke bottle and it hit Leroy square in the side of his head. When the bottle splintered it cut a huge slash in his head and he was bleeding like a stuck pig. We stopped playing. Some of the guys were pissed as hell; they wanted to raise a ruckus, but with about 2,000 whites in there I figured it wasn't the time to take a stand, so I cooled everybody down. But Leroy was in bad shape. We took him to the back, and the other guys were ready to call it quits. Leroy said, "Hell, no. We came here to play music and we're gonna finish. These folks are not going to run us out of this town with a coke bottle, man."

We wrapped some bandages around Leroy's head and went back out and finished the dance. The next morning we found out that it was the police chief's son who had thrown the damn bottle. This kid comes over to where I was staying and says, "I'm truly sorry, Mr. Calloway. I just got drunk and threw the bottle and didn't care where it went. I wasn't trying to hurt anybody." Well, what could I say? "That's okay. Forget it." But I was angry as all get out.

Of course there were some funny things, too. We were the first Negro big band to play a white nightclub in Miami. No Negro band or entertainer had ever worked Miami Beach and none would for a couple of years until they booked Bill Robinson in there. My band became the second Negro group to play Miami Beach, soon after Bill. But in 1931 we went into Ft. Lauderdale not far from Miami. They had white cops all around the place in Lauderdale, although it was a Negro club and there were quite a few white people in the place.

The gang that owned the Cotton Club in Harlem also owned some clubs in Miami Beach, and when I got to Ft. Lauderdale, some of the guys I knew from the Cotton Club in New York came over to meet the band. The cops had roped off an area in front of the bandstand to keep the crowds back, but when my white friends from New York came into the place, they walked right over the ropes. The cops couldn't believe it. They had strict rules about whites and blacks mixing in public. One of the lower-level guys in New York gangs was named Fudgie. We all liked the guy; his wife used to hang around the Cotton Club, so we all knew her too. Well, we were up on the bandstand when these Miami people came in, and Fudgie's wife ran over the ropes and to Benny Payne and gave him a big hug and kiss. Everybody stopped playing.

Everybody stopped dancing. I could hear the guys in the band whispering, "What the hell is she trying to do, get us lynched?"

The cops ran up and pushed her back behind the ropes and told us to start playing again. I got the band playing again, and people started dancing, and the place cooled down. I could hear the guys sigh in relief.

We made another trip through the deep South the following year. The guys were less nervous, but we still had to play different dances for Negro and white crowds, or in some places like Winston-Salem and Atlanta they had a rope down the middle of the dance hall with the Negroes dancing on one side and the whites on the other.

When I think back about those trips through the South, I suppose they taught me a lot. I was only in my mid-twenties, and learning the entertainment business. This was the first trip where I was in charge. The Alabamians had been a smaller band, and since it was a cooperative we had shared the responsibility. Now I was beginning to learn what it means to be a responsible professional. No matter what the circumstances, we had to overcome them, go out on the stage, and do what was expected of us—and do it well.

When that white boy cracked Leroy Maxey on the head with the bottle, we could have packed up and split. But we were professionals and went back on the stage and performed. "We're the best," I used to tell them. "Let's act it." I've always tried to impress the same idea on my daughters Chris and Lael, both of whom are trying to make careers for themselves in show business. Dammit, I've told them, no matter what problems you have personally, or what obstacles might be thrown against you at a performance, go out there and do your thing.

In the fall of 1975, Lael opened her solo act at the Riverboat nightclub in midtown Manhattan. Lael didn't have the experience of her older sister, Chris, so she was nervous as hell. Her third night there she contracted a very serious case of laryngitis. I didn't say a word to her, I just watched. It would have been easy for her to call it off. But she worked on her throat every day, went out there every night, and did a damned good job of it. I was proud as hell of her. "Go on, gal," I thought to myself. "Do it the way your old daddy would."

One time in Memphis during that second trip South, we were in a big nightclub and all six stagehands went on strike. They refused to set up the bandstand for a Negro band. Some of the guys in the band were ready to pull out; to hell with this crap, they said. But I took a different approach. The white stagehands were sitting over by the side of the stage, grumbling and scowling. I walked over to them and sat down. A couple of the moved away, the rest stayed.

"How about a drink?" I asked them. A couple of them said, "Yeah." The rest were silent. I got the manager to open up the bar and we started drinking. On the second round the rest of the stagehands joined in, and by the fifth round some of the guys in the band had come over and we were all talking and laughing together like we had been buddies for years. By that time I was so drunk that I didn't care what I said. "What's this crap I hear about you guys not setting up the bandstand for us?"

"Aw, hell, man, we didn't mean nothin'. We figured you guys was some slick New York musicians and we said to hell with that. We ain't settin' up for no New York City niggers. But you all are just regular guys. Shit, we'll set up for you." And they went ahead, stoned drunk, and set up the bandstand.

Well, if I had let negative thinking prevent me from doing what I knew I had to do, we would never have played that Memphis dance. However, when positive thinking and simple human discussion fail, I am not beyond knocking some guy on his can. Like that time in Kansas City when Lionel Hampton was playing in an all-white theater and the usher wouldn't let me in to see him. I tried to talk to him at first, but when he got obnoxious I hit him on his jaw.

When we came back to New York City after the first trip South, we were greeted at the Cotton Club like heroes. It was a hell of a big welcome. We went into the club first, and then I took the band back out on the theater circuit around New York.

Around this time I figured my band ought to get into films. I was cocky as hell after the trip South, and we were such a big success around New York that it was pretty clear we were making it. And Irving Mills and Herman Stark were helping to add to the band by bringing in some really top musicians. So I decided the time was right and went into Frenchy DeMange's office in the Cotton Club. As I said, these guys liked me. I was loose and open and from the streets. I could drink and swear with the best of them, and I loved women and a good time. We got along well. And I never meddled in their business. They would have meetings at the Cotton Club with mobsters from all over New York and the place would be guarded like Fort Knox. I'd be around there, but I'd mind my own business. I kept my mouth shut and my nose clean, as we used to say in those days. Anyhow, one day around this period I went into DeMange's office and told him that I'd heard Al Jolson was doing a new film on the Coast, and since Duke Ellington and his band had done a film, wasn't it possible for me and the band to do this one with Jolson. Frenchy got on the phone to California, spoke to someone connected with the film, and the next thing I knew the band and I were booked into Chicago on our way to California for the film *The Singing Kid*. We had a hell of a time, although I had some pretty rough arguments with Harold Arlen, who had written the music. Arlen was the songwriter for many of the finest Cotton Club revues, but he had done some interpretations for *The Singing Kid* that I just couldn't go along with. He was trying to change my style and I was fighting it. Finally Jolson stepped in and said to Arlen, "Look, Cab knows what he wants to do; let him do it his way." After that, Arlen left me alone.

And talk about integration: Hell, when the band and I got out to Hollywood, we were treated like pure royalty. Here were Jolson and I living in adjacent penthouses in a very plush hotel. We were costars in the film so we received equal treatment, no question about it. And the balcony on my penthouse was so damned big that in the afternoons when we weren't shooting I would gather the band together on that balcony to rehearse. We really lived in style; it was a hell of an experience.

After we did *The Singing Kid,* we went back to the Cotton Club and the old New York circuit. Harold Arlen and Ted Koehler were still writing those great revues, and just about every new revue had a hit song in it. In the twenty-first edition of the Cotton Club revues—there had been a minimum of two a year and sometimes as many as four since the mid-twenties—the hit was "I've Got the World on a String," and a sequel to "Minnie," written by Arlen and Koehler, called "Minnie the Moocher's Wedding Day." And in the Cotton Club revue in 1932, Ted and Harold wrote two songs that told a lot about the climate around the Cotton Club and some of the patrons: "Wail of the Reefer Man" and "The Reefer Man."

For the next two years we were in and out of the club, doing the theater circuit around New York and the Northeast, and each year there were two national tours. In the summers we did a circuit through the Midwest, and we did a tour through Texas that broke all the box-office records. In fact, just about all of our shows during these heyday years of the big bands were breaking records.

We were also doing benefits around New York City. One of our fa-

"After we did The Singing Kid, *we went back to the Cotton Club and the old New York circuit."* Frank Driggs Collection.

vorite benefits was at Sing Sing Prison in upstate New York. We would go up there with the whole damned show, and put on a performance that would knock your eyes out. It wasn't strictly altruistic. The Cotton Club boys arranged these shows three or four times a year because all their buddies were up there. As soon as we got inside the gates we'd be mobbed by guys we'd known at the Cotton Club.

It's a funny thing about benefits. I've always hated to do them. I don't know if it's because I was poor and came up on my own that I have this attitude, but it's a possibility. I've done a thousand benefits in my life. I have given my talents to every kind of cause you can imagine. Benefits for blacks, benefits for whites, benefits for blacks and whites. I've done them for forty years, and it took me all that time to realize that the benefit game is the phoniest business in the world. If I do a benefit and they raise $40,000 for cancer research or if they raise $150 million for cancer research, the cancer researchers get the money, or maybe part of it; they get their salaries and run their laboratories; and the next year, sure as I'm sitting here, dammit, 150,000 people are going to die from cancer anyway. The awful thing about benefits is that you work your tail off and you never get to see any results.

I had the greatest fight in my life because of a benefit. It was in the 1930s, and Bill Robinson came to me and said that there was a group somewhere in Queens that wanted the Cotton Club show for a benefit for some deceased artist. During those days, we didn't have the kinds of unions that entertainers have now, so if an artist died we all got together and did a benefit for him. Well, I told Bill to go straight to hell; I was tired of running around doing benefits and I wasn't going to do this one. Of course I had the Cotton Club band at the time, so Bill needed me. He got mad as hell and called me a cheap son of a bitch, and I got pissed at him and we had the damnedest fight right on the floor of the Cotton Club. And of course that was something, because Bill Robinson even then was quite a man in New York City. He was the first black man to break down the barriers and become a popular star, and I was still just a kid in the Cotton Club. Hell, Bill was called the Mayor of Harlem. Everybody knew him, and I was only beginning to make a name for myself. But he was also a vulgar, tough man. All those stories about Bill carrying a gun and shooting and fighting are true. He told me, "Listen, little jerk, don't think you can go anywhere in this business without me. I can make you and I can break you, you son of a bitch, and when I say we're going to do a benefit, we're going to do it.'' So we fought. It was a quick and beautiful fight, and neither of us really won. Except that we wound up doing the benefit. Bill Robinson became one of my greatest friends in the world. He guided me and did a lot of things for me. He was wonderful.

But I was still against doing too many benefits—at least the kind that raise money for distant organizations. There were other kinds, though, that seemed all right. Every Christmas, the Cotton Club would do a benefit show for the poor people in Harlem. We'd all give our pay for a week, and folks from Harlem would come by the club during Christmas week, and we'd give them a basket full of turkey, cranberries, potatoes, celery, the whole thing. That was something that was real for me. I loved to do that benefit. It was altogether different from the phony ones they do today. Another thing the Cotton Club did that I enjoyed was to provide the talent for organizations trying to raise money for things like college scholarships for colored boys and girls. That made sense to me, but these big benefits they do today I can't go for. You never see where the money goes or if you've done any good.

The climax of the Cotton Club period was, of course, our trip to Europe in 1935. At that time, only a few big bands had gone to Europe. Duke had been a great success in 1933, but the only other Negro big band that had gone to Europe as far as I know was Sam Wooding's. Sam was a pianist at the Club Alabam in New York, and several of the men in the band that he took to Europe in 1924 eventually wound up with my bands, namely Doc Cheatham, Ed Swayzee, and Garvin Bushell. All three of those men—Cheatham on trumpet, Swayzee on trumpet, and Bushell on sax—plus Al Morgan on bass, Walter Thomas, De Priest Wheeler, Benny Payne, and Harry White, were with me when I took fifteen pieces to Europe. It was quite a band. But except for Doc Cheatham, not one of us spoke a foreign language. Doc had picked up some German while he was with Sam Wooding.

Traveling to Europe has become so commonplace these days that it's difficult for me to tell you how excited I was. A kid from Baltimore, with a little Chicago and New York slickness on the surface, and suddenly I was going to places that I had read about in school but never expected to see. We were headed for London, Manchester, Amsterdam, The Hague, Antwerp, Brussels, and Paris.

I was so happy and excited about going that I did something I would not normally have done—I took my wife, Betty. She wanted to go badly, but she was not in the habit of being around a band, or of being on the road with a bunch of rough, energetic, slightly crazy musicians. Betty liked to move in different circles. Maybe she was trying to compensate for her background or something, but she was seeking out friends who were doctors and lawyers and people in Negro society. I said, to hell with that, my friends are hard-drinking, rough-talking, down-to-earth people. No middle-class bourgeois folk for me.

But in a moment of weakness I agreed that she could come with me to Europe. Musically the trip was a fabulous success. But as far as Betty and I were concerned, it was a disaster. We fought our way across Europe. It was agony. After a performance I would want to go hang out with the band—get some drinks, relax, and have fun. Some of the other guys had brought their wives with them, and their wives would always hang out, but not Betty. After a concert or a dance she wanted to go straight back to the hotel. And if I said to her, okay, go ahead, but I'm not coming, she would raise hell. I knew that she was a jealous woman, but it really came out when all those white women in Europe started coming around the band. Every time some woman looked at me or came up to me after a show, Betty would carry on and accuse me of being unfaithful. Frankly, I was, from time to time, but I could never understand why she raised so much hell about it. It was nothing new to her. It was just my way and she knew it. If I saw a fine chick and I had been on the road for weeks, what the hell. I'm a man just like any other man, as far as that goes.

What finally brought the whole thing to a head between me and her was an incident in Paris. After our final show, we were all in a bar having a drink, and this fine young French girl across the bar was making eyes at me. At first I ignored her, but we were all drinking hard, and after a couple of hours, with the fine chick just staring and smiling at me, I couldn't take it. When she got up from the bar and went towards the toilets—of course in Paris at that time, men and women used the same toilets—I followed her. We were in a corner making out hot and heavy when in walks Betty. Lord, did we fight! The French chick ran out and Betty came after me, screaming and swinging. I swung back. The guys in the band had to pull us apart, and we both wound up with black eyes. We didn't have much to say to each other after that. We got the boat train to Le Havre and the trip back was very silent as far as the two of us were concerned.

Musically, it was a completely different scene. We opened up at the London Palladium in Picadilly Circus. This was a command performance for the Prince of Wales, who was one of my biggest fans. He had visited the Cotton Club when he was in New York and came over afterwards and told me that he had heard our records and loved them. The prince's guest that evening was the king of Greece. They had quite a gala affair going and that was some thrill for me. Because the prince and his friends were there, they had decorated the Palladium with balloons and streamers of all colors. You may have the impression that English royalty is stodgy. Well, you're wrong. Some of them can swing with the best, and the Prince of Wales and his party were damned good examples. They did the contemporary dances that we were doing in Harlem just as well as the hot set at the Cotton Club.

One thing that I really dug about Europe, especially London, was the accommodations. In New York at that time there were a lot of hotels where Negroes were not welcome, and anywhere south and west of New York was just hell. London was wide open. Betty and I had a suite at the Dorchester Hotel, a very fancy place, if I may say so. Some of the guys in the band stayed in hotels in Soho, the Bohemian section, and a few others stayed at the Cumberland Hotel. Everywhere the accommodations were beautiful and the treatment the same.

In the States, if you went to a fancy restaurant you stood a good chance of being put in the rear in a dark corner. In London, the restaurants put us right out in front and treated us like ordinary people. I was living as a human being for the first time in my life, and I felt free. Free. That is the only way I can express it. Sometimes we received special treatment because we were celebrities; other times we were just ordinary people. In America it was impossible for a Negro to feel like an ordinary person.

I had heard other guys talk about this feeling before I went to Europe. Musicians like Ed Swayzee would come back from a trip and say, "Man, you got to get to Europe. They don't give a damn what color you are over there. In Scandinavia the women will swarm all over you just because you are black." We had all heard how free we would feel over there, and it turned out to be true.

After two weeks in London we went to the Palladium in Manchester. You would have thought we were gifts from the gods. People climbed all over the stage and then tried to tear our clothes off as we left the theater every night. People think rock stars today get special treatment.

Shoot. Forty years ago we got the same kind of reception as Elton John or the Rolling Stones do today.

We were in Europe for five weeks, and I thought that Holland was the most beautiful of all the countries we visited. I loved the atmosphere, the customs, the people, and the beauty of the tulip fields as we drove through them. Betty and I went down to Volendam one day. They were still wearing native Dutch clothing with wood shoes then. They would leave their shoes on the front step so you could tell who was home and who was out.

Everywhere in Europe the people were enthusiastic and so—how else can I say it?—so foreign. At least they seemed foreign compared to any-one I had ever met. They were so open and free and direct.

There was one funny thing about European audiences, though. For all their enthusiasm, they were a little uncritical. They had heard so little jazz and were so unfamiliar with our kind of entertainment that the slightest thing brought them to their feet. It was great for the musicians. Every time an instrumentalist soloed the crowd would be on its feet, cheering. In the States, people didn't come to their feet unless it was re-ally something par excellence.

The money on the European trip was good. We got $7,000 a week for the band, and I got my $500 a week plus a cut at the end of the year in profits from the corporation.

One of the best stops in the tour was Paris, our last gig. We had a ball. We found out where the expatriate Negro musicians and artists were, and the guys in the band all headed there. We met Sidney Bechet, and some of the guys went up to Montmartre to Bricktop Davis' nightclub. In fact, it was at this club that I got into trouble with Betty over that Frenchwoman.

The trip back was hell. We had come over on the *Majestic* and were going home on the *Ile de France*. She was a huge, fine liner, but we hardly noticed. The night before, everybody had gotten loaded, and most of us missed the boat train from Paris to Le Havre, so they held the damn liner up.

That first day out was really something. I was drunk and sore after fighting with Betty the night before, so as soon as I staggered on the boat, Benny Payne and a couple of the guys put me into a bathtub filled with champagne and ice cubes. I was sitting up there hung over as I could be, and the guys all came down one by one and drank champagne out of the tub while I sat in it feeling rotten as hell. Then just as soon as my hangover was gone, the damned seas started rolling and I got seasick. That was one long five days coming back, let me tell you. Till this day, you can't get me out on a boat. Nuffie has asked me countless times to accept invitations from friends who have boats. I say no every time. I don't want no part of any boat.

After Europe, we came back to the Cotton Club for a while and then we went out on a tour through Texas. When we came into Dallas a high school band met us at the train station, paraded us through the downtown area, and then up through the Negro section. It was a hell of a welcome.

The crowds on this Texas tour were fantastic. We lined them up for blocks at every show, four shows a day. We set all kinds of records for that tour. The gross was $65,000 to $75,000 a week, and the prices were only $1 or $1.50 at night and fifty or sixty cents in the afternoons. That's how much business we were doing.

In Houston, there was such a demand that we did midnight shows, too. Five shows a day, and we still had to turn them away. After the first four days at the Majestic Theatre in Houston, they had to open up the mezzanine to give the Negro audiences more room. They had never before allowed Negroes into that section of the theater. There was the "colored balcony," as they used to call it, and the whites had the mezzanine and the orchestra, but the black folks came out in droves this time and the mezzanine was empty, so they opened it up. It wouldn't be the first time, or the last, that I learned that lesson—the power of the buck. It'll sometimes do more for you than all the protesting and hollering in the world. You put a $10,000 profit up in front of the man's face, even in a town as segregated as Houston was in those days, and the man will open doors quicker than you can blink.

I was very impressed with the way Negroes in Texas were living. I had never seen Negroes with that kind of money. The people who had money in the North were mainly entertainers and a few doctors or dentists, but there were very few of those. In Texas Negroes who had owned a little piece of land suddenly became rich when oil was discovered between 1900 and 1930. When the oil boom hit, there were lots of very rich people buying huge cars and $500 suits and $100 boots and building nightclubs, concert halls, theaters, and gambling houses.

And they paid handsomely. We had a guarantee and a percentage of the gate as well. Our expected gross was $50,000 a week, and the band got something like $15,000 of that first $50,000 plus 10 per cent of anything above $70,000. Of course we had plenty of expenses. We had rented our own Pullman train plus a baggage train, but the money was rolling in, and sometimes we'd be out on the road for six months at a time, mostly through the South, Southwest, and Midwest. In addition to a seventeen-piece band, we had three acts that traveled with us—a comedy team, a dance number, and one other—plus a couple of soloists. It was a hell of an operation. We were one of the few bands at that time that traveled in its own Pullman car.

Although we had this private car, in most cities we still stayed with Negro people in the community. In Houston, I stayed with Ann and Bill Robinson. They ran a haberdashery and were socially prominent in the Negro community. Ann was light-skinned. The Robinsons lived about five miles outside the business district in Houston, and Ann would drive Benny and me into the city every day. One particular day, Ann didn't get dressed, but drove us in her bathrobe. She said to us, "You all better be nice to me now, because all I have to do is holler rape, and that's it for you; every white man within a hundred miles will be on your back." Benny and I laughed because we knew she was right. Don't get caught messing with a white woman in the South. It'll be your tail.

Bill and Ann were wonderful to us; on days off they took us riding through the country or gave parties for us, and one day they took us to Galveston, where a whole bunch of colored folk gave a beach party for the band. Texas was really lovely to us.

All the guys in the band had arrangements like this with local families in each town. The hotels in these cities were strictly segregated: no Negroes allowed unless they waited on table or swept the floor.

Of course, there was another trip we made to Texas that didn't work out quite as well. In 1939, I took the band down to Longview, Texas, to play during the Dallas Centennial. We were there when Max Schmeling beat Joe Louis. I heard it over the radio and ran down the hall shouting, "He lost, he lost! Jesus Christ, Schmeling beat Joe. Jesus Christ!" The guys in the band couldn't believe it. But the worst thing was to have to announce it to the audience. They were out on the fairgrounds in this town. The crowd cheered and clapped while the guys in the band softly moaned and groaned.

During that trip we played a big bash in a little roadhouse on the outskirts of town. We went out there in our Pullman and took taxis to the roadhouse. It was a white dance and the folks were heavy Texas drinkers. They were drinking whiskey before we even got going. This young white girl was dancing right near the bandstand, and she had eyes for Benny Payne. Of course Benny was as handsome and dashing as you can get. Benny just kept playing the piano, trying to ignore the chick. Finally the little girl wouldn't stand for being ignored. She walked right up to Benny and said, "Hey, want a drink?" Benny looked at me and I looked at him, and we were both scared as hell.

Benny said, "No thanks, I don't drink."

"You're going to tell me you ain't going to take a drink? You refusing my drink?"

Benny was damned if he did and damned if he didn't. So he accepted the girl's drink, and sure enough, the guy she was with got mad.

"What are you doing drinking my old lady's whiskey?" And he hit Benny in the mouth.

Now, I was up in front just hi-de-hoing to beat the band, because there was a rule in Texas at that time—I don't know if it was the law, but it was the practice—that a white man could hit a Negro in the mouth if he wanted to, but he had to pay a $300 fine. These people had plenty of money, so there was no problem paying the fine. Lots of Negroes got hit in the mouth because of that law, and Benny Payne was one of them. But Benny was no sissy. He stood up ready to beat the crap out of the guy, and then somebody in the band grabbed Benny and held him. But by this time the joint was in chaos.

The white man who was running the dance ran over to me and said, "I'm gonna try to save you niggers, if I can." People were surging towards the bandstand while the cops were trying to hold them off, and the guy opened a trap door in the middle of the stage and we all ran down the ladder to the basement. Man, it was wild. The place was going crazy. Once we were out of the way, with the cops and this white guy keeping the crowd back from the trap door, the folks were so drunk they started fighting with each other. We were sitting on crates and sacks in this dark basement with a whole hullabaloo of a riot going on above us. The building was shaking so hard we were scared that if they didn't get through the cops to get us they would bring the whole building down on top of us. The racket went on for a good hour before they wore themselves out and began to leave.

Finally, when things got quiet, the trap door opened and the manager came down and led us out. We got into our taxis and raced out of that town back to our Pullman with a police escort howling in front of and behind us. When we got inside the Pullman, we locked all the doors and proceeded to get plastered. Longview, Texas, is one place I will never forget.

I also learned during those national tours every year that while we were in the Cotton Club, the national radio networks were building up a national following for our band. College kids throughout the Midwest, Southwest, and Far West used to stay up into the wee hours of the morning to listen to the Cotton Club show. We had become pop heroes around the country without knowing it. In the summers of 1933, 1934, and 1935 I took the band on tours of Texas, Kansas, Ohio, Illinois, Tennessee, Missouri, and Oklahoma. We played theaters mainly and met many, many wonderful students who came out to see in person this bad, hip New York City band they had been hearing on the radio. One such student was Alex Peebles, a young man my own age, who joined the band the summer of 1933 in Kansas City and put himself through law school at the University of Kansas selling programs throughout the Midwest with our band. Alex also got us into a bad jam one summer. It was either 1933 or 1934. We were booked into Memphis, where racial prejudice was awful, and we were going to play the Fairgrounds Park, a colored concert in the late afternoon and a white dance in the evening. Alex was selling some programs at the edge of the dance floor when two young husky white fellows came up and asked him what he was doing traveling with a Negro band. These guys were half drunk and very insulting, and this led to that, and in a minute Alex and some of the guys in the band had taken those guys on and the place was in pandemonium. Well, they had to carry us out of that park on a flatbed truck with carloads of young whites chasing us and the state troopers trying to keep them away. We finally made it back to our Pullman, and, once again, got good and drunk. That was probably our closest call. But Alex Peebles is now one of the top lawyers in Kansas City, and a very good friend of mine to this day.

There were times like that, but they were few and far between. I found that most people loved music and loved the entertainment that we brought to them. And they appreciated the fact that we put out one hundred per cent. They respected what we could do and they enjoyed themselves dancing and clapping and singing "Hi-de-ho" along with me and the band. The few rough times were more than offset by the many great performances and the excitement of turning a crowd on—North or South—and feeling the joy of the people no matter whether we were playing in a classy nightclub in New York or Chicago, in a tobacco warehouse in South Carolina, in a shack in some small town in West Virginia, or in a roadhouse in Texas. If the music is right, the people will appreciate it.

A lot of it had to do with the kind of band that we had between 1936 and 1942, the time that the big bands were drawing enormous crowds everywhere. I say 1936 because that's the year that Milt Hinton joined the band. Then, in July 1937, I hired Chu Berry away from Fletcher Henderson's band. We called Milt "Fump" because the fump-fump of his heavy bass gave the band a depth it hadn't had before, and Chu, of course, was one of the top two or three saxophonists in the country. He brought a melodic quality that our band had not had before.

Fump was a funny little guy when he came with us. I was in Chicago with the band on a trip through the Midwest when Al Morgan, our bassist, decided to leave for California. He was tired of the tempo of the East. I needed a bassist quickly, and somebody told me to go over to the Three Deuces to hear this little bassist out of Vicksburg, Mississippi, who was playing with Zutty Singleton's band.

To hear Fump tell it these days, having me in the Three Deuces was like a visit from the heavens. I didn't see it that way. I was a celebrity in terms of the public, but inside of myself I was still a guy who used to hustle newspapers in the streets of Baltimore and stood in awe of talented musicians. Fump was one. As soon as I heard him play, I wanted him, but he tells the story differently.

FUMP REMEMBERS CAB

Well, we all knew Cab had come in town. Shoot, Cab's band even at that time was one of the greatest in the country. It was quite an honor having a guy like that come into the club. As usual when a celebrity came in, the band was on. We played our tails off that night. Cab had just come back from making The Singing Kid *in Hollywood, and that was quite a thing because only Duke*

"Well, we all knew Cab had come in town. Shoot, Cab's band even at that
time was one of the greatest in the country."

Ellington had made a movie at that point. And Cab had a way of strutting, you know, all New York hip in a big coonskin coat and a beautiful derby. He was the toast of Chicago. That was where he had gotten his start, and everybody knew it.

Cab walked in and sat down, and Zutty and he had a drink. And after one set he called me over.

"How you doin'?" Cab said.

"I'm doin' fine," I said.

Then Cab said, "We're leaving tomorrow. If you want to join my band the train leaves from the South Street Station at nine in the morning. Be there and you've got a job."

Man, I didn't know what to say. Oh my goodness, what was I going to do? Here was a chance to get with one of the top bands in the country, and I was hooked up there in Chicago. I never dreamed of joining a band like Cab's, and the opportunity looked like it was going to slip right through my hands.

"I don't know what to do, man," I said. "I have a contract with Zutty and I can't just walk on him."

But Zutty saved me. "No, Milt," he said. "You go on with Cab. I'll get another bass player. You can't pass this up. This young cat got a good thing going. Go on with him."

Man, I wanted to jump through the roof. I was so happy. I didn't even ask Cab how much he was paying me. I was making around $35 a week with Zutty and that was the best job in town. I played the rest of that show at the Three Deuces that night and the next morning I was down at South Street Station at eight. I had a green suit on and a little canvas bag with all my worldly possessions. I got on the train and there's all these guys, man, Ben Webster, Claude Jones, Garvin Bushell, Keg Johnson, Benny Payne, Mouse Randolph, Lammar Wright. I couldn't believe it. These guys were heroes to me—the greatest jazz musicians in the country. I was awestruck by the whole thing. Ben looked at me and laughed. "Who in the world are you?" he asked. "You're so thin if you turn sideways nobody will be able to see you." Cab had just come onto the train, and they were all standing around cracking up. I was so happy, I didn't give a darn.

Then Cab told them, "This here's Milt Hinton, our new bass player."

"The new what!" Ben screamed. "Oh, my Lord. We won't even be able to see this little cat behind that bass. Cab, what in the world got into your head, man?"

That was one clowning band, one happy bunch of guys. Next thing I knew we were underway. I was in the band for six months before we hit New York. We traveled the road, playing one-nighters mainly, all through the South and Midwest and Southwest. I couldn't get over the band traveling in its own Pullman—strictly first class, all the way. There's never been any band, black or white, that traveled any finer than Cab's band did. Behind the Pullman was the band's baggage car with all the H & M trunks in it. Everybody in the band had the same kind of H & M brand of trunk. When I looked into the car for the first time my eyes nearly popped out. And in the middle of all these trunks and instruments was Cab's big green Lincoln. Right in the baggage car. Everywhere Cab went he took that beautiful car with him, and when he got into a town the rest of us would get taxis but Cab would roll that old Linc down off the train, with his coonskin coat on and a fine Homburg or derby, and drive off into town looking for the action.

That band was really something to see. We were the tops and we knew it and we acted it. Arrogant as all get out. The guys dressed to kill—all the time. The first thing I did was to take $600 and buy a whole closetful of suits. I had to. It was embarrassing traveling with those guys unless you were suited down.

The first gig I played with the band was in Des Moines, Iowa. It was a big theater, and the people had jammed the place. I had been playing with little three- or four-piece outfits, never in front of a crowd of a couple of thousand like this one. That first night

"Everywhere Cab went he took that beautiful car with him, and when we got into a town the rest of us would get taxis but Cab would roll that old Linc down off the train, with his coonskin coat on and a fine Homburg or derby, and drive off into town looking for the action."

was frightening. I had studied the music, but knowing the score is one thing, getting the feeling of the band is something entirely different. And Cab's band was playing such a high caliber of music I wasn't sure I would cut it.

We opened without a rehearsal. As the band warmed up, I was afraid all that sound would blow a little guy like me right off the stage. Cab started calling the numbers, and I was coming down all right and beginning to relax. They had placed me right up front, in the crook of Benny's piano, and Benny was calling the chords out to me if I couldn't find the music in time; this was one fast-moving show. So I'm up front and Benny's calling out the chords and I'm making the changes okay and feeling okay except that I had on Al Morgan's jacket and Al was about a foot and a half taller than I and it must have looked pretty funny. You couldn't even see my hands.

About halfway through the show, Cab called a number that featured the bass. It was an Al Morgan special. I knew about it because I had heard Al play it on records. In fact, I had studied it and his style of playing for some time. The tune was called "The Reefer Man," and as soon as Cab called it all my relaxed feeling disappeared. This was going to be some baptism, especially since that band played along such clean, clear lines that any error would stand out like a sore thumb. I looked at Benny and Benny said "F, man, just start in F and keep going." So I started in F and kept on going. The band started and Benny's calling the chords and I'm playing, and after about five minutes into the tune the band stopped and Benny hollered, "Keep on. You got it, man. F, F." And I played F chromatic and just let it swing and it felt good. After a few minutes Benny said, "Okay, man, now just fall into my arms." And he brought the piano in behind me and then the rest of the band came in and the whole place was rocking. The music was swinging, the people were hollering and dancing in the aisles, and I had a smile on my face wide as a mile. When we finished the people stood up and called for more. Cab sure put me on the spot that day. I loved it. I was with his bands for the next fifteen years, but that was the biggest moment.

LIFE WITH THE BAND

Fump was one hell of a bass player. He was so little you could hardly see him up there behind that big bass, but he brought a sound to the band that even Al Morgan hadn't had.

Milt Hinton's name is well known now. He's recognized as one of the great jazz bassists of the century, and he's won the *Down Beat* and *Metronome* polls as the tops in the country over and over. He was with my bands until 1951. Then he worked around New York City with Joe Bushkin, played with Jackie Gleason's orchestra, went with Count Basie for a time, then with Louis Armstrong, Benny Goodman, Teddy Wilson, Russ Case, and Jimmy McPartland. In other words, he's played with some of the best.

There's one other thing about Milt Hinton. He was a lousy gambler. I have never known a guy that had such bad luck gambling as Fump did. You gave him fifty-fifty odds and he was probably the only guy living who would lose ninety-nine times out of a hundred. Fump liked to gamble as much as I did, but he had a worse problem because at least I would get my share of winnings. Fump could play the hell out of a bass, but don't put a deck of cards or a pair of dice into his hands.

One year in the late thirties, we were in Columbus, Ohio, playing at the Colonial Theatre. I always paid the band on Thursdays. And I have never in my career missed a payday for a band. In any case, on this particular Thursday my road manager, a guy named Hugh Wright, gave the guys their pay envelopes. Every week, five minutes after Milt Hinton got his bread he would be upstairs in the theater dressing room shooting craps with the guys, and ten minutes after that he would be flat broke. Sure enough, this time the guys are all on the dressing room floor shooting Thursday night craps when in walks Milt. Lord, they loved to see him coming. In five minutes, Milt didn't have a quarter to his name.

At that time, Mona, who is now his wife, was traveling with Milt. He went to her and borrowed $100 and five minutes later he had lost that, too. So Fump comes back downstairs and asks Mr. Wright if he can get an advance. Wright says, "I ain't gonna give it to you, son. You're just gonna go back upstairs and lose it and that'll be next week's pay."

Milt was a stubborn cat. The next thing he did was to come up to my dressing room and ask me if he could get an advance; Mr. Wright had said no, he told me. I told Milt, "Get the hell out of here, man, before I lose my temper. All you're gonna do is lose it gambling again."

The next thing I know, Mr. Wright is at my door telling me that he has given Milt the $1,000 I okayed. Milt had gone back downstairs and told Wright that I said it was okay to advance him $1,000. I was so damned angry, I ran upstairs to the band's dressing room. Sure enough, there was Milt with a wad of bills in his hand getting ready to lose that, too.

That was the end of that crap game. I told the cats, "Listen, I don't interfere with how you guys spend your bread, but you know that Milt is a fool when it comes to craps. He don't know how to drink and he don't know how to gamble and he can't win. The crap game is over. Anybody who shoots any more craps in here with Milt can just get out and go home." I really didn't like the idea of those cats taking advantage of Milt like that. Then I got Milt downstairs and read the riot act to him for lying to Mr. Wright, and got the $1,000 back from him.

Things were very quiet in the dressing room for a while after that. I didn't go after the band often, at least not about personal things. I'd get mad as hell if they missed a rehearsal or if somebody wasn't playing up to snuff, but it was unusual for me to get into their personal business, so they knew I was serious. After a while I heard the dice rolling again, but I knew they wouldn't let Milt back in. His money wouldn't have been worth a dime in their game because they wouldn't have let him play. Besides, he didn't have any more money.

Milt never gambled again. That night Mona was ready to leave him. "It's the dice or me," she told him. "If you want to spend your money like that, it's your money. But I don't want to be around you." Milt really dug Mona. They were up all night in the empty theater hassling it out and they made an agreement that Milt would play the music and Mona would handle the money. They've kept it like that for more than thirty years. Milt will go out to Las Vegas to this day and walk right through aisles of gambling tables and slot machines without batting an eye. He was lucky that way; he solved his gambling problem early. It took me many years and tens of thousands of dollars to kick the habit. I had it bad.

Benny Payne could gamble some, too, but Benny liked to bet other people's money. We were in a small town somewhere in the early forties and Benny heard about a horse at a local racetrack named Jeffersontown. Hilton Jefferson was playing alto with the band at the time. I was a real heavy horse player and I knew that Benny didn't know a thing about this horse. It was strictly a hunch bet. But I went for it and called my bookmaker in New York, and I placed a $1,000 bet on Jeffersontown to win. You may think that a $1,000 bet to win on an unknown horse is a lot of money, but for me at that time it wasn't at all unusual. I don't know how he did it, but this time Benny had the horse right on the nose. That old Jeffersontown nag came in first and paid $17 or $18. They brought my money in a satchel and the band had one hell of a celebration that night.

I feel like I could go on and on about these guys. When you live with a group of men day in and day out for years and years, you get to know them pretty well. Men came and went. Some I knew I would miss and some I was glad to see leave. As the years passed, the original Missourians left the band or were replaced by better musicians. By the late thirties, little of the sound or the feeling of the Missourians was left. I had taken the band and molded them into the kind of orchestra that I wanted. In 1939 I had a full shakeup, and changed the whole band around. Of the old band only Benny Payne was left. Benny is the only musician who was with the band from the Cotton Club shows of the early and mid-thirties when we had a dynamite show and dance band, to the late thirties and early forties, when we had one of the top jazz bands in the country. I made that transition because I saw the handwriting on the wall. When Prohibition ended, the mob became less interested in running clubs uptown where they could sell bootleg booze out in the open. And I think that people's tastes were changing, too. The Cotton Club moved downtown in 1936 and it closed four years later.

When the Cotton Club closed I took the orchestra into the Club Zanzibar and we continued the road tours, but bands were beginning to play more jazz, which the people seemed to want to listen to. Since that was my natural inclination, anyway, I began to move in that direction. The only problem was that jazz is much more demanding than show and dance tunes. It requires a greater degree of musicianship. So I made changes in personnel. Perhaps the guy to tell you about those changes and what the band was like in those days is the one guy, besides me, who lived through it all—Benny Payne.

BENNY PAYNE REMEMBERS CAB

This is the kind of guy Cab Calloway was in those days. You could get drunk with him and bring him home on your back (and I did that many a night) but the next day when he raised his hand for the downbeat, he didn't want to know nothing about what had happened the night before. He was there in time and ready to make music, and he wanted every man in the band there and ready too. Leave your personal problems in the wings, man. And please don't make a mistake. "Fellas," he would say, "I don't want no individuals; if there's a mistake, I want to hear seventeen mistakes."

That band was like being in school all the time. We learned about music, we learned the responsibility of being professionals, and we learned about life. We had great individual musicians and arrangers. When a guy like Benny Carter was rehearsing the band it was like a class at Juilliard. Or a guy like Buster Harding. He gave a music lesson at every rehearsal. Occasionally, when Cab didn't rehearse the band, he would sit on a stool by the side, half crocked with his bottle of Mount Vernon whiskey, and smoke three packages of cigarettes while we worked our tails off to get the

"This is the kind of guy Cab Calloway was in those days. You could get drunk with him and bring him home on your back (and I did that many a night) but the next day when he raised his hand for the downbeat, he didn't want to know nothing about what had happened the night before."

music together. It didn't bother us. We knew that while we were
taking it easy Cab would be stone cold sober negotiating
contracts, figuring the books, or getting a new show organized
with a theater manager.

I learned a lot from a man in the band named Walter Thomas,
who had learned it all from Jelly Roll Morton. Walter, who we all
called Foots—he had the biggest feet you ever saw—was with
Cab's bands until 1943, and he did a lot of our arranging. I came
into the band with classical training and a pop tune background
but with little feeling for gut-bucket blues or jazz. Foots would tell
me, "Benny, to get the syncopation right just keep your foot
moving. Do anything you want with it but keep it moving." Once I
learned that I lost that one-two-three-four rhythm forever. Then
Foots got me writing arrangements. I could never write shout
arrangements for the band, but I could write the pretty stuff, and
the more I wrote the better I got. We had guys in the band,
though, whose ears were so good they could write boys whistling.
Don Redman was one. He'd be sitting on the bandstand and a tune
would come to him and he would say, "I've got to have that
arrangement." And while we were playing he would be arranging
in his head. In between tunes he'd be writing. By the end of the
night Don would pass out the arrangement and we'd all sit around
for an extra hour rehearsing his new tune.

Andy Gibson was another one. He was originally a violinist,
taught himself trumpet, played with Lou Redman's (Don's brother)
band in Maryland in the twenties, and then came to New York and
joined a band led by Cab's older sister Blanche Calloway. Andy
could write a complicated arrangement in a minute, but he was
unreliable as all get out. One time Cab got angry because Andy
was supposed to do a new arrangement of "St. Louis Blues." As
the days went on Andy kept getting drunker and Cab kept getting
angrier. Finally Cab said, "Andy, if you don't have an
arrangement of 'St. Louis Blues' by tomorrow morning you can
pack ass." Andy didn't know what to do. At that moment he was
already loaded. Couldn't write a line. Three of us sat up all night
and got him sober. He wrote and we played and in the morning he

had it. I can't say that it was the greatest arrangement of "St. Louis Blues" but I ain't never heard no better. Andy was in such a hurry he wrote the thing without a score sheet. It had three singing choruses in addition to the orchestra instrumentation and three solo choruses for Chu Berry on sax. It was some piece of writing.

At one point Cab had a smart drummer named One Arm Fats. He was good, but he used to get on everybody's nerves because he was arrogant and boasted all the time. Several times I personally wanted to knock the guy's block off, but Cab had a better idea. Jo Jones was just getting out of the army—this must have been in the early forties—and he came down to the theater in New York where we were playing. Cab asked Jo to sit in on drums for one show. Jo had never even seen the show, never mind the music, but he went home to get the shoes that he always wore when he played, and then he played the show and put the band into near destruction. He was all over those drums. Afterwards, Cab went over to One Arm Fats and said, "When you're that good, then you can raise hell. Until then don't give me no more trouble." And he didn't.

Cab's band only played Las Vegas once that I can remember, and that was in 1933. Vegas didn't like the dark of the moon at that time. I played Vegas with Pearl Bailey once when both of us had to stay in our dressing rooms because no hotel wanted anything that looked like us. If we hadn't cottoned up to the gangster Bugsy Siegel we'd really have been in trouble. Vegas then wasn't what it is now, and there were only three little joints and a whole lot of white cowboys off the prairies who didn't care much for Negroes. When I went back to Vegas in the late forties with Billy Daniels, the people at the hotel said Billy could come in but not me. Billy was so light-skinned he looked white. But Cab never went back after that time in 1933 because we had to come in the back door and go out the back door and in between nobody wanted to see us in or near that town. Cab wouldn't stand for anybody denigrating his band like that.

I've known Cab since the thirties. They talk about the Depression, but I don't know anything about it because I was

*hustling in speakeasies in New York and then I went on the road
with Cab in* Hot Chocolates. *Cab and I used to hustle the old
Railroad Club in Boston; he'd sing and I'd play the piano behind
him and we'd take whatever coins the people would hand out. We
weren't rich yet, but we were making it. That was what the
Depression was like for us.*

*Now, some of the guys in the band, six or seven of them,
smoked tea every day of their lives. Some of them would smoke it
like other people smoke cigarettes and you never knew it. They
could play better high than straight. Cab used to tell them, "I
don't have anything against anybody smoking tea, but if you
intend to bring it into the theater, that will be your job."*

*About women. The band was so famous in the thirties and
forties that everywhere we went the women used to clamber after
us. Cab most of all. Man, Cab had so many women you couldn't
keep track of them. And the rest of us didn't do badly either. There
was a theater in Iowa where the guys used to sit on the fire escape
and wink at chicks passing by and some of the girls would come in
and they'd have a time. The one thing Cab always demanded was
that we try to be cool. Some of those bands would come into a
town, screw all the broads they could get their hands on, wreck
the hotel, and leave the people resentful as hell. Not Cab
Calloway's band. Cab always told us, "Go ahead and do what
you want to do, but there are two rules. One, when we come out
on that stage every man is one hundred per cent ready. Two, be
cool about what you do off the stage. You reflect on the band every
time you cause a ruckus, and too many ruckuses and you're out of
this band." There has never been a town where Cab's band
wasn't welcomed back because somebody disgraced himself,
though there were a couple of places where racial incidents
occurred—in the South mostly—where we chose never to go back.*

*Cab's band was the first of the big bands to have its own baseball
and basketball teams. We bought uniforms and balls and bats, and
every town we went into, we'd have a game scheduled with the
local semi-pro team. We'd play charity games in the local*

"Cab's band was the first of the big bands to have its own baseball team. We bought uniforms and balls and bats, and every town we went into, we'd have a game scheduled with the local semi-pro team."

stadium. I think we were playing integrated semi-pro baseball long before the major leagues started letting Negroes in. A few years after we put a team together, Tommy Dorsey got one of his own, then some of the other bands, and it became a common thing. This was in the forties, and we had a pretty good bunch of athletes on the team. Cab was a darn good shortstop and he could hit pretty well, too. Having the team was good for our spirit; it helped to build morale in the band. Those road trips were sometimes as long as six months, and believe me, it could get pretty wearing.

Cab's bands were studying bands. Sometimes we would go out on binges drinking, and we had guys who smoked tea all the time, but we also spent a lot of time listening to music and learning about it. There wasn't a man in the band who didn't want to improve his skills. We used to set up a record player in the hall where the dressing rooms were and we'd all sit around and relax and try to learn something from the music. Sometimes we'd argue about the instrumentation, sometimes the musicianship, sometimes the arrangements, but we were all listening and learning. A band is like a family. Everyone is related and the relationships are always in flux. Different people gain influence and their thing becomes the band's thing, like when Doc had us all become Masons or Cab got us started on baseball. But the one thing we all had in common and which, in fact, Cab demanded and expected of us was that we were first of all musicians.

For example, whenever we were in Chicago, Foots would go over to a little theater in the Negro section there on the South Side, where an old man he knew played flute in the pit band. This old man made that flute sound like pure honey. Foots would spend days at a time listening to him and talking to him and learning from him. In different towns different musicians had their favorite teachers, and they were usually old men you would never hear about, who could play their instruments far better than we could. But these old guys never had the break when they were younger and segregation was tighter.

We used to call Cab "The General" behind his back because he was such a stickler for discipline. To his face we nicknamed him

*"Fess," short for Professor, because he was always teaching us
and helping when we had a problem. He taught us to work
together. And for some of the guys, the younger ones or those who
came from small towns, Cab was almost like a father. He taught
them how to dress, hold their booze, gamble, and deal with the
women who were always running behind the band. And he taught
them how to be professionals. From A to Z, Cab did it.*

*For example, Cab bought all the uniforms. We had three or four
different changes, usually white tails or tuxedo jackets, and for
more formal affairs we had traditional black tuxedos. Cab insisted
that we keep them clean and wear them properly. This meant that
on some days when we were playing four or five shows we had to
change three times a day. We'd do an afternoon show, two
evening shows, and a midnight show. Occasionally we would have
a record date or a charity benefit in the middle. One week in 1933,
in fact it was Christmas week, we were playing at the Apollo
Theater in Harlem and Fred Waring came up to ask Cab if he
would bring the band into the Paramount Theatre downtown
because Waring and his Pennsylvanians had a conflicting date that
week. We were already playing five shows a day at the Apollo, but
the Paramount was big-time and we were just beginning to make a
name for ourselves, so Cab said yes. For four days we played
eight shows a day. I never will forget that. We played two shows
at the Apollo, got taxicabs downtown to the Paramount, ran back
uptown just in time for the next show at the Apollo, jumped in cabs
again to get downtown for the second Paramount show, came back
uptown, then downtown again, then back uptown for the midnight
show at the Apollo. And those theaters were hot as all get out. We
must have changed five times every day, but Cab wouldn't have
anybody on the stage looking rumpled. If somebody had a hole in
his shirt, for example, Cab would put his finger through it and
pull; there went your shirt, baby, and you had to replace it, not
Cab.*

*We didn't stand for anybody having B.O. or anything like that.
In a lot of the places we played we didn't have any showers. We
would come off-stage and have to be back for another show in
thirty minutes. Imagine three guys in a tiny dressing room and*

only a bowl and tap. One guy would use the bowl and wash while the others were changing their suits; then we would rotate and in thirty minutes we'd be ready, some fine-looking, fine-smelling cats.

Things got really wild when Dizzy Gillespie joined the band in 1939. He liked to cut up a lot and I knew Cab wasn't going to stand for that—at least not up there on the bandstand. Dizzy would sit in the back with the trumpet section and throw spitballs at the trombone players down front. The spitballs would go ping *off the trombones and everybody would crack up, but Dizzy would just sit back there with that innocent look of his on his face.*

Dizzy liked to cut up but he was an ace musician. Man, could he toot a horn. He and Cozy Cole and Chu Berry were the stars of the band. Dizzy worked with Mercer Ellington around New York and played Europe before Cab hired him, though nobody had heard much about him.

There was always a state of conflict between Cab and Dizzy. Cab wanted everything orderly and set; Dizzy was wild, and he wanted more improvisation. In all Cab's bands the brass section was the most important. He relied on it heavily to carry the melody and to give the music its tonal quality. Well, Dizzy would take the whole brass section aside and have a meeting. He'd tell all the cats, "Listen, let's liven this music up a little, let's get some bop in this thing, let's cut loose. We shouldn't be held in by these written scores, man." He wanted the rhythms to change and the trumpets to double everything, to pick up the tempo and hold it there while the rest of the band kept the original tempo. In other words, Dizzy wanted Cab's band to play bebop. And from time to time, during a performance, Dizzy would just take off in double time. Man, it was wild. The people in the audience didn't even hear it most of the time, but Cab was very meticulous about music and he would get mad as hell. "What the hell you tryin' to do with my band!" Cab would holler at Dizzy. Dizzy would just smile, and all Cab could say was "Just play it the way it's written."

Their conflict never did get resolved, and there was always tension between them. Dizzy was only around twenty-two years old when he joined us, Cab was ten years older, and he didn't like this wise kid messing around. I could see a blowup between the two coming because Cab has never been the kind of man who will stand a lot of crap, but Dizzy got away with it for a while because he was such a good musician.

There was another guy who gave Cab a lot of crap and he didn't last long. His name was Kansas Fields and he was a drummer. We wondered from the start why Cab had hired the cat. In rehearsal, Cab would call a tune and Kansas would holler, "I don't want to play that." There would be a silence. Then Cab would call the tune again and Kansas would say, "I don't want to play no jumpin' tunes, man. Let's play something soft." That happened about four times, and the fifth time Cab walked over to him, took the music off his stand, and pointed to the door. That was the end of Kansas Fields.

Well, not quite the end. In spite of his attitude, Kansas Fields was quite a drummer. He played with Ella Fitzgerald, Benny Carter, Charlie Barnet, and with the great Charlie Parker and Dizzy Gillespie band of 1942. After Cab bounced him, he went with Eddie Condon, Willie "The Lion" Smith, and Roy Eldridge. It wasn't that old Kansas couldn't play drums, Lord knows he could, but Cab just wouldn't accept any stuff from people, no matter how talented.

The big bands were always very competitive, and the toughest competition was between the white bands and the Negro bands. Benny Goodman used to bring his band up to the Savoy from time to time, and the story was that Chick Webb, who had the regular Savoy band, would give Benny and his band a little face-washing and send them back downtown. There was no way that Benny Goodman's band could stand up to Chick Webb's. It was reputed that Chicklet had three different books, or types of musical program. The third was mild stuff, number two was hot stuff, and number one would blow you away. Chick used his number three book on Benny Goodman; he and his band didn't even work up a sweat. But if Earl Hines was in town playing with Chick, then Chick would have to dig into that number one book and bring out the hot numbers. Earl was the only one who could put any pressure on Chick for sheer showmanship, musicianship, excitement, and energy.

Nobody could put pressure on Cab, though. There was only one boss in Cab's bands. That was Cab. One time Herman Stark, who ran the Cotton Club and taught Cab a lot of what he knows about managing a band, began to call for rehearsals. Cab let it pass the first time and the second, but the third time Cab walked out in front of the band, right with everybody there and listening, and he says to Stark, "Herman, no more rehearsals. That's it." And Cab walked away. Herman stood there red-faced, but Cab had made his point. Everybody knew who was running that band.

It was not unusual in those days, either, for a theater manager to come to a rehearsal and figure that since he knew the theater and the crowd he could tell the bandleader how to play the show. Not with Cab. He didn't stand for it. He would tell any theater manager, "I'm running this band. Don't give my guys no orders." He was very protective of us and very jealous of anyone usurping his role.

THE GUYS IN THE BAND

Benny left the band in 1945 to go into the army. It was a sad day for us. We were playing somewhere in upstate New York when he got his invitation to join Uncle Sam. We gave him a big farewell party, got him totally polluted, and put him on a bus for New York. Benny and I ran into each other a couple of times during his army stint. He was stationed somewhere in the South playing in an army band led by Tony Martin, and my band was on the USO circuit. We played the armed forces installations in different parts of the country, and we got a heck of a reception from the servicemen. One day, when we were playing in St. Louis, Benny came into town and sat in for one show. He got a standing ovation. The war spirit was high everywhere and they just loved the idea of this guy in an army uniform playing with us.

When Benny got out of the army Dave Rivera was playing piano for me; naturally Benny expected his old job back. It was a very hard decision because Dave Rivera was a fine musician and a fine person as well, but I had made the commitment to Benny and Dave had to go. Benny only stayed with the band for a month, though. He was very unhappy with us. The army had changed him, and the band had changed while he was away. He was accustomed to big production numbers; he remembered the days of the big colorful Cotton Club shows. In October

of 1947 he couldn't miss the changes. Benny was also going through some changes of his own, complaining all the time about the music and the schedule, and hassling with some of the other musicians. He was not the same buddy who had gone into the army two years before. I couldn't figure out what was wrong with him. I sent him down to Philadelphia to visit with a friend of mine who was a physician and who counseled Benny. After a couple of weeks, Benny rejoined us but he left soon afterwards, this time because he and I argued over money. He was making $200 a week and he wanted $225. The band wasn't doing very well then, and I just couldn't afford to give him more money because then I would have had to give the other musicians more money. I couldn't afford it; we argued bitterly and he split. It was our worst fight. He called me a cheapskate and a lousy friend and a lot of names I'd rather not print. He joined Pearl Bailey and eventually wound up with Billy Daniels.

Maybe it was better that we split, but it was many a year before he and I exchanged a civil word. Today we're the best of friends again.

I've always had a hard time letting guys go, especially guys like Benny, but through the years I've learned the hard way that business is one thing and personal friendships are another. I don't want that to sound too harsh. I've given guys money and help of all kinds when they needed it. Even when I wasn't all that sure of the next booking. There were some pretty rough times after I broke up the big band, but I've put myself out to help friends when asked. With Benny I guess the timing just wasn't right. I couldn't afford to make a commitment to him for more money than I was paying Dave Rivera when I wasn't all that sure of what the future held.

I think I made the right decision about Benny, although we argue about it to this day. But there is one guy who I owe an apology to. His name is Dizzy Gillespie. Benny is right when he says that there was always a kind of tension between Dizzy and me. I mean, Dizzy was a pain in the neck and if he wasn't such a great musician he wouldn't have lasted as long with the band as he did, but he was a great musician. To this day, when I listen to some of Dizzy's solos on records he did with the band I am flabbergasted. The clarity of his tone. The line. Man, the cat is something else.

But when Dizzy was with the band we didn't appreciate what he was doing. He always wanted to double everything on his solos and in the trumpet section. He was trying to get us to play bebop, and I didn't understand his ideas. It was as simple as that. Years later, he got together with Charlie Parker and Max Roach and Miles Davis. I don't feel too bad about missing Dizzy's message in the early forties. A lot of us missed what was happening to jazz when it changed from the era of the big bands to bebop. One of the musicians who was Dizzy's—and bebop's—strongest critics was Louis Armstrong. But I didn't fire Dizzy because of his playing, I fired him because of his clowning. Lord, did he clown. Like Benny said, he would sit up there in the back row cutting up and throwing spitballs. One night, during a performance, I was hit with two spitballs. Normally Dizzy limited his kidding to the other guys in the band, but this time it seemed to me that he had overdone it. After the show, I was steaming. I walked into the musicians' dressing room and confronted Dizzy.

"You hit me with those spitballs, man. That don't go in this band."

"What?"

"You hit me with those spitballs and you're fired."

"But I didn't do nothin'," he said.

"You're out, man." I wouldn't hear anything else. Dizzy was out.

Fifteen years later, my friend Milt Hinton and I met in New York. We were having a drink and Milt said, "There's something I've got to tell you, Cab. It wasn't Dizzy that hit you with those spitballs in '41, it was me. But you were so angry I was afraid you'd fire me instead of Dizzy."

Well, by this time I'm around forty-eight years old and Milt is around forty-five and we're pretty mellow gentlemen, you might say. I looked at him; he looked at me. And we both broke up laughing. Sorry, Diz.

Milt Hinton also reminded me when I saw him recently of another story. One evening in 1938, after the Cotton Club had moved from Harlem down to Forty-eighth Street and Broadway, old Milt, who could clown some too, got into a jam with Chu Berry. Now, 1937 was the year that Chu won the *Down Beat* and *Metronome* polls for tenor sax; he was quite a celebrity around New York. But more important for Milt, he was an ex-football player, weighing about 250 pounds. Picture him matched against Milt Hinton's 150 pounds. Apparently the guys had had a few drinks before the show and Milt was feeling no pain. The saxes were sitting down front in this show and Milt was up in the back behind Benny Payne. Milt had brought with him a pocketful of fried rice from a Chinese restaurant, and he reached into his pocket and pulled out a few grains and threw them down the bell of Chu's horn. Now, Chu had a short fuse. We were in the middle of a show, and when Milt did it a second time Chu turned around and whispered, "You do that again, Fump, and I'll slap the you-know-what out of you." The entertainment ended, and just as we were about to go into the dance numbers, Milt threw some more rice into Chu's horn.

Now the club was packed, and people were coming out onto the dance floor, but that didn't stop Chu. He put his horn into the rack and jumped up and went after Milt. Boy, was he mad. Milt leaped up out of his chair and headed down the back stairs with Chu on his heels. Next thing I know they're hauling tail up Broadway, Fump running his little tail off and Chu lumbering like a freight train. Fump knew that if Chu ever caught him he would clobber him. They ran all the way up Broadway to Fifty-second Street, but by that time they were both exhausted. Fump was too tired to run any more and Chu was too tired to whip him. They both just stood there on the corner of Broadway and Fifty-second Street holding onto the lamppost and puffing and blowing. Then Chu pointed a finger down at Fump and said, "Dammit, if you ever do that again I'll murder you."

All this time, I didn't know what was going on, until Bill Robinson came into the Club and said he had seen them running up Broadway.

"What those fools doing running up Broadway in the middle of the night, Cab?" Bill asked.

The Bands

The Missourians band that was scheduled for that fateful Plantation Club opening and that eventually went into the Cotton Club and later became Cab Calloway's Cotton Club Orchestra was obviously very different from the bands that toured the country and broke records everywhere in the late thirties and early forties. As soon as I got into the Cotton Club I began to change some of the personnel. R. Q. Dickerson, Thornton Blue, and Earres Prince were replaced by Ed Swayzee, Eddie Barefield, and Benny Payne. Walter Thomas took George Scott's seat in the sax section. Doc Cheatham was added to the trumpet section. Harry White was added to the trombone section. Al Morgan took over bass

"Now, 1937 was the year that Chu won the Down Beat *and* Metronome *polls for tenor sax; he was quite a celebrity around New York."*

from Jimmy Smith. At every stage of the band's development I was satisfied that I had the best men behind me that I could find for the money; as the money got better I could afford better musicians. My best bands were between 1939 and 1943. But of all of them, I think that 1941 band really put it together.

This was what it was like.

Saxophones	Chu Berry, Jerry Blake, Hilton Jefferson, Andy Brown, Walter (Foots) Thomas
Trumpets	Dizzy Gillespie, Jonah Jones, Lammar Wright
Trombones	Keg Johnson, Tyree Glenn, Quentin (Butter) Jackson
Piano	Benny Payne
Bass	Milton Hinton
Guitar	Danny Barker
Drums	Cozy Cole

Fifteen pieces of utter madness. God, could those men play.

Keg Johnson, for instance, is a trombonist that few people have heard of today, but if you listen to the 1933 version, the famous version, of Louis Armstrong's "Basin Street Blues," that's Keg Johnson's trombone solo. Keg and Tyree Glenn split most of the trombone solo work in my 1941 band, and if you listen to any of my old records, the 78's or any of the newer re-releases, it'll be either Keg or Tyree on those solos. Tyree was actually the star of the trombone section. What can I say about that man? First, we were pretty close buddies. He was a Texan with a Texan's heart, big and full and generous. People loved him. He joined the band in 1940 and stayed until around 1945. He eventually got into studio bands around New York and even did a little acting. He was a warm, sensitive cat who rarely gave anybody any trouble. Tyree died of cancer in 1974. Man, I was heartbroken over that. It was so unexpected. After working nearly all of his life he had finally reached a time when he could relax some and boom! He was gone.

The backup trombonist was Quentin Jackson, but to call him a backup really isn't fair. He got the nickname "Butter" from the mellow way he played that trombone. Quentin was one of the best in the business with a plunger mute. In 1948 he went with Duke and later on he did the famous trombone solo in Ellington's "Black and Tan Fantasy."

Sax player Jerry Blake is another guy you'll find doing a lot of the solos on my records. He had been tutored by Sam Wooding and he was right up there with Chu Berry and Walter Thomas and Hilton Jefferson. Jonah Jones, Cozy Cole, Dizzy, Milt Hinton, Danny Barker, Lammar Wright—all of these guys were fabulous.

In 1941, the composing was done mainly by Andy Gibson, George Little, Artie Shaftel, and Sonny Skyler. In 1942 I tied in with Jack Palmer and I even did a couple of tunes with my friend Willie "The Lion" Smith, a pianist and composer who I greatly admire. Nat Cole and I did a couple of tunes together that year, too.

The real change came in 1943. His name was Buster Harding and his arrangements brought a whole new feeling into the band. Buster and I wrote lots of songs together—"The Jive's Been Here and Gone," "We the Cats Shall Hep Ya," "Don't Falter at the Altar," and "Foo a Little Bally Hoo"—but Buster's main contribution was in the way he worked the sections against each other, the tonal arrangements he brought in, and the way he could place the music underneath the soloists to bring out the best quality of the solo.

There were other bands that I liked a lot too, beginning with the 1934 group.

Here are some of those bands:

1934

Saxophones	Eddie Barefield, Andy Brown, Arville Harris, Walter Thomas
Trumpets	Lammar Wright, Doc Cheatham, Ed Swayzee
Trombones	De Priest Wheeler, Harry White
Piano	Benny Payne
Bass	Al Morgan
Guitar	Morris White
Drums	Leroy Maxey

In all of my bands, the guys often doubled. Eddie Barefield on clarinet and both alto and baritone saxes, Andy Brown on bass clarinet and again both alto and baritone saxes. Arville Harris doubled on clarinet, Foots played flute and clarinet, and Morris White doubled on banjo.

My band in 1934

My band in 1940

1940

Saxophones	Chu Berry, Hilton Jefferson, Andy Brown, Jerry Blake, Walter Thomas
Trumpets	Dizzy Gillespie, Lammar Wright, Mario Bauza
Trombones	Tyree Glenn, Quentin Jackson, Keg Johnson
Piano	Benny Payne
Bass	Milt Hinton
Guitar	Danny Barker
Drums	Cozy Cole

For that 1940 band, I hired Tyree away from Benny Carter, and he stayed with me until 1946, when he joined Duke. I hired Quentin Jackson from Don Redman and he was with me from then until 1945, when he left to rejoin Redman for a European tour; then Quentin rejoined me for a year before going with Duke. Hilton Jefferson had been playing in Harlem with several bands, including Fletcher Henderson, Claude Hopkins, and Chick Webb. He stayed with me until 1951 and then he—you guessed it—joined Duke.

By 1942 the war had begun to take its toll of jazz musicians. Several of the guys were drafted around that time, and by 1945 the band looked like this:

Saxophones	Hilton Jefferson, J. Chabama, Andy Brown, Ted McRae, Walter Thomas
Trumpets	Jonah Jones, Russell Smith, Paul Webster, Shad Collins
Trombones	Tyree Glenn, Quentin Jackson, Keg Johnson
Piano	Benny Payne
Bass	Milt Hinton
Guitar	Danny Barker
Drums	Cozy Cole

Shad Collins had replaced Dizzy in the trumpet section; you know what happened there. Ted McRae had replaced Chu Berry in the sax section. That's another story. A sad one. This newspaper clipping from the *New York Times* of October 23, 1941, tells it all:

> CONNEAUT, Ohio, Oct. 27 (AP)—Leon Barry [sic] and An-
> drew Brown of New York, saxophonists with Cab Calloway's
> orchestra, were injured when their automobile struck a concrete
> bridge abutment south of here today. Barry, the driver, was
> taken to a hospital with a possible skull fracture, cuts and
> bruises. Brown was treated for bruises.

Leon "Barry" was, of course, Leon Berry, who we all called Chu
Berry. He died on October 31 from those injuries. He and Andy were in
a car going from one gig to another. The rest of the band was traveling
in separate cars. We had been doing one-nighters all over the Midwest,
and everybody was exhausted. Then suddenly, this beautiful man was
gone. That horn that played with so much feeling would never do it
again.

It's hard for me to explain what happens to a group of men who have
been working and traveling and drinking and arguing and gambling
together for years when one suddenly dies. It's not like the normal
working relationship where at the end of the day the guys go home to
their separate families. We were the family. For some guys Chu was
like a brother. Many of the young musicians looked up to him like a father, and some of the older players looked on Chu like a son. His death
struck each of us in a different way. For me, it was like losing a
brother, someone I had joked with and hollered at. There was a quiet
around the band for weeks, and we left his chair empty.

Death is something I have not yet come to terms with. To this day
when a close friend passes, it gets very quiet around our house. Nuffie
and the kids understand and stay out of my way. I don't talk about it—
unless I get plastered drunk, and then I might loosen up some. But generally I'm not a guy with a lot of words. I keep most of my feelings inside. As far as my own death is concerned, I've often thought that I'll
probably go during a performance. That's the way I'd like it.

Chu was playing with Fletcher Henderson's band, where he and trumpeter Roy Eldridge were the main soloists, when I hired him. Everybody knew about him; he was one of the toughest sax players in New
York. I didn't know if he would leave Fletcher to come with me and I
felt a little guilty about trying to steal him from my friend, but, well,
business is business. At first Chu wasn't particularly receptive to my
offer.

Then he said, "Okay, Cab. I'm interested. But there's one condition."

"What's that?" I asked.

"As long as I'm with you, don't never play that damned sax of yours."

I thought I would bust a gut, but Chu was totally serious. Every now and then I would pick up my sax during a performance and play a little solo. I was no sax player. I could hold a tune and follow the rhythm, but I was strictly a vocalist when it came to music. I knew it, and the guys in the band knew it, but we treated it lightly. Not Chu. No more horn blowing for Cabell Calloway the Third if Chu Berry was on the bandstand, and that was it!

"Okay," I said. "No sax." And I had him.

Chu sat in Webster's seat. Ben had left the band the year before, and after I tried a few substitutes I decided that only Chu would be able to hold Ben Webster's chair down. So I went after him.

Chu was a big guy and he sometimes wore glasses that hung on the end of his nose. His suits never quite fit him right and he had a way of half-smiling and looking down his nose at you through those glasses. And when he got up on the bandstand and opened up that horn. Lord. We didn't have another really exciting sax player until Illinois Jacquet joined the band in 1943.

What else can I tell you about those big bands? They were spectacular to see and more spectacular to hear. I loved working with them.

Sometimes I sit around the house and listen to the records from those years. I hear a clear, sharp, crisp sound with strong musicianship. I hear a rhythm section that rocks, a brass section that always hits exactly when it's supposed to hit, a reed section that is all over the place, just beautifully toned, and when you put it together all I can say is that it leaves me feeling good inside. Fifteen, sixteen, seventeen men who have practiced hard and work together like parts of one instrument. And the feeling is communicated to the people in the audience and all of a sudden people are clapping and feeling good. Feeling good! That's what those bands were about.

The critics liked us during those years too, but one of my favorite reviews was written more recently by the French jazz critic Daniel Nevers. It seems that our music, Negro music, is always being underestimated in this country and appreciated more fully in Europe. (That's me speaking as a lover of honest-to-goodness jazz, not as the entertainer who has been treated beautifully by the American critics.)

> Cab was a man who seemed to feel imprisoned by the limitations of words; he hence sought to break them down, to distort and extend them in all directions, so as to be able to reconstruct them to fit the melodic line and the mood of the moment. The existence of multiple takes bears witness to the extent to which Cab, a born improviser, varied his performances in the best tradition of even the most imaginative instrumentalists. The logical result of this process was "scat," a form which Cab did not invent any more than Louis [Armstrong] did but which—like Louis, yet along a different path—he developed to perfection. Cab exploited the idiom better than anyone, brilliantly using the vast range of his amazing voice to switch from pure sentimentality to the wild excitement of the most frenetic, yet always carefully-measured outbursts. Cab's very evident sense of humor was closer to that of McKinney's Cotton Pickers in their early days than it was to that of either Louis Armstrong or Fats Waller, and one of its immediate consequences was the emergence of vocalized bop; this evolved into the very spirit of bop itself, of which Cab was one of the first precursors. The public was immediately won over, but learned critics were outraged and deplored what they termed Cab's "braying." They were incapable of realizing the true meaning of his style, which did not seek to be part of the established scheme of things, but on the contrary, an escape toward something different, a move toward liberation.

I like that one, but so much for being immodest. It was not me alone. The band behind me made all the difference. I was up front. I had a beautiful voice, a fine trained tenor voice, but behind me were fifteen men, some of them individual giants, others just ordinary good musicians. We made music like a family, and Lord, do I miss it.

We're all getting on now. The era of the big bands is long gone and a lot of the musicians of those years are dying. A couple of times a year I hear of another one who has gone. The Fletcher Hendersons and Duke Ellingtons are gone. The era is gone and so are the bands. Tommy Dorsey, Jimmy Dorsey, Glenn Miller, Chick Webb, Harry James, Earl Hines, Lionel Hampton, Ray McKinley, Charlie Barnet, Jimmie Lunceford, and Louis Armstrong—they all belong to the past. And it was some past. It was a heck of a time for music. And for people who loved great joyful music.

PH-6-4

"*In the simplest terms, we were raising hell in those days. We were in and out of the movies, making records, smashing attendance records everywhere, and doing national radio shows. Lord, were we riding high. Beginning with Jolson's* The Singing Kid *we did about ten films.*"

In the simplest terms, we were raising hell in those days. We were in and out of the movies, making records, smashing attendance records everywhere, and doing national radio shows. Lord, were we riding high. Beginning with Jolson's *The Singing Kid* we did about ten films. My favorite was *Stormy Weather* in 1943. *Stormy* has become a classic. It was written by Ted Koehler, once of the Cotton Club, and Fred Jackson. It starred Lena Horne, Bill Robinson, Fats Waller, the Nicholas Brothers, Katherine Dunham and her dancers, and me and the band. Ada Brown, Zutty Singleton, Mae Johnston, Flournoy Miller, and the comedian Nickodemus were all in it, too. The movie was natural for me; all I had to do was my usual thing and I loved it. And I loved that cast.

My second-favorite movie was *The Cincinnati Kid,* written by Ring Lardner, Jr., and Terry Southern. The cast included Steve McQueen, Edward G. Robinson, Ann-Margret, Karl Malden, Tuesday Weld, Joan Blondell, Rip Torn, Jack Weston, Jeff Corey, and myself. It was a wow. I guess a close third, though, would be *St. Louis Blues* in 1957, with Nat King Cole, Eartha Kitt, Pearl Bailey, Ella Fitzgerald, Mahalia Jackson, Ruby Dee, Juano Hernandez, and Billy Preston.

In addition to those full-length films, the band and I did many short subjects. My favorite was a funny version of "Minnie the Moocher." Other shorts were *Hi-De-Ho Cab, Jitterbug Party, Manhattan Merry-go-round,* and *Old Man of the Mountain.*

In our heyday we were so busy we hardly had time to breathe. There was the famous benefit in December of 1937, featuring me and the band, Bill Robinson, and Rudy Vallee at the Alhambra Theatre. That may have been one of the few times, if not the first, that Rudy Vallee came uptown to Harlem. Man, the town turned out. The receipts went to needy children in Harlem. Another of my favorite benefits was the 1947 Madison Square Garden concert given for the Negro National Day Committee, the United Negro College Fund, and the Damon Runyon Memorial Fund, for cancer research, I believe. That show featured Eddie Anderson (who later played "Rochester" on Jack Benny's television show), Duke Ellington, Lucky Millinder, Willie Bryant, Lionel Hampton, Louis Jordan, Larry Steele, Billy Banks, Doles Dickens, Dorothy Donegan, and me and my band along with four or five other acts. We turned the place out. As I said before, I don't much like doing benefits, but those two were special.

When the Cotton Club closed I took the band on the road for an ex-

"When the Cotton Club closed, I took the band on the road for an extended tour."

tended tour. We played in the Casa Mañana in California, the famous Panther Room of the Hotel Sherman in Chicago, the Lookout House in Cincinnati, and a lot of others between. Everywhere there was standing room only. When we came back into New York, we got a fabulous reception. For two weeks at the Paramount Theatre people paid a total of $84,000 to see us. It was an all-time summer performance record.

In 1943 we played the Cocoanut Grove in New York for a couple of months, and packed the place every night. Then we went into the Meadowbrook supper club in Cedar Grove, New Jersey, and after that the Zanzibar Club at Broadway and Forty-ninth Street in Manhattan. Everywhere we played, we packed them in.

During all of this time I was still writing and publishing and doing radio shows. I guess that my favorite activity of all was the Sunday night "Quizzicale" shows that we did for about a year in 1942 over NBC's Blue Network. The "Quizzicale" was a Negro parody of the Kay Kaiser "College of Musical Knowledge." We had loads of fun with it and turned it into a vaudeville show, which was quite a jump from the straight question-and-answer show that was popular around that time. NBC aired the show without a sponsor. We auditioned for dozens of backers, but it was impossible for Negroes to get a regular commercial sponsor in those days. In fact, that problem didn't change until recently. Even in the fifties Nat King Cole's variety show was canceled when the sponsor pulled out and just about admitted that it was because of pressure from the southern affiliates, who didn't like the idea of a Negro show. It was all right if we came on as entertainers on a white show, but we couldn't have a show of our own. "Quizzicale" lasted for less than a year, but during that time we proved that if you put the talent together a national audience—unlike a sponsor—will accept you.

"Quizzicale" was basically a road show. We broadcast from little towns like Morgantown, West Virginia, or from big cities like Philadelphia and Pittsburgh and New York. In each show we picked participants from the audience and rolled dice. The dice gave the numbers of the questions they were to answer. They were all questions about songs or musicians or musicals, but the real fun was the clowning that went on by several vaudeville characters who were created by members of the band. I played a character called Professor Calloway who was the moderator and headmaster-type. Eddie Barefield created Brother Treadway,

" 'Quizzicale' was basically a road show. We broadcast from little towns like Morgantown, West Virginia, or from big cities like Philadelphia and Pittsburgh and New York.''

a fumbly, exuberant guy who always made mistakes with the way he used words. There was another character called Brother Sixty-two Jones. Lord only knows where that name came from, but either Milt Hinton or Eddie Barefield played that one. Brother Jones was always insulting the rest of us, talking about the way we were dressed or the way we talked. We had some funny routines, and the band loved it.

A lot of the work that we did in the late thirties and early forties was based on Negro slang, the super-hip language of the times. Dizzy Gillespie was a past master at hip talk, but even he would admit that Professor Calloway himself was the hardest jack with the greatest jive in the joint. You hep to what I'm puttin' down?

I mean that old Cab Calloway had a hard spiel and a kopasetic line that was a killer-diller. You would never hear me comin' up on the wrong riff or talking in dribbles or coming up with no off-time jive. And if I ever did melt out I'd just blasé up and say, "Mash me a fin, gate, so I can cop me a fry." Then everything would be straight, with my fry and my fine vines and my main queen on my arm.

I absolutely refuse to translate, but for those of you who don't understand I've included one each of my *Swingformation Bureau* and *Hepster's Dictionary* pamphlets as an appendix. So if you want to get hip, turn to the back of the book.

HARD TIMES AND SOME MORE HIGH TIMES

Sometimes I think that if I could only be out on the stage, performing, all the time, life would be perfect. When I'm out there my total concentration is involved; nothing else in the world exists except me and that audience. I become so tuned into an audience that I can sense their mood; I can tell just from the feel whether they want up-tempo stuff or slow, moody, sentimental stuff. And I adjust my program to meet their desires. I can read an audience like the palm of my hand, but it takes complete concentration. Maybe I'm so sensitive to an audience because the worst feeling in the world for me is to flop. When I go out on a stage and the audience doesn't respond it's like something inside me dies. Maybe I'm so afraid of that feeling that I tune totally into an audience to make sure that I'm giving what they want.

In 1937 I was thirty years old, not a young man any more, but not a fully grown man either. In between. I was on top of the world. I had all the things that money could buy, and then some: women, clothes, cars. You name it. I also had fame. Lord knows I've had my share of fame. It was a lot for a man of thirty to handle. Maybe I handled it well, maybe I handled it poorly. I don't think about it very much. My goal is still to live every day as well as I can. "Live long and well," as they say.

By 1947 I was forty years old, and things had begun to change. I was a lot more mature by then. You men will know what I mean when I say that at a certain point in my life it really didn't matter which woman I woke up next to. Gambling, drinking, partying, balling through the night, all over the country. I knew that women were interested in me because I had fame and I had a lot of money and I would show them a good time. Man, those women would jam the stage doors of theaters all around the country just to get a look at me. Sometimes they would go crazy and tear my clothes off, screaming, and the cops would have to escort me to my car. I was a wild man on the stage, energy personified, singing, dancing, moving, always moving, getting that tremendous audience response, getting everybody worked up singing "Hi-de-ho" and clapping and dancing in the aisles. I guess they all figured I'd be a wild man off stage, too. Sometimes I was. But often, as I got older, I would want to retreat and be alone. I guess by the time I was around thirty-five I began to realize that I needed more than just the high life.

Some of the other guys in the band had wives or girl friends who traveled with them; some of the guys had wives who were faithful and stayed at home waiting for them. In a way I envied those guys. It seemed that they had something solid and I didn't. We were on the road as long as six or seven months at a time. Betty stayed home, took my money, and was my legal wife, but she liked to live her own way. There were lots of parties and she had a pretty good social life. She knew a lot of men and I can't complain; I had my women. We had been married since 1927, but by around 1939 we had stopped having a marriage relationship. I visited her when I was off the road, but by that time I had stopped living at home in Fieldston when I was in New York. I preferred living in hotels in New York City.

Betty had always been jealous, and we argued a lot about rumors that I was having an affair with this or that woman. She hassled me to the point where it wasn't worth coming home any more. When I came off the road I was tired, and being hassled was the last thing I wanted. By 1939 our marriage was null and void as far as I was concerned.

The big band era came to an end for me in 1947, and the years after that are not easy to talk about. I went through some very rough times. I went from a guy whose gross was $200,000 a year to someone who couldn't get a booking. No work at all, and no money coming in. Jesus, that was demoralizing. I'm a proud person, and damned independent. To be in a position where I don't know where my next buck is coming from hurts me to the core. I guess I became a little bitter. I saw Woody Herman and some of the other white bands still going strong, being booked in the big rooms, and the best I could do was some small hotel rooms and nightclubs. And those were the good days. Other times there was nothing at all. I had spent hundreds of thousands of dollars on my friends. Now I was alone with nothing. Only Nuffie got me through. Nuffie and her love, encouragement, understanding, and support—all of the things that Betty would not or could not give me, Nuffie did.

The one point in my life when I did look back sadly at all the money I once had was in the late forties. I realized that living life a day at a time can lead to problems. A little planning for the future may be needed in there somewhere.

The crunch came in 1947. Movies were in, small combos were in, bebop was in, and big bands were out. I just couldn't get the bookings for the big band, so I called the band members together.

"This is one of the worst things I've ever had to do," I told them. "But the bookings are not there any more. I've got to let most of you go. The big bands may come back, but right now it's not happening. Anybody who needs work, I'll do what I can to help you find something. It's been real, man, and I hope we're all together someday."

That was it. There were a lot of long faces in the room that day, but I think they all knew it was coming. I know I did.

Then came the rough years. From 1947 until 1950 there were times when I wasn't sure that I would make it. But Nuffie has often said to me that I am the most resilient man she knows. "Cab, I don't know what it is, but when one career ends, something else always seems to come along to get you going again."

In 1950 something big came along. I was asked to play the part of Sportin' Life in a revival of *Porgy and Bess*. That was one heck of a break, brother, let me tell you. The interesting thing about *Porgy* is that George Gershwin used to spend a lot of time in the Cotton Club during the thirties and the characterization of Sportin' Life was drawn directly from my performances. In fact, in 1935, when *Porgy* was first produced, I was asked to play the part of Sportin' Life but I turned it down because I was too busy with the band and the club. That 1950 revival was something, a smash from start to finish. The cast was Leontyne Price as Bess, William Warfield and later Leslie Scott as Porgy, John McCurry as Crown, and I played Sportin' Life. Even the supporting

players were fantastic: Howard Roberts, Helen Thigpen, Georgia Burke, Jerry Laws, Kitty Ayres. *Porgy* ran for three and a half years, including a great year in London.

After *Porgy* I went back with a small combo. We toured South America, the Caribbean, Europe, and the United States.

In 1967, at the age of sixty, mind you, I did another Broadway show. I played Horace Vandergelder opposite Pearl Bailey in *Hello, Dolly!* Like *Porgy, Dolly* ran for more than three years. But that's where the similarity between the two shows ends. One was a tremendous pleasure; the other was a series of hassles.

Pearl is one fantastically talented woman, but I found her to be very difficult to work with. Much as we all love her, she was the most unpredictable performer I've ever met. I never knew when she was going to show up and whether she would be on time and ready to perform, or how she was going to feel. She came up with heart attacks when it was convenient, or when she wanted to grab a lot of attention. During the entire two-year run of the show on Broadway Pearl's understudy did about ninety shows. It pissed me off because, hell, when I make a commitment to an audience I mean it. A professional performer has a contract that's a lot more than what's on paper. We make a deal with the audience: You pay for your ticket and give us your whole attention and we'll give you all our talent and energy. I've always believed that. So Pearl's attitude really steamed me up.

What capped it was the way she closed the show down. For three and a half years we had had a terrific run everywhere. Then on a Saturday we were leaving Houston and due to open in Milwaukee on the following Monday. Well, Pearl came back into the dressing room after the show and said, "Carol Channing closed the original *Hello, Dolly!* here in Houston so I'm going to close here too."

No one paid any attention to her. Pearlie was always being overly dramatic about something. I figured she just meant that we were closing down Houston. So we all moved on to Milwaukee, the whole company and all the scenery. By Monday night the sets were all hung up, and we were ready to go with $75,000 in advance sales and great publicity— and no Pearl Bailey. She never came. The show never opened in Milwaukee and it never opened anywhere again. Pearl had decided, on her own, that she wanted to give it up.

We later heard that that very night, Pearl was in Sardi's restaurant in

"In 1950, something big came along. I was asked to play the part of Sportin'
Life in a revival of Porgy and Bess. *That was one heck of a break, brother,*
let me tell you."

New York City, having a natural ball, and David Merrick, the show's producer, walked in. He had a fit right there in the restaurant, and the two of them made a heck of a scene out of it. He was burned to the gills; she had quit the show and not informed anyone, not even him.

The next night, Pearl was out in Shea Stadium at a ball game, while the theater in Milwaukee was dark. They had to bring the whole cast back, and the theater in Milwaukee confiscated the scenery and all of the music and props until Merrick and the backers paid off the loss. And that was the end of that show.

I couldn't understand her doing a thing like that. People, families, careers, and livelihoods were involved. Hell, what kind of justice is that?

If Pearl was hard to work with, the Harlem Globetrotters were just great to work with. I knew Abe Saperstein from the Chicago days when he had a Negro team called the Harlem Five and was trying to hire players to work up an act. That act eventually became the Harlem Globetrotters. In 1965, when Abe and I ran into each other in Chicago, he was looking for something to spice up his halftime intermissions. As soon as he saw me he said, "Cab, you're just the guy I've been looking for."

I began to travel with the Trotters doing the halftime shows. The Trotters had two teams, the East Team and the West Team, and I would switch from one to the other throughout the season, traveling all over the country. Those were some of the sweetest, most natural guys you'd ever want to meet—Sweetwater Clifton, Meadowlark Lemon, Marquis Haynes. They were wonderful men. And they loved life just like I did. We would do a show, go back to the hotel and sit up all night playing poker and drinking booze, then board the bus in the morning, get to the next town half asleep, do another performance, and start the whole routine all over again.

The halftime show was a new kind of experience for me. I would walk out into the middle of the court, and they would roll a piano out with me and my pianist and I would let them have it. All the old tunes, all the pop tunes. The whole auditorium, 15,000 to 20,000 people most of the time, would be hushed and listening to see what I was going to put down, and by the end of the halftime, I would have the whole damned place echoing with "Minnie." I could feel the mood of the crowd even in a huge auditorium. And it was a ball, me just swinging and swaying with my hair flopping down on my forehead and my arms

"In 1967, at the age of sixty, mind you, I did another Broadway show. I played Horace Vandergelder opposite Pearl Bailey in Hello, Dolly!*"*

stretched out, singing my heart out. There's no feeling like that for me in the world. I don't care what the setting is. You put me in front of a mike, with a little instrumental support and a crowd, and I will perform. I love it.

Porgy and *Dolly* put an end to the hard times professionally, but I still had a lot of personal problems to wade through in those years, and most of them had to do with Betty. In 1937 we decided to have a child. Well, really it was Betty who wanted the child. I was already beginning to dislike the marriage, but she pressed me and I agreed. There was one problem; she was unable to conceive, so we agreed to adopt. But Betty couldn't admit to her society friends that we were adopting a baby, so in 1937 she left the country to "have" our two-month-old daughter. We named the child Constance. We soon found out that Constance was mentally retarded. Betty was heartbroken. So was I. It was awful. We sent Constance to special schools and to specialist physicians of all sorts, but they finally agreed there was nothing anybody could do. She would probably always be somewhat retarded.

The baby hadn't helped our marriage, and Betty and I were moving further and further apart. I tried to stay in touch with Constance, but Betty made it difficult. So did my schedule. I was on the road a lot and it was hard to sustain a family when the real love did not exist. I haven't seen Constance for about six years now. She is in Chicago somewhere, I think, maybe with her mother. She would be thirty-eight years old now. I hope she is all right. Constance is an aspect of my life that makes me very sad. I've completely lost touch with her. When her mother and I finally divorced in 1949, almost all contact was broken. I sometimes wish that during Constance's early years I had been around to give her more love. It might have made a difference. Or it might not. I'll never know. And it's too late for my regrets to make any difference. I guess my memory of her as a sweet, dark-haired little girl struggling to cope with things will have to remain the best I have of her.

From 1939 to 1949 Betty and I were separated in fact if not by law. It was during that time, in 1942 to be exact, that I met Nuffie. A mutual friend, Mildred Hughes from Washington, gave me her number because I was headed for a gig there. When I got into town I called her, and that whole week I was seeing Nuffie in between shows. She had an apartment where she'd cook dinner and I could just get away and relax. I liked her a lot right off. I was thirty-five years old at the time, with plenty of money and plenty of women, but there was something about

Nuffie that caught me. She was not the run-of-the-mill woman I met on the road. She was proud, and aloof as all get out, and very intellectual. She kept me at arm's length, but she was also very warm and friendly. I couldn't quite figure her out. She was impressed by the money that I had—not many Negroes had that kind of money—but on the other hand her family, her mother especially, had a strong dislike of entertainers. To her, entertainers were not quite acceptable people. Matter of fact, Nuffie wasn't sure at first that she wanted anything to do with me. And that was something new for me.

After I left Washington, we corresponded regularly, and every now and then when I had a day off I would run down to Washington to see her. Occasionally she would come up to New York to visit me. She loved the band, and she loved being around me and my work. It was exciting as hell to have found a woman who was intelligent, interested in my work, in love with me, and who would spend hours and hours with me without any hassles. By 1943 we were pretty much living together, and I knew I had found the woman I wanted. It was then that I began efforts to get a divorce, but Betty used every trick in the book to keep me on the ropes and milk me of as much money as she could. The divorce laws were much more stringent then and that woman wanted both my arms and both my legs. It must have cost me $25,000 in lawyers' fees alone to get rid of her. One problem was that one of my legal advisers really screwed me. Every time I turned around there was a new "problem" in getting the divorce. He needed more money for this or that. Well, I was anxious to get out of the marriage and by 1943 Nuffie and I were tired of hiding our relationship from Betty. Nuffie traveled a lot with me and was around constantly, so the guys in the band knew, but we kept it secret from Betty. By 1944 Nuffie and I wanted to have a family of our own and I would have given just about anything to get out of that marriage. I finally got Betty to agree to a legal separation, but I paid dearly for it. That year I had a gross income of $48,000, with expenses of $29,000 and net income of $18,000. I had already paid Betty $3,000 for the separation and $5,000 in cash to agree to a settlement. I paid her another $3,900 when she signed the settlement and $7,700 when she signed the final decree. Besides all that I gave up the house in Fieldston, which was worth $150,000, and two apartment houses that I owned in Chicago. And I've been paying alimony for the last twenty-six years. Man, what money I gave up to get away from that woman.

This book has created some problems for me and my family because I

"Besides all that I gave up the house in Fieldston, which was worth about $150,000, and two apartment houses that I owned in Chicago."

promised myself I was going to be honest about the whole thing. It took so long to get the divorce that two of my children were born out of wedlock. In 1945 Nuffie became pregnant. We tried to push for the divorce, but Betty wouldn't settle. Of course, she never knew the real reason I was pushing so hard. Nuffie and I wanted to have a normal family, but it just wasn't working out. Both Chris and Lael were born before the divorce came through and before Nuffie and I were married. Nuffie and I had never told the children about this. Maybe we should have, but it just never seemed necessary. They were both conceived and born out of great love and that was all that mattered. Nuffie and I argued for several weeks in 1975 on how to approach the problem. My idea was, hell, just call them up and level with them. Chris and Lael are both women now, and so is Cabella, our youngest daughter. Don't make a big deal out of it, was my argument. Nuffie disagreed. She wanted to get everyone together and have us all sit down and talk it through, but I got stubborn about it and refused to participate in any such thing. Finally, in September 1975 I had a gig out in Chicago with Lael, and Chris, who is now living in Los Angeles, joined us there. Nuffie simply told them, as she had told Cabella before we left for Chicago.

Perhaps these are old-fashioned attitudes. We felt no shame when the children were born out of wedlock, but we, especially Nuffie, weren't quite sure how the girls would take it. They handled it like I knew they would, with maturity. Nothing to it.

In 1949 the divorce came through, and Nuffie and I hustled down to Leesburg, Virginia, and were married by a justice of the peace. It was a great feeling to be free and open about everything. As soon as we exchanged vows we laughed and hugged and Nuffie wept. It was wonderful. We were finally together for real and totally and fully.

I have five daughters now. There is Camay from my teen-age relationship with Zelma Proctor. There is Constance. And there are three daughters by Nuffie and me: Chris is now thirty, Lael twenty-eight, and Cabella twenty-three. Five daughters and no sons. I get a lot of kidding around here because of that. But I got my own back. I have five grandsons. I've already told you about Camay and Booker's two boys. Lael has Todd, who is nine, and Sean, who is six, and from Chris and her late husband, Ruppert Crosse, there is Osaze, who is three. By the time you read this book I may have another grandson, or my first granddaughter. Cabella and her husband Andrew Langsam will give birth any day now.

"In 1949 the divorce came through, and Nuffie and I hustled down to Lees-burg, Virginia, where we were married by a justice of the peace."

That's my family. From 1947 on, whatever I've been through they've been through. For good or bad. I want to give you a closer picture of them, but I learned some time ago that I cannot speak for them. Lord, these children are independent. And Nuffie is more independent than all the girls put together. People in this family speak for themselves. Believe me.

I never will forget when I did the "Person to Person" show with Edward R. Murrow in 1958. He brought an enormous television crew up to the house in Lido Beach to spend an hour with the family. It was quite an event to be on national television in those days, and of course Edward R. Murrow was one of the greatest broadcasters of his time. We all prepared for days. The whole family was to be there, Camay, Constance, Chris, Lael, Cabella, and Nuffie. The girls were to do little numbers of their own. Lael was to do a tap dance or something, Chris was to play the piano, and Cabella was just to answer a few questions like a nice little girl of five or six should. Well, Lael did her dance and Chris played a little tune on the piano and then Murrow came over to talk to Cabella. She wouldn't say a word. He asked her a question and she looked like she wanted to hide in her mother's belly. Nuffie was pulling on her arm and trying to get her to talk, but no, Cabella had made up her mind she did not want to be involved and that was it.

For a while Lael wasn't much better. When she was eight, my manager and I dreamed up an idea for me to do a father-daughter routine with her. In fact, I cut three records with her—one of them, "Little Child," became quite a hit—and I took her with me up to the Catskills a couple of times for shows. She was a big hit, but she hated it. She hated having to study the lyrics from a record and she hated getting all dolled up in frilly dresses and tight patent-leather shoes. She was not ready for a professional career and she made it obvious whenever she had a chance. She would pout and grimace and frown every time we had to get ready to do a performance. After about five months we gave it up.

"Nuffie," I said, "this child just does not want anything to do with entertainment, so let's forget it." That was one happy child when she went back into her play clothes for good. No show business for her at that time.

So you can see they are all independent. They speak for themselves. In their own words.

"When Lael was eight, my manager and I dreamed up an idea for us to do a father-daughter routine. In fact, I cut three records with her. One of them, "Little Child," became quite a hit."

NUFFIE TALKS ABOUT CAB

People have asked me what attracted me to Cab. Well, he was personable, it was as simple as that. He had a warmth and a charisma about him. And he could make people feel wonderful. He could make an audience feel what he felt. He made me feel what he felt when we met. He killed me with charm.

My dear friend Mildred Hughes, now Mrs. David M. Grant of St. Louis, introduced us. I was living in Washington when she called and said, "Now listen, I have a very close friend who is coming to town tomorrow and I want you to meet him because I think you will really like each other. You're both peculiar."

"Well, thanks a bunch," I said. "But any friend of yours is welcome in my house, you know that." My southern training was coming out. "Who is he?"

"Calloway, Cab Calloway," she said.

"Cab Calloway! I do not want to know any show people."

"Look," she said, "he's not show people like Isabella's (that was my mother) connotation of show people. He's from a nice Baltimore family."

So I agreed, and the next night Cab came over after he finished the show at the Howard Theatre. Of course I didn't go to the show. Those were my Mona Lisa days when I wore my hair very straight and pulled back severely.

Cab was very polite. I had heard that he was something of a Don Juan, and a high liver, but the first thing he asked me for was a glass of water. He was very charming and I was more than a little confused because the way I was brought up one simply did not associate with show people. But Cab was very handsome—and almost shy, so that he didn't seem like show people.

*The next day he called me and asked to come over again. I was
still hesitant because he was in show business, but I said yes and
we began to see each other every day. We talked about the
symphony and about the kind of theater that I enjoyed. I was
surprised that he was so sophisticated and knowledgeable about
all sorts of things. And it developed from there.*

*To this day I hold Mildred responsible for what has happened.
Whenever Cab and I go to the White House, which we have
several times, I call Mildred and say, "You know, if it hadn't been
for you, girl, I wouldn't be going to the White House." And when
Cab and I have a fight, I call Mildred and say, "Dammit,
Mildred, if it weren't for you I wouldn't be in this mess!"*

*Cab was very famous, at that point. Everywhere he went he was
a sellout, and he was booked a whole year in advance. This was
during the war and he had an exemption because he had an
enlarged heart. In order to make up for that he did an awful lot of
work for army bases, bond drives, and that sort of thing. He
played in all the major defense plants, and in order to perform for
all the shifts he did six or seven shows a day.*

*The late Moms Mabley, the famous Negro comedienne, worked
those shows with him. She always called me her wife-in-law
because she used to say Cab was her husband. In addition to
Moms the show in those days included the dancers Stump and
Stumpy, the Peters sisters, and a line of beautiful chorus girls.*

*Cab was booked so tightly that it was impossible for him to get
a vacation. His managers were cracking the whip, and he didn't
have a free minute. They were hectic years, but they were good
years.*

*Then there came a time, in 1947, when the big bands no longer
drew crowds. Cab had been used to adoring mobs standing
around the bandstand, watching him and listening to him and his
music. Now he would have an engagement and there might be only
a handful of people. It was a traumatic experience. Cab knew it*

"People have asked me what attracted me to Cab. Well, he was personable, it was as simple as that."

was time to change, but the band had been so much a part of Cab over the years that it was difficult for him.

But that's getting ahead of my story. To go back to my early acquaintance with Cab: In 1942, when we met, I was twenty-seven and he was thirty-five. I was a college graduate, working as an administrative secretary in the Department of Housing (it was not easy for a Negro woman to make much headway in those days), and I had previously worked as typist and researcher for the Swedish social scientist Gunnar Myrdal on his classic Carnegie Foundation study of the Negro problem, An American Dilemma. *I was not looking to get married. I was independent and enjoying an active social life; I had plenty of men friends, my own apartment (against Mama's wishes), and I was very much a rebel.*

Cab simply bowled me over. He was a new kind of man for me. He was probably the least "intellectual" but wisest person I had ever met. He was gentle and warm and solicitous with me, but strong and firm at the same time. I have, in the years since, seen Cab as a sweet, generous man with a fierce temper when he or one of his is insulted or hurt. I've seen him knock people down with his fists for getting out of line.

But beyond the personal side of Cab, was the world he was in. It was exciting and dangerous and tantalizing and intimidating for me. Mama, bless her, had always told me: "Nuffie, you stay clear of show people, they're no good." That was her attitude and the fact that she felt so strongly about it made the whole business a bit titillating for me when I met Cab; Cab was nothing like I expected a showman to be. And when he took me backstage that first week at the Howard Theatre in Washington and I met the other guys in the band, I was nervous and fidgety. Of course, I didn't let Cab know; he would never have understood that kind of an attitude, that kind of fear. The first time I ever saw Cab perform was there in Washington, at the Howard. I had heard of him, of course; Cab Calloway was a household name in America then. But I was very much involved with classical music and with Negro classical music—gospel, jazz, and so forth. It had never occurred to me to seek out a popular, commercial entertainment.

Cab absolutely blew me away that first night at the Howard. This quiet, gentle man, when put up on the stage, had a beautiful, clear tenor voice; he could carry a schmaltzy ballad or a hell-raising jump number with equal force; and he had an energy and an intensity about him that was almost frightening. He moved with a wildness and a sureness that was unbelievable. By the end of the performance I was perspiring. And the band he had behind him was not just a bunch of ordinary musicians. These men obviously knew their instruments, and the show was highly organized and colorful and entertaining from start to finish.

Afterwards, Cab took me backstage. I was anxious to meet his friends, but I was very nervous. My mother had implanted this idea about entertainers so firmly in my mind that I felt guilty going backstage. I remember meeting Benny Payne and Milt Hinton especially. These guys were so warm and gentle and loving; I felt totally accepted and appreciated. In the following months, as Cab and I saw each other more and more frequently, I got to know these guys, and their wives, well. Dizzy and Lorraine Gillespie are still among my best friends in the world. And Benny and Alice Payne and Milt and Mona Hinton are too, even though Benny and Alice now live in California and I don't see them often.

I later found out that the men in the band were all surprised that Cab had chosen me for what was to become a permanent relationship. I was so different from Betty, who had really looked down on them in an almost personal sense and who, apparently, never came to the theater or invited the men in the band into her home.

I guess it's one of life's paradoxes. I was taught that show people are evil, low life, and inferior, but Mama also brought me up, as a Christian, to respect each individual as a person. That was paramount. So when it came down to it, and these men turned out to be loving people and gentlemen, my better instincts prevailed and all my prejudices melted. I became fascinated by the entertainment world. Whenever I could I went to Cab's shows and afterward you would always find me backstage talking to the men, laughing with them, enjoying their feeling for life.

My world, the world of Washington's Negro intellectual class, was as different for Cab as his world was for me. And he was just as intimidated by my friends as I had been by his. I tried to get him involved in the parties and functions of my group in Washington. He resisted; he didn't like the idea of parties where the people stood around making delicate, intellectual small-talk and smoking pipes and discussing politics. Cab was a gambler, and while gentle, his natural milieu had been among rough, tough-talking, earthy folk. I felt very cut off from my former friends. Then, in 1943, about a year after we started seeing each other, Cab agreed, at great insistence from me, to go to a typical D.C. Negro upper-middle-class party. It was the turning point in our relationship.

I don't recall whose house the affair was at. But I could feel Cab withdraw as soon as we walked into the place. Cab has always been a pretty flashy dresser; these guys were all collegiate types and many of them worked for the government—so they were dressed conservatively. And, as a matter of fact, they did tend to stand around talking about government policy and Washington politics, subjects that Cab couldn't have cared less about. He quickly found himself a strong drink and a quiet corner.

But Walter White and a small group of men were standing near Cab talking about racial discrimination around the country. And of course Cab had experienced some of the worst of it—his was the first major Negro band to make the great deep-South circuit. So Walter or someone asked Cab about his experiences and Cab suddenly became the authority, and boy did he open up. Before the evening was over just about every man in the place was huddled around Cab listening to his stories about traveling with a big band through the South.

They had, in effect, acknowledged Cab's wisdom and intellect. This was very gratifying for him because his first wife had always belittled him in front of her so-called intellectual friends. Walter did love and respect Cab greatly, and years later, when some of the Negro organizations protested the revival of Porgy and Bess *as demeaning to black people, Walter White spoke out most strongly that* Porgy *was a folk opera and that it should be a source of pride.*

I'm trying to remember just who was present at that party. It's important because many of these men subsequently became friendly with Cab. Frank Horne, Lena's uncle, had been my boss in the Department of Housing. Cab and Frank became very close after that party. So did Judge William Hastie, who later became the governor of the Virgin Islands and dean of the Howard University Law School; and William Trent, head of the government's racial relations department; and Abe Harris, chairman of the Department of Economics at Howard University; and Sterling Brown, of Howard's English department; and Eugene Holmes, of Howard's philosophy department; and Claude Barnett, founder of the Associated Negro Press and a close friend of mine from childhood; and Clarence Johnson, who headed labor relations in the race-relations section of the Department of Housing.

These men were all at this party which was so important to my relationship with Cab—for the first time our lives became fully intertwined. I had established friendships with his friends and he had established friendships with mine.

Cab was on top of the entertainment world in those years: from 1942, when we met, until 1947, when he had to disband the seventeen-piece orchestra. That began the low point of his career: from 1947 until 1950, when Porgy and Bess *came along. In 1947 the other bands were cutting down, and it wasn't until it was financially impossible to go on with sixteen or seventeen pieces, plus a bandboy, a valet, and a road manager, that he decided to reduce to seven pieces.*

We talked about it often. The only advice I could give him was, "When one door closes another one opens. When it's time for a change God will show you the way."

When he cut the band I felt terribly sorry for him. It was like giving up a part of himself, like losing a child or something that was inside of him. And you also have to realize that in cutting down on the band he was risking his image. But he did it.

Cab bought a big Chrysler that would seat nine people and we had a driver who was quite a character. We would put the luggage on top and the bass drum inside, plus the seven fellows and their instruments. The group was very successful, but then even that format became less popular. And every time he had to acknowledge within himself that the thing he was trying wasn't working, it was a whole new trauma. He became less talkative and began to live deep inside himself. I don't know precisely what he was going through in the late forties, but I had the feeling that he thought he was retrogressing. After being the toast of the town and the country he had begun to feel that he was going backwards, that he was losing something.

Then he went from seven pieces to a trio. It was another devastating blow. I always tried to stay out of his business, simply to bolster him and encourage him, but at this time his agents and the people who were booking him put him into some places that I did not approve of.

One place in Chicago, next to the Chicago Theatre, was a little club where a lot of musicians played, but I didn't like it for Cab. I didn't speak up then as I do now, but I did say to him that he had once played in the Panther Room in the Hotel Sherman, which was three blocks away. He had opened there every New Year's Eve when he was on top. Now he was being booked into this little place three blocks away. It was an insult, and it hurt him deeply.

There were other places they could have booked him. It made me mad because I felt that it was because he was black—or Negro, as we said at that time—that they didn't try to push him into the elegant spots. That engagement in Chicago in 1949 was the low spot in his career. From there we went into Brown's Hotel in Denver, and it was there that Blevins Davis came to him and talked about him appearing in a revival of Porgy and Bess.

Cab had a lot of mixed feelings about it. He had been away from the stage since he did Hot Chocolates *in 1929, and he didn't know if he could do it. It's funny, but sometimes I can communicate with Cab and sometimes I can't. When he was trying to decide about* Porgy *we talked openly and freely about his fears. Finally he agreed to try it.* Porgy, *of course, was a great success in the theater, but as far as Cab was concerned he felt at first that it was something of a disaster for him. He was not used to working in relationship to other people on a stage. He was used to working directly to a whole audience. But he was such a marvelous performer and so talented that his natural ability to project overrode his reservations and he carried it.*

Porgy *made it in Dallas, where it opened, but a couple of critics picked up on the problem Cab was having in adapting. In Chicago Robert Breen, the director, really began to work with Cab and to teach him techniques of working with other people on the stage. He would tell Cab, "You are not one-to-one out there, you are with these other people."*

It took a little time for the lessons to sink in, and meanwhile Cab remained a little depressed and unhappy with his performance. Any time Cab goes out on a stage he wants to give the best that's in him. That's the root of his being. In Porgy *it worried him that he couldn't. But God bless Robert Breen. He was fantastic, and he knew how to get the best out of Cab. In a while, Cab's spirits began to lift; he got into the feeling of the work and his depression disappeared like magic. Once he felt he was really performing at his best, that was all he wanted.*

When Cab was going through these changes it meant stress and strain at home. He eventually left Porgy *partly because he felt he was needed at home. Chris, Lael, Cabella, and I lived in London with Cab for the year that* Porgy *played there. It was a very happy time. One of the first times that we were a whole family together. But after the London performances, he was on the road again and we missed him terribly. The children were getting older and he was getting older and weary of the road.*

I don't want to paint too grim a picture of these times. Cab had some tremendous successes with the seven-piece band and with the trio. His three tours of South America and the Caribbean in the 1950s were all smashes; everywhere we went the crowds hung on his music and his singing. In 1950, for example, he reconstituted the old big band for a three-week stand in Uruguay during Carnival time that broke South American records for jazz and pop and opened up the whole Latin continent to American musicians for years to come. And his 1947 performances in Havana were simply superb. One of the mistakes I think that people make when they think about Cab Calloway is to ignore the possibility that inside that energetic, vibrant, vital man projected from the stage beats the heart of an ordinary man who can feel disappointments deeply, who is in his own way very shy and who has been through changes that would have broken a weaker man.

As I said, we felt the pressures at home, but whatever we had going for us helped us to survive and overcome. It was not always easy. I guess that the strength we both had, whatever it was that we were sharing, helped us. And besides, Cab is a wonderful father. He drank heavily sometimes and was hard to get along with sometimes and sometimes he got a little stretched out with the horses—well, truthfully, at times it was worse than that, at times it got downright hairy because of the horses—but we stuck it through and we all grew together into a strong, damned exciting family.

As far as Cab and the horses go, that's a lifelong love affair. Whenever Cab isn't working, unless he has things to do around the house, you can bet your life that he's out at Belmont or Aqueduct. And when we're on the road, the first place he heads for on a day off is the local racetrack. One of the first rules of etiquette that my daughters learned around the house, all at an early age, was that when they answered the phone and it was a call for Daddy while he was at the track, their answer was, "Sorry, Daddy's not home. He's at the office." When Cabella, our youngest daughter, was around twelve years old, a man called looking for Daddy three days in a row. On the third day he said to

Cabella, rather crossly, "I've been trying to reach him for three days and he's never home." "Well," Cabella said, "he's actually taking a novena and it takes nine days for a novena."

In 1949 and 1950, when the big bands were dying, Cab was gambling heavily and we had no money. He never told me how much he owed the bookies, but it got so bad that those guys, who really loved Cab, refused to take his bets. They didn't want to see him go any further into debt. He owed them thousands of dollars. Maybe more. A series of events led up to a confrontation between Cab and me over this. A couple of times when Cab came home from his booking agent and they had no bookings for him, he had only $2 in his pocket. Literally only $2. He'd go to the bookie there in Long Beach, Long Island, near Lido Beach where we were living, and he'd put that $2 on a horse. When the horse won—and it often did—we had money for dinner. When he would get a gig, Cab would get back into gambling heavily again. He probably figured that one big hit would solve all our problems. It didn't work that way, and for years we stayed right on the brink of financial disaster.

One Sunday afternoon I mustered up all my courage, picked up the baby, Lael, in my arms, and walked into the living room where he was studying the racing form. They didn't allow horse racing in New York State on Sundays then, but the Mexican government had just opened up Sunday racing in Mexico City, so Sunday had become a day for the horses, too. I stood in front of him and said as calmly as I could: "Cab, I can't take it any more with the horses. I'm going to pack up, take these children, and leave. Then it'll be you and the horses. It's become an addiction with you that will ruin the family if you don't stop."

"Oh, baby, it's not that serious," he said.
"It is that serious," I said. "I'm that serious. I can't take it any more."

Without hesitation, he said, "Okay. Okay. Okay. I'll stop. I'll quit." And he walked away. He wasn't happy about it at all, but he meant it. Cab didn't bet on another horse for four years. Not a

208 / NUFFIE TALKS ABOUT CAB

dollar. I suppose that he realized it must be serious for me to confront him like that. I never questioned him in those days.

In 1954 or 1955, when we had recovered and things were going well financially, Cab and I talked about it again. "Cab," I said, "I don't mind your betting on the horses, on one condition. That you take the $300 or so we would spend in a nightclub and go to the track and bet there; not with the bookies, where you can bet more than we can afford and get into another hole."

We made a deal that day that is still in force. Cab goes out to the track as often as he can. It's his pleasure, his relaxation, and his satisfaction. His troubles fade away and he loves the racetrack crowds and they love him. He has dozens and dozens of photographs of himself presenting trophies to the winners of stake races. But one reason that I think he gets such pleasure out of it now is that it is no longer an addiction. It's a hobby, thank God.

The entertainer who has become one of my most durable friends is Lena Horne, and I met Lena in 1942, some months before I met Cab. I was in New York visiting some friends; they invited me to a party in Harlem at the Theresa Hotel and Lena was there. I knew, of course, who she was, mainly for the name she made singing in the Cafe Society Downtown in New York. But she had also made several films by then, including Blackbirds of 1939, *and worked with Charlie Barnett's and Noble Sissle's bands. In 1942 she was traveling with the USO, entertaining the troops, and she had just finished the film* Panama Hattie.

Our first meeting, at the Theresa, was not exactly friendly. Lena is the first one to admit that she can, at times, be a little cold towards people she doesn't know or doesn't like. When we were introduced, I sensed a certain sharpness towards me; we immediately began that kind of female sparring that some people would call cattiness. In her autobiography, Lena, *she described that exchange like this:*

> *We clashed immediately. [Nuffie] was very light-skinned and I am very thin-skinned and I thought she was some white hanger-*

on. I had all the proper prejudices too. You see a white girl hanging around with a Negro man, you immediately think she's a tramp. . . . We picked each other out immediately and started dueling the way women will. I had to give her credit—she was bright and I was always attracted to brainy people. I admitted that even before I found out she was Negro.

I had to go away to work and when I came back she was still with the group. I drew one of the men aside and said, "What the hell is that white bitch doing here?"

The guy was amazed. He said, "Don't be silly, Nuffie ain't white." . . . I went up to her and admitted my mistake, and apologized. I was especially ashamed and I had to admit—as both of us cracked up—that I thought it was only white folks that couldn't tell what we were.

A couple of years later, Cab and I were in Los Angeles with the band. Cab wanted to go by a friend's house. He wouldn't say who. He went up to a house in a section of Hollywood and rang the bell. Lena answered the door and they hugged and kissed like old buddies. Then Cab turned to me and said, "Lena, I want you to meet my wife, Nuffie."

Lena looked at me and I looked at her and we cracked up, again.

"Meet your wife!" Lena screamed. Then she ran down the steps hollering, "Nuffie! How the hell you been, girl? I didn't know you two were married!" And Cab, obviously, didn't know Lena and I knew each other. He stood there wide-eyed.

Cab and Lena had met years before, in the Cotton Club. Cab still claims to have "discovered" her—"I pulled her out of the chorus line because she was so beautiful and so talented," he recalls. And while she was in the Cotton Club, Lena credits Cab with protecting her, as a young sixteen-year-old, from the roughs around the club and with giving her "realistic guidance on how to behave." They worked together on and off over the years, their most memorable being the film Stormy Weather *in 1943, in which both starred.*

In 1945 I was pregnant with our first child, Chris, and I was traveling with Cab on the West Coast. Cab had to go back on the road with the band, and we were sitting around talking with Lena one evening.

Lena said, "Nuffie, you're too far along to be running around the country with this cat. Why don't you stay here with me?" I stayed with Lena for four months, and when my time came it was Lena who drove me to the hospital. Lena and I became very close during that time; and she is Chris's godmother.

Lena has a lot of the qualities that Cab has. She's tough when she needs to be and she's gentle when she wants to be. Both of them have fierce tempers, both of them have a kind of singlemindedness when they're performing, and both of them have managed by their dedication and talents to survive several careers and to span several eras of music and entertainment. Even though I don't see Lena as much as I would like these days, the basic love and loyalty of our friendship remains.

What continues to amaze me about my husband, Cab, however, is that durability. The man spans three or four eras of music and entertainment and he can still go into the Concord Hotel in the Catskills and slay 2,500 people, get them standing up, singing hi-de-ho, clapping their hands, and stomping their feet. He still has the charisma. I appreciate it, respect it, and am awed by it. More important to me personally, though, is that Cab through all the years, and with all his grand successes and dispiriting disappointments, remains the warm, somewhat shy, charming, strong, sometimes rough and crude but always human man that I met in Washington and still love deeply.

People often ask me what kind of life it's been with someone so independent and proud, along with being so talented. Well it's been difficult at times and it's been glorious at times. Chris was born in 1945, and in 1947 Lael was born. We were beginning a family and I wasn't able to travel as much. Cab was away for long periods, in and out of their lives. They knew him mainly from a

"More important to me personally, though, is that Cab through all the years, and with all his grand successes and dispiriting disappointments, remains the warm, somewhat shy, charming, strong, sometimes rough and crude but always human man that I met in Washington and still love deeply."

distance, as a kind of hero who the kids at school would ask them about with some reverence but about whom they knew little of a personal nature. The best year for us during that period was 1953. Our youngest daughter, Cabella, was born in October of 1952 and six weeks later I took the family, including little Cabella, to London, where Cab was in Porgy. *We were together for a year; Cab was at home all the time. He would walk Chris and Lael to school and pick them up whenever he didn't have a matinee. We were a family for an extended period for the first time. It was just fantastic. The children got to knew him and he got to know them.*

After that year in London, Porgy *went to Paris and we all went along. After Paris,* Porgy *came back to New York for a run at the Ziegfeld, and then Cab went on the road again. It was like that for the next fifteen years, with Cab on the road much of the time and us at home, until Chris and Lael got a little older and I could leave them. Then Cabella and I would sometimes join Cab in Mexico or Cuba or California. I suppose the times the children remember best are the great family reunions at Christmas and other holidays when Cab was home. Friends and relatives would come over, I would cook turkey and ham and spareribs for the whole gang.*

Camay, Cab's oldest daughter, by Zelma Proctor, was in and out of our lives during those years. She will tell you about that with her own words. She fills out the immediate family.

There is one other person I want to mention, to whom Cab and the rest of us have become deeply attached—so much that the girls all refer to her as "sister Liz." E. Simms Campbell, the wild genius of a cartoonist, and his wife, Vivian, who Cab and I spent many joyful, often-plastered hours with over the years, both died within three months of each other: Vivian in October 1971 and Simms in January 1972. They had one daughter, Elizabeth. She is now thirty-six years old and she lives nearby in White Plains. When Viv and Elmer passed, in that short space of time, Liz was absolutely devastated. She was their only child and was very close to them both. During the same period, Liz was going through a divorce. It was a difficult time for her, and since Cab has taught us all to open our hearts and our arms when a friend is in need, Liz became a surrogate Calloway. In the years following, this loving, vital woman and her daughter, Leslie, have become as close to all of us as if she had been born into the family. And she has brought with her into our little circle her husband, Bryant Rollins, who, coincidentally, has coauthored this book with Cab. Between Bryant and Andrew Langsam, Cabella's husband, Cab seems now to finally have found the sons he never had.

That's the family. It's a pretty independent bunch, especially the five girls Camay, Chris, Lael, Cabella, and Liz. But you judge now for yourself.

LAEL REMEMBERS DADDY

What kind of family was it? It was an organized family. Everything had to be highly organized. Nuffie saw to that. Daddy was on the road a lot so it was up to her to set the tone of things. We each had certain chores and we had better get them done or the punishment was swift and sure. You bet your life. I missed many a sunny day outside or many a visit from school friends because my chores weren't done.

There were good times and there were bad times. But the good times far outnumbered the bad. We wanted for nothing. I've never known Daddy to say no to me when I asked for something, no matter what it was or how lean things were for him. There was a feeling of life around the house, especially when Daddy was home from the road; a feeling that everyone was living life to the fullest. Talk about celebrations. Christmas was also Daddy's birthday and we used to have some slam-bang Christmas parties. We moved from Lido Beach to White Plains when I was about eight and I remember the times at White Plains much more clearly. We would have huge Christmas dinners. The whole family would come in, from wherever they were—Chicago, Baltimore, Philadelphia, California—and we'd have fifty people sitting down to dinner. Nuffie always insisted on doing her own cooking but we kids had a slightly different slant, because afterwards we had to clean up. But the dinners and the Christmas Eve parties were always a hell of a time.

Daddy was out traveling a lot when I was young, and we missed him. We knew, though, that if we ever messed up we would have to deal with him whether he was there or not at the moment.

It wasn't always easy being Cab Calloway's daughter. All I wanted was to be treated like anybody else, but I found that I had to earn that. I had to let other kids know that my father does what he does, but I'm still me. I still like to play games and do whatever any other kid does.

In 1952 we left Lido Beach to live in England for a year while Daddy played in Porgy and Bess. *That was a wonderful year. On most days Dad would come to the school and pick us up, and whenever it was foggy he would walk us to school. You know the English fog. We would have to follow the curbstone to find our way.*

We went to public schools all the way through. I was never a great student, but I was doing okay until my junior year in high school. Then I really messed up, and part of the reason had to do with Daddy. That year I had a lot of problems I hadn't worked out. I wasn't going to school regularly, and when I did go I was there only physically, not mentally. Because I had done so badly I knew that my report card would be a disaster, so I got hold of a blank report card, filled it in, and gave it to Mom. Of course Mom and Dad found out what I had done. Daddy had just come in off the road and he didn't understand at all. He and Mom kept hollering and screaming at me and I was just sitting there shaking. I couldn't defend myself. Then when I completely lost control of my body they knew something was seriously wrong and they stopped hollering. They sent me to see a psychiatrist, and it wasn't

"What kind of family was it? It was an organized family. Everything had to be highly organized. Nuffie saw to that."

until then that I began to realize that the problem could be worked out but that it was a problem.

What I found out about myself was that I had built up a fear of my dad. He was my dad but he was distant from me. I had always figured that as long as I didn't bother him it was cool. We had a relationship but we didn't. He was my dad, he made sure that I had everything, and I knew that he loved me, but I never really related to him. I never sat on his knee, for instance, and talked to him. The thought never even crossed my mind.

I had a lot of hangups about color, too. I am the darkest member of the family, and for a long time my grandmother, Nuffie's mother, who lived with us in Lido Beach and for a while in White Plains, would tell me that Cab and Nuffie didn't love me because I was dark. Lord, was she fouled up. And it had an effect on me.

I also found out that I didn't want to be my father's daughter; I didn't want to be an entertainer's daughter. Why should I have this burden on me? Why can't I go to Joe's Bar on the corner or do the things my friends do just because I'm my father's daughter? These were the kinds of problems I had and the things I found out about myself. Mom and Dad and I had all played a part in setting up these problems, but once we discovered them things began to change.

We all decided that it was time Dad and I spent some time together and got to know one another. It was difficult, just as difficult for him as for me. This was when Dad and I drew closer together, and it happened through sports. I've always liked sports, and of course Dad is a sports nut. We started going to basketball and football games together and to the racetrack. Then, all of a sudden, this man who had been so distant became a close-up father. I began to love him in a new way, not automatically because he was my father but in a personal way because of his warmth and gentleness and understanding, because he recognized a problem and responded to my need.

My problems were not entirely over, though. It's never that simple, is it? I became pregnant by a boyfriend while I was in high school. I was horrified. I went to Mom first and she offered to handle Dad, but I said no, it was my problem and I would talk to him. I went to him and it was one of the first times that I was not afraid to confront him with a serious problem. I was in a mess, but he just told me to do whatever I thought was the right thing and he would stick by me. Very few words, but a whole lot of feeling.

I also learned that when Daddy says he will back someone up, he means it—to the hilt. I decided to get married, and Daddy cosigned with my husband and me for a mortgage on a house and for a car, and when the marriage ended four years later, as it was doomed to, Daddy was left holding that mortgage and some other bills. He never said much, just went ahead and stuck behind me as he said he would.

There is one more episode. At the age of twenty-six, having completed nurses' training, and with a job of my own and two sons for whom I was responsible, I became involved with a man who was quite a bit older than I and who, in fact, had once worked as Daddy's valet. Charles Bethel was his name. Charles had left Daddy after a short period and gone on to make quite a lot of money. We struck up a rather innocent friendship that, over time, developed into love, and finally we began to live together as man and wife. I loved Charles deeply and he loved me. He took care of Sean and Todd and me with a kind of tenderness that I had never known, but I was very nervous about how my parents would react. Even though I was an adult I was still influenced a great deal by their opinions, and I did not want to lose their love and respect. Mom and Dad soon learned about our relationship. Charles and I had all their love and support. That's the kind of tolerance that my father has set as a standard for our family.

In the summer of 1974 Charles died after a long and difficult struggle with cancer. It was an awful blow to the family, and it hit Dad hard because he had known Charles for so long and had helped him when he first came to New York from Florida. As I grow older I hope that I can be as tolerant, loving, and understanding as my dad. He has such a positive attitude toward life and people. Even when he gets angry it is almost always because that optimistic sense of his is being blocked by narrowness or intolerance on the part of someone else.

I've decided to try a career in show business and Dad has been more than helpful. I know that a lot of the jobs, maybe most of them, that Daddy accepts now he does because he wants to help me. We're working together as a team, and it's great traveling with him. We have a wonderful, mature, father-daughter friendship and lots of love, and he's taught me so much professionally. But I don't want to be a burden on him any more. In September 1975 I opened at the Riverboat in New York City for my first solo gig. It was more than just a debut in a major club; it meant that I'm on my own. Daddy doesn't have to feel obligated to take care of me or support me. That's what I want. For me and for him.

CABELLA LEARNS ABOUT DADDY

I was born on October 11, 1952, in New York City. I'm told that when I was about six weeks old they wrapped me up and hauled me over to London, where Cab was in Porgy; *that's the first time he saw me.*

I saw little of him when I was growing up. I'll put it this way: Mother became very, very competent at reintroducing him to all of us when he came home off the road. That's how much time he spent away. She was also very good at keeping him in our minds as the man of the house, as the breadwinner, as a father who loved us. Still, to me he became a kind of omnipresent person who was rarely actually there. We would talk to him from Paris or Venice or Rome or Mexico City or California. He would call in the

"I've decided to try a career in show business and Dad has been more than helpful. I know that a lot of the jobs, maybe most of them, that Daddy accepts now he does because he wants to help me. We're working together as a team, and it's great traveling with him. We have a wonderful, mature, father-daughter friendship and lots of love, and he's taught me so much professionally."

*middle of the night or early in the morning and everybody would
be rousted out of bed to talk to him. And this voice that sounded
vaguely familiar would come across to me on the telephone as
always happy, always loving.*

*I was a sophomore in high school in 1968 when Daddy did
Hello Dolly! on Broadway. I was becoming more aware of mother
and of him, and when he came to New York with Dolly I really
began to learn about him. He was living in White Plains with us
and commuting to New York City for the show every day. Chris
and Lael were away; Lael was married and living with her
husband and Chris had her own apartment in New York. So there
were only the three of us—Mother, Daddy, and me. That's when I
began to know him as a person, to experience his various human
traits and idiosyncrasies. He became real.*

*The small things stay in my mind. I remember sitting out on the
sun porch drinking orange juice and watching the baseball game
on TV with him. I remember sitting in the big bed with him and
Mother in the evening, all of us snuggled close together, watching
TV. There was a period, when I was in high school, that he
and I would go frequently to the racetrack. We'd sit in a box
together and he'd teach me about the horses and the racing. Then
we'd go down to the paddocks, where he knew all of the jockeys
and all of the trainers. We'd share a beer and he would tell me the
faults and the strengths of all the horses, which ones he would bet
on and why. I always wanted to learn to walk the hots, as he had
when he was a kid. But Cab has always been very protective with
me. He wouldn't allow it; he was afraid I might take a fall.*

*I also learned about him by going down to the theater. I
learned, for one thing, that he was a living legend. I never had
realized what this mania was about my father, but when I saw him
in Dolly it sent goose bumps down my spine. There he was,
basically the same as the Beatles, who I was into at the time. He
would come out on the stage and just destroy the place. The joint
would just collapse behind his performance. I loved it, and I was
so proud of him. I suddenly understood why he was away so much*

*of the time and why Mama took so much care to let us know that
his reasons for being away from home were special ones. Now I
suddenly knew the reason was his incredible talent and genius as
an entertainer.*

*He has always protected me in a career sense, too. He never
allowed me to even entertain a thought about going into show
business. Chris and Lael, at different points, both went into show
business. When I was very young, six or seven, I seemed to have a
natural inclination as a dancer. George Balanchine was a good
friend of Daddy's. Balanchine told Daddy to send me to him to be
trained. Daddy refused. I didn't find out about Balanchine's offer
until I was seventeen years old. By then I had decided for myself
that I wanted to take ballet seriously. I wanted to go to France to
study, but Daddy always found an excuse for keeping me away
from it. At one point, when I was in college, I wanted to work with
the Hartford Ballet. I would be teaching underprivileged kids in
Hartford as part of my studies there. I was pretty well trained and
taking classes at the Boston Conservatory. But Daddy said, "No
Hartford Ballet, not even to teach. I just don't want you to go into
any kind of entertainment field."*

*I said to him, "But I have the genes, Daddy. I have the feelings.
I can't ignore them. I have to go in the direction my feelings lead
me. You always did; and my tendency in this direction comes from
you."*

*He finally relented and I was allowed to study and teach at the
Hartford Ballet for a year. But Cab was adamant that I was
always to teach, never to perform. It's something I have never
understood: why he prevented me, the youngest, from going into
the field that he had been involved in all of his life.*

*One summer, while I was still in high school, I went with Daddy
to California, where they were beginning a Cotton Club revival on
film. I had heard all about the Cotton Club, of course, and seen
pictures of it. But this was the first time it was brought alive for
me. It was tremendously exciting to be on the set with him. I knew*

every lyric to every song, and after that, when he left Hollywood for a series of performances in the Catskills, I went with him and helped carry the music and sometimes drove for him.

Slowly during this period it dawned on me that this was the only thing that my father did. This was his whole life— entertaining and playing the horses. And I studied him closely and found, as I understood him better, that he is really a rather complex man, difficult to know well, and very stubborn. He rarely says much about himself and his deepest feelings, except when he gets loaded. He isn't so great with words and he uses songs to express his feelings.

Daddy has always been a very quiet person. You can ride in the car with him for miles and he won't say a word. But if you're used to it you realize that he isn't unhappy or bored or not enjoying your company, he's just relaxing and enjoying himself.

Many times he used to get absolutely ripped drunk. He would get me up at three in the morning and want to talk truth about sex and life and Mama.

He also has a pretty good temper, although it takes something pretty outrageous to trigger him.

Now I'm married and pregnant and happy. When Daddy first learned that Andrew and I wanted to marry he just looked at Andrew and shook his head: "Well, son, good luck, but I don't know. These Calloway girls aren't too good when it comes to marrying." He was referring to the difficult first marriages that Chris and Lael had.

But he and Andrew have become close friends now, and Daddy is utterly hysterical that he's going to be a grandfather again.

Money has always been a problem—not a serious one in my lifetime, but a problem. Daddy would be away for two months and

*he'd come home and there would be a stack of bills on his desk.
And he'd start hollering, "What's this! What's this one! Who the
hell bought this!" But he would always pay them and we always
were secure that he would provide fully for us. He is a little stingy.
He would go away and leave Mama what he thought would be
enough money to run the house. Of course it never was, and
Mother and I would always wind up manipulating that little
money. We always managed, so maybe Daddy knew what he was
doing!*

*In recent years I've seen Daddy hurt a number of times, mostly
by the deaths of close friends, people he's known for years and
years. On the other hand, the relationship between Mama and
Daddy seems to have blossomed just within the last year. Now all
us girls are out of the house on our own. As a result Mama and
Daddy have had to stop and look at each other for the first time in
years. For the first few months after Chris left in 1974 they
were by themselves and they fought constantly. But then they
seemed to mellow. They touch each other with great warmth now,
and sit and talk for hours.*

*I see a softness and a tenderness between them that I had never
seen before. Daddy's home a lot and Mama has finally let it sink
in that she doesn't have to feel responsible for her daughters
twenty-four hours a day. As long as they don't let any of the
problems us kids have interfere with them, their relationship will
keep getting healthier and healthier. I just love to see that
happening.*

CHRIS DISCOVERS "CAB"

*Hello, I'm Chris, and I was born on September 21, 1945. I was a
little apprehensive when I was asked to contribute to Cab's book. I*

haven't been sure where to begin. I realize that a lot of my childhood was fundamentally happy. I didn't have a lot of bad feelings. I was Cab and Nuffie's firstborn child, and in a way that has been the core of my relationship with Daddy. It has been said by members of the family and by friends that for one reason or another I am his favorite daughter. The whole situation around my birth, with Ma and Daddy going through so much, has probably reinforced that idea for me and for the family. And that has led to a very intense, complex, and passionate relationship between me and my father. I guess my story of the early years is a lot like Lael's and Cabella's. Cab was on the road so much that I never really got a chance to know him. As we used to say around the house, Daddy's coming home, get out the good tablecloth and the best silverware, we're eating in the dining room. It was always quite an occasion. So when I was young I was very confused about exactly who Cab was. When I was in junior high school, he was in Porgy *and* Bess *and at home for a long stretch, but by then the patterns of our lives had already been established. Mama, in her desire to keep the family unit whole and tight, sometimes built Cab up and covered up for him; she made excuses and created him to be something that he really wasn't. By the time that I was thirteen or fourteen I felt like I was just that kind of love object to Cab that children become when a parent hasn't spent day after day dealing with the rather ordinary things of life.*

To this day Cab and I don't have what I would call a warm, physical kind of relationship. We love each other, and there's tremendous respect on both sides. But for instance, we don't hug each other very often, or touch each other. It's not the kind of thing where your father is always tousling your hair with the kind of feeling that comes from the times that he used to change your diapers. It's not the kind of relationship where I would come to him with a problem and put my head on his shoulder and say, "Oh, Daddy, I hurt," and have him say, "It's okay, baby, it's okay, just let it out, it's gonna be better." It seems that when I was younger the most he could give when I had a problem was to clam up and get very stern and grim and say, "Oh, come on now." And dismiss the problem.

He's a very introverted man; he has all the love in the world to give, but for some reason in personal relationships he keeps a lot of it inside. He'll do anything in the world for the people he loves; our family always came first, and we never wanted for anything.

Growing up in America is a unique situation anyway; growing up in a black upper-middle-class type of environment also has its unique qualities. And growing up the daughter of a public figure makes all that other stuff seem ordinary. For me, it's been a slow process of understanding. I first began to become aware of the meaning of what Dad did when I was in junior high school. I can remember seeing him on television, and one eveing Lael and I accompanied him to a performance of his act. I was stunned as I began to appreciate him and to react to him on another level, for it suddenly became clear to me that the man who was quiet and introverted at home became outrageous and charismatic on the stage. I was inspired, moved, deeply affected by the experience and I wanted to try myself, or perhaps found a sudden warmth in my father on the stage and desired to emulate him for that.

So, by the time I was a sophomore in high school I became very involved with the drama club, and participated in several high school plays. A local producer and friend, Pat Iozzo, had seen me in one of those plays and he asked me to work with the White Plains Summer Theatre in a production of Bye, Bye, Birdie. *I was to play Rosie Alvarez, a part created by Chita Rivera on Broadway. It was like a button finding a buttonhole. I prepared fervently for it. Daddy was unaware of what I was doing, and I wanted it that way. It meant a great deal to me to show him what I could do. I supposed I hoped it would bring us closer together on a level on which he was more comfortable, open, and facile.*

Finally opening night came, and for me it was the biggest night of my life because my father was there. And for the people in the audience it was a big night because "Cab Calloway" was there. It must have been very difficult for them to try to watch me and watch his reaction to me at the same time. It was a glorious night. I raised hell in that performance, singing on top of the tables, kicking my legs, and my father was absolutely stunned. After it was over he came backstage and rushed up to me and threw his arms around me; it was one of the warmest moments that we had. He was earnestly pleased and proud. He told me years later that that was the first time he saw in me the light which shines so brightly in him.

Now that I had gotten my feet wet, I began to study his craft. He was doing a production of Porgy and Bess *at a summer theater in Connecticut. The whole family went; it was a chance for us all to be together in the country even as he worked. Lael and I went to the theater every night, and it was at this point that I began to learn how it happens. Night after night after night my sister and I watched our father live his love. It was magic. He gave that love and the people gave it right back—Cab as Sportin' Life, slipping and sliding and and singing and dancing across the stage. And when he took Bess away, singing, "There's a boat that's leaving soon for New York," then sashayed off the stage like nothing I had ever seen, well, I can remember feeling elation and joy, a dynamic fullness swelling inside of me. And he did it every time. He threw himself into what he was doing at that moment on the stage and succeeded through the discipline of vocal technique, stage presence, timing, and pure charisma.*

My growing awareness of his craftsmanship and my increasing desire to perform brought me to the realization that I wanted to go into show business. This was my junior year in high school, so I went to my father and told him how I felt, and I'll never forget what he said to me: "Well, okay, if that's what you really want to do, but it's one of the rottenest businesses in the world. I don't know if you're strong enough to take it." Many years later we had occasion to work together in Hello, Dolly! *and, after my husband, Ruppert Crosse, died, as a father-daughter nightclub act. Lord, talk about conflicts. We're both very strong-willed and stubborn, and of course he's the old pro and I'm the first offspring to follow in his footsteps. So for a while, all of his pride and passion as an entertainer became focused on me. He taught me all that I know about the business, and what a hell of a teacher. From A to Z, this man has been through it all and done it all. You want to know how a singer can go out night after night and sing over the top of a bad cold or laryngitis, just ask Cab Calloway, he knows all the secrets.*

"*He taught me all that I know about the business, and what a hell of a teacher.*"

On the other hand, though, I've resented him, and I've worked against him at times. I didn't like the way that he tried to put me into a special world, up on a pedestal, a little beautiful bird in a gilded cage with cellophane on top so it couldn't breathe. All of his hopes for my success sometimes felt like a yoke around my neck. He wanted success for me so badly that whenever I tried to grow in a direction that he didn't approve of we would tangle.

One bad time was when I decided to drop out of college. I was going through some bad changes. I had gotten involved with a guy who wasn't the best sort and things seemed very screwed up there in Boston, far from home. I became depressed and took some aspirins or sleeping pills or something. I really didn't know what I was doing. I left school and came home and tried to explain to Cab. But in my emotional state, the more I tried to explain the less he understood, the more emotional I became, and the more violent became the encounter. He couldn't understand my dropping out of college or having emotional problems. He had worked all his life so we kids could go to school and have what we wanted; what the hell was I doing throwing it all away? It was a typical father-daughter argument.

The final thing about Daddy is this: All of us in that family know that he may holler at us and even become violent, but when we are in trouble he will be there, to help. A few years ago, I was separated from my first husband, Hugh Masakella. It was a very rough separation for me. I left New York and went out to California half crazed out of my mind, junked up on just about every kind of pill you can think of. I stayed for three days alone out at Hugh's house in Malibu, but Hugh found out I was there and called and told me to get the hell out, he never, ever wanted to see me again. I had no money, I was out of my head on pills, I had no friends to call. So I called Daddy. There was no pity in his voice, he was his usual stern self. He just said, ''Okay, girl, there'll be a ticket at the airport, get on a plane and come on home.'' And when I got home there was none of this hugging and stroking, he was angry because I had gotten myself into such a situation and because I had resorted to pills. He told me so. And that was it. Then he began to help me get myself together.

I suppose the worst confrontation he and I have had was when I left the Broadway hit revival of Pajama Game. *Cab had helped me to get a pretty good part in the chorus and I was understudy to Barbara McNair. Cab saw it as the greatest chance in my life. I saw it differently. The producers and backers of the show were a pretty unscrupulous bunch as far as I was concerned. The company was being treated like crap; the producers and backers were getting their money up front while at the same time the cast was being asked to take pay cuts. And besides that, I didn't like the way Cab was being treated. They had threatened that if he didn't take a salary cut they would close the show. So he took the cut and the next day they posted a notice that they planned to close the show, anyhow. To me that was an insult, and it left me free to leave the show to protest the way he was being treated. As a result, Father and I had a confrontation. He wanted to know why I had decided to leave the show, and when I told him he got very angry.*

"Goddammit!" he hollered. "This is the biggest mistake of your damned life. How damned ungrateful can you be? How the hell can you do this to me?"

First I felt hurt. Then I got angry. "Man, I'm breaking my ass trying to be what you want me to be!" I shouted. "And I just can't seem to do the right thing. What the hell do you want from me?"

By now my father was screaming and shaking his fist at me, and Nuffie had come downstairs and gotten into it, and it had turned into this incredible brawl, with him finally standing at the back door hollering after me, "Don't you come back here neither!"

Well, eventually I did, and in a while we were reconciled again. Now I'm living in California with my son, Osaze. I am very independent and very happy. I'm studying Buddhism and training myself for that "right" opportunity—that musical, that film role, that nightclub opening. It's hard work and sometimes frustrating, but I love it. I talk to Cab and Nuffie on the phone often, and whenever Cab's in the vicinity he's sure to check up on me. Either I will make it in show business or I won't. I know I have the talent and the spirit, it's largely a question of the right opportunity now. I know that Cab has given me all that he possibly could, as a father to a daughter and as a old trouper to a beginner. It's been rough at times, but it's always been out of love.

CAMAY

I was born in Harlem Hospital on January 15, 1927. As you know by now, my mother, Zelma Proctor, and my father, Cab Calloway, were not married when I was born. They were just kids, really. She was around seventeen and Cab was about nineteen. Not long after I was born, my mother brought me back to Baltimore. During those early years Cab would sometimes bring his band into the Royal Theatre in Baltimore, and whenever he was in town he would come by to see me. I was very afraid and overwhelmed. It was always a big occasion around the house when he was coming. And I was a very distant child, so he had to work hard to bring me out. He was sending money to my aunts and to my mother for my support, but when he came to visit he always wanted to do something special. One year, I remember asking him to give me a coat just like his. Well, this must have been around 1932 or so; Cab was in the big-time by then, and two days later I received a lovely little camelhair coat with a big collar and a camelhair belt that tied around the waist—just like his.

When I was about eight years old, Mama brought me to New York City, and I stayed in New York pretty much straight through college at New York University, except for one year when I lived in California with Cab and Nuffie, at Lena Horne's house.

I saw Cab quite a bit during those New York years. He would often ask me to come over to the Cotton Club or to the Apollo Theatre to see the shows.

The Cotton Club was simply the most fabulous place you can imagine, but what I remember most are the chorus girls who, after a matinee, would take me into their dressing rooms and talk with me or make me up with lipstick and rouge. And as I reached my early teens I got to know people like Bill Robinson and Pearl Bailey pretty well and some of the musicians like Milt Hinton and Benny Payne. But I was always sort of gangly and awkward. I thought I was out of place among all those beautiful women and talented entertainers.

It strikes me, though, that while I was around Cab quite a bit during those years there were only two occasions when he and I were alone. I mean, he was my daddy, and he provided for me and always was happy to have me around, but there was always a valet with us in his dressing room, or a half-dozen people with us when we went out to eat. We truly never sat together alone and just talked to each other. Not until I was around fifteen years old and he called me down to the Zanzibar Club and, in his dressing room, told me that he planned to marry Nuffie. I hadn't met her, and since Cab and I never, ever talked about personal matters, I didn't have any idea how to react, so I guess I was not as enthusiastic as he would have liked.

The second time that he and I talked, just the two of us alone, was much more important. It formed the basis for the rather close relationship that he and I have had since.

Here's the way it happened:

I was a pretty good student. I graduated from Morris High School in the Bronx with a 91 average and was admitted, in 1945, to Hunter College. After a year there I decided Hunter was not for me, so I accepted Cab and Nuffie's offer to spend the year with them in California. Chris had just been born, and they could use me to help with the baby. So I accepted. After a year, we returned to New York and I entered New York University. Cab was paying my tuition, as he had at Hunter, and providing a little (I do mean little) allowance besides. And I was living for the most part with them out at Lido Beach. But one weekend when they were away I brought a bunch of my friends from college out to the house at Lido Beach. I must admit that my friends at NYU were sort of a ratty bunch. When Cab and Nuffie returned they just knew that there had been a wild party at the house.

They called me in and read the riot act, telling me how terrible it was that we had raised Cain out there and drunk all their liquor and so forth.

I thought they were being pretty high-handed about it, even if I had messed up. They were making me out to be such a horrible person and they were acting so superior and righteous. So I said, "If that's the way you feel, there's nothing for me to do but leave." So I left.

I refused to accept any of their money. I worked two or three jobs to stay in school. I got a dormitory apartment in Judson Hall at New York University and for two years I had nothing to do with them. I completely broke off communications. If they wanted to be so righteous about a lousy weekend party, then I would show them that I didn't need them.

After a while, of course, it became sheer stubbornness on my part. I just wouldn't give in, even though I began to miss them and wanted to see them. And I later found out that Cab was periodically checking with the people at the dorm to make sure I was all right. He missed me, too.

While we were in California I became very close with Lena Horne. She was interested in me and she liked me. One day about two years after I had had this break with Cab and Nuffie, Lena called me. She was playing at an East Side nightclub in New York and she wanted to talk to me. I got dressed and went over to the club. Lena was very upset.

"Look," she said, "you and your father have got to stop this shit. You love each other and it's crazy for you to be acting like this. Why don't you cut it out and act right." She went on like that for a couple of minutes, quite emotionally. Then she told me that she had asked Cab to come down to meet with me, and she opened

the door of her dressing room and there he was. Well, I hadn't seen Daddy for two years and my heart pounded. He walked in and Lena told him the same thing she had just told me; then she told us that we really needed to be alone to talk it over, and she left.

We stood there for a moment looking at each other. Then he started to talk, but he was so subdued and his voice was so uncertain and halting that he seemed like a completely different person from the man that I had known.

"Listen," he said "how you been? You all right? I'm sorry that we had a disagreement. I'm sorry that Nuffie and I were so hard on you. Do you need anything? You got enough money? You know, I missed you. You know, I love you. You are my first child and you are my daughter, and we shouldn't be apart like this for so long."

Well, I was stunned. He had never before talked to me in that way. I don't think he had ever told me that he loved me; he had never been so explicit about his feelings. I just broke down and cried. I was so happy. I was sitting in this little dressing room, with Lena's telegrams and flowers all around, just crying. And Cab came across the room to me and put his arm around me and just held me. We sat there for a while, just talking quietly, then Lena knocked and came back in and we all went out to where Nuffie was sitting. Nuffie has always been very demonstrative, and she broke down and cried and I cried some more and we had a hell of a reunion. And Lena capped it off with, "Now I don't want to hear about no more of this kind of shit from you Calloways."

That incident seemed to open up something in my relationship with him. Since then he and I have become very, very close. He has at times taken me into his confidence about problems that he's had; he's talked quite openly about his relationship with my mother when they were both just kids. I often come up to White Plains to visit, and whenever he's in the Washington-Baltimore area I go to visit with him.

What I have found out about this man is that he is really a super-sensitive person. Even though he gives a lot of veneer about being tough, he is really easily hurt. Even though he gives this appearance of being carefree and not caring what other people think about him, he really cares very deeply what other people think about him.

But because he is so sensitive and aware, he can say things that really come to the core of situations. But his moods change quickly, and a lot of his varied feelings and changes really have to do with his genius as an entertainer, with his great abilities, with his sense of timing, with his charisma. It is all effortless and natural for him and that makes him a real genius. And he knows it, he knows what he has and he uses it well.

If he would allow himself to, Cab could be a very loving, personally attractive person—he is always like that on the stage; he is only sometimes like that off the stage, where he tends to become self-protective and aloof.

I think, though, that he is happy most of the time, but he is maneuvered by a lot of people, and when he becomes aware of it he can get very angry.

I guess that I worry about him quite a bit now. His mood changes seem to be stronger than they were. He's capable of being a recluse without too much effort, but I hope that he doesn't go in that direction because he should keep alive what he has to offer people in the world and not surrender.

Cab taught me about life. I grew up with few male images around me. I decided a long time ago that I would not want to marry someone like Cab—I wanted a more homebound person—but he is so earthy and for-real that I used him for a long time as the only real male image in my life. And for that, as well as everything else that has gone into our relationship, I love him very much.

MINNIE THE MOOCHER
AND ME

One thing that has probably come clear to you is that I actually had two families: my family of two-legged relatives who lived in White Plains and my family of four-legged animals that lived at Aqueduct Park and Belmont Park and Saratoga Springs or anywhere that there's a racetrack, some ponies, and a crowd of people with money in their pockets.

My love for the ponies goes way back to Pimlico in the early 1900s, when I used to walk the hots as a kid. I remember the old grandstand at Pimlico, before the fire ruined it. For a long time, after I left Chicago until the late thirties when I began to make the real long bread, I left the horses alone. I was too busy with my career. Then, in the late thirties, as the band traveled around the country, I had the time—and the money—to bet, and I did.

I was the first Negro allowed into the grandstand at Hialeah. All over the country, to this day, racing men know me. The owners and trainers love to have their pictures taken with me in the winner's circle presenting the trophy after a stake race. I must have seventy or eighty photographs of me presenting trophies to owners. They love it and it's a pleasure to me, because for me racing is truly "the sport of kings."

Part of my creed is that I never pay to get into a track. I've given a hell of a lot of time and energy and talent to the sport. I've entertained

at tracks everywhere to help promote racing. I was the first entertainer to perform at the Preakness. Until then, 1962, it was unheard of for a performer to sing or play before a major race, but in 1962 Lou Ponfield, president of the track, asked me if I would bring the band out to the Preakness to entertain before the race. I said, "Hell, yes, Lou. I'd be honored." The crowd loved it, and nowadays pre-race entertainment is a standard thing.

The sport has changed recently. In New York State they have something called off-track betting. There are betting parlors all over Greater New York. Man, you couldn't get me into one of those places with handcuffs. I hate them. They take people away from the tracks. I mean, after all, it's not just a betting sport, it's an outdoor sport and the horses are beautiful to watch. And half the pleasure comes from the roar of the crowd as the horses make the run to the wire.

Of all the owners, my favorites are Sig Sommers and his wife Viola. They're fabulous friends. Viola and Sig own about 150 thoroughbred horses, and they race them all over the East Coast, from Massachusetts to Florida. They win a quarter of a million dollars a year in stake races and are about the smartest horse traders in the country. It is obviously a business as well as a sport for them.

I happen to be closest to Sig and Viola—I usually sit in their owners' box at Aqueduct and Belmont Park—but I also have a great deal of respect for a number of other owners; not just respect, admiration and affection too. People like the Dreyfus family and their Harborview Stable; Alfred Vanderbilt; Cornelius "Sonny" Whitney, Liz Whitney Tippett, and Colonel Cloyce Tippett; Elliott Birch; the Frankels; the Jacobsons; John Olin; John Picou; Penny Tweedy and her beautiful Meadowbrook Stable which bred Secretariat; "Big Red," Fred Hooper, owner of the Clarion Farms Stable—they're all my friends. The trainers too—people like Reggie Cornell of Calumet Farms and Woody Stephens and Allan Jerkins of Hobo Farms, the trainer of Onion. Chester Ross, Johnny Nerud of Tartan Stable, Homer Pardu, Frank Martin, W. C. Freeman, Buddy Hirsch of King Ranch, Everett King, Tommy Heard, Johnny Campo, Jim Conway, Joe Traveto, Laz Barera, and Clifford Scott, the famous black trainer from Chicago and New Orleans. They're more than just names to me. They're guys I have known from years of hanging around the stables, of watching them work their magic with these fine animals, of talking and drinking and laughing and kidding each other.

These trainers are serious men who enjoy their work and who give horse racing the competition and the high quality that has kept it one of the top sports in the world. It's a difficult business just like any other. Perhaps even more, because horses can be such finnicky animals. You can buy a well-bred horse for $500,000 that will be a complete and total bust, and you can buy a horse that nobody ever heard of for $10,000 that will become a million-dollar winner. Who knows? That's why it's such a wonderful sport. Millions of dollars won or lost in a fraction of a second on a fraction of an inch.

I've seen some of the great races. I was there when Secretariat was beaten and I was there when Ruffian was beaten. There's no thrill like an upset and there's no thrill like watching a big horse like Secretariat gallop with those enormous, graceful strides. The jockey and horse ride as if they were one, the horse all muscle and the jockey floating up on top. There's nothing like it.

There is another group of people at the tracks that I love and respect. These are the regulars—some of them pretty eccentric characters—who come out to the track day after day. They know the horses' records, the jockeys' records, the stables, the trainers, and the tracks inside out. They are always out there, riding every stride whether they've got $2 on it or $2,000.

Every track has guys like that. Around New York it's people like Greasy Jerry, whose real name is Jerry Beck, and who will give you a tip a minute if you let him. And there's Willie Bananas, and Manny, and Horse Steele, and Little Mickey and Slick. Every race for them, and for me too, is a whole new start, with its own long shots or its own "sure things." And each guy has his own system. The system never fails. Instead there's always an excuse, like a bad ride by the jockey, a bumped turn, or a slow start. Each guy cries the blues when his sure thing finishes out of the money and each guy buys drinks for all the others when his long shot comes in with the money. That's the atmosphere around thoroughbred racing. Every guy is sure that someday he's going to make that big hit that just never seems to come. The disappointments, the surprises, the frustrations, the happiness. That's what it's all about, and I love it.

A few years ago, I invited a few of the jockeys up to the house in White Plains for a Sunday barbecue. Angel Cordero, Braulio Baeza, Jacinto Valasquez and their agents came up, with their wives and kids.

We had a ball. They were thrilled, because they had met Nuffie and me at the track and seen me on TV and in movies and nightclubs but they had never been close to me in a personal setting.

I love to cook barbecue. Ribs, chicken, hamburgers, hot dogs, fresh roasted corn along with a fresh salad and wine, beer, or hard liquor— whatever your poison is. I'll cook up a barbecue at the drop of a hat, for family, friends, or neighbors. And when I'm cooking a barbecue, don't expect to see me in a zoot suit and wide-brimmed hat with pointed shoes and a long key chain. I usually wear raggedy old slacks, a banlon jersey, and the worst-looking shoes you have ever seen. They're black loafers about ten years old, and spattered with ten years' worth of chicken gravy and rib grease. That's how I greeted these guys and they couldn't believe it, because at the track I'm always dapper. We laughed and ate and drank and told horse-racing stories for hours.

The same year, I had a barbecue for some of my black friends from the track, the regulars from Harlem. Horse Steele came up, and a few others. They were just like the jockeys. They couldn't believe that I was dressed in those old clothes. They were dressed to kill, and it took them about an hour to get out of their neckties and jackets and really get down to the grits.

Whether it's a Sig Sommers, an Angel Cordero, or a Horse Steele, I feel the same kind of affection for people who love the horses as much as I do. We're all brothers. We're all kin. So I guess that maybe Nuffie and the girls do have something to worry about. Maybe I do have another family at the racetrack.

If I do, the lady who was and still is my all-time favorite is Chicken Sadie. Chicken Sadie is dead now, but she was a lovely black woman who traveled the New York State racing circuit year after year selling fried chicken and other goodies to the regulars. Sadie started out feeding the jockeys and stable workers. Fifty cents would buy you two pieces of chicken, two pieces of bread, and a soft drink, and her chicken was absolutely delicious. At first Sadie would make it around with just a basket, but in the early sixties she got herself a cart and began to sell sandwiches and cakes and things. In the mid-sixties Stevens Caterers, which had the state concession to sell food at all the racetracks, tried to get Sadie removed from the tracks. Her food was strictly soul food and the jockeys and stable workers dug it more than the packaged stuff Stevens was selling. The track people raised hell and the State Racing

Board made a special ruling that gave Chicken Sadie the right to sell at the tracks. She was the only exception to Stevens' concession.

Sadie loved Nuffie and me. Many a night she would pack up a bag of chicken for the kids and send it home from the track with me. Whenever I brought home a bag of Chicken Sadie's goodies there was a celebration at Knollwood Road.

Chicken Sadie became ill in 1966 and went into a hospital. She never came out alive. There isn't a jockey, trainer, stable worker, or regular who doesn't miss her.

Racing has given me some of my happiest, most relaxed moments and some of my best friends. I love everything about it. Being out of doors, the clean, rich atmosphere of the tracks, the thoroughbreds themselves, the jockeys, the betting, the gambling—the whole thing is just a gas.

One person with whom I shared a lot of happy moments at the tracks was Freddie Rosenblatt. Everyone in the family called him Uncle Freddie. I met Freddie when I was up in Saratoga Springs playing at a hotel in the fifties. He just came up to me and told me he liked my singing and had liked it for years, and we started talking. He bought me a drink, I bought him a drink, and from that time on we were buddies. He and I started going out to the Saratoga Springs racetrack together. He loved the horses as much as I. His wife, Mary Ann, loved the horses too, and she and Nuffie hit it off. Freddie owned a chain of theaters and was a major real estate developer in upstate New York. He had money, but he was cool, unostentatious, tasteful, and full of warmth and friendliness. Just a regular guy. Freddie, Mary Ann, Nuffie, and I made several trips together. We went to Acapulco, Mexico, and we all loved the casinos, the clubs, the beaches, the people, and the beauty of the country.

Last August, Nuffie and I went up to Saratoga Springs for another combination work-vacation. I was singing at a local resort nightclub. Nuffie and I stayed with Freddie and Mary Ann. He'd been hospitalized a couple of times with a heart condition, and on a Sunday night while we were there he had a mild seizure and spent the night in the hospital. On Monday, he was released. On Tuesday night we all sat up until around one in the morning talking and drinking and laughing about old stories. Then we went to bed. At around two in the morning Mary Ann banged on the door of our bedroom.

"Freddie and Mary Ann and Nuffie and I made several trips together."

"Something's wrong with Freddie!" she hollered. "Come quick!"

Nuffie and I jumped out of our bed and ran into their bedroom. Freddie was on the floor, struggling to breathe. Somebody called the police and I did what I could to make him comfortable. But I really didn't know what I could do. He looked awful and could hardly get air into his lungs. Nuffie was trying to calm Mary Ann, who was hysterical. I massaged Freddie's chest and tried to talk to him, but I could tell he was in very serious difficulty, and as I held him, massaging him, stroking his forehead, trying to talk to him, he seemed to stop breathing. The police came and carried him out, but Freddie was dead when he arrived at the hospital. That old bugaboo death again. I suppose that death is so hard for me to accept because I love life so much. Nobody escapes it, but damned if I can accept it.

I suppose the hardest death to accept was my mother's. Of course, I had been very close to her. When I left Baltimore and went to Chicago she was heartbroken. I was her oldest son, and I had been the family's main support when she and Papa Jack broke up. And I guess she knew that if I left home I would probably never get to law school. In the forties, Mama moved to Philadelphia, where John and Camilla were living. She got to be immensely proud of my success and she used to kid me about quitting college.

In 1943, Mama became very ill. She had a stroke and she was hospitalized for a long time. When I went down to visit her, she was very weak and it was hard for me to handle. About a month later I was playing at the Zanzibar and my sisters called me from Baltimore to tell me that she had passed. I knew that she was very sick, but I didn't know she was going to die. It hit me like a boulder. I had never had a feeling like that before. She was the first person close to me who had died. I had barely known my father. When she died there was such a hollow feeling. I mourned for her for months. I just kept thinking about her and about how good she had been to me and how hard she had worked for us kids and all that she had taught me. I kept thinking about all the times we'd had together. There were so many memories and they kept coming back for months.

I'm sixty-nine years old now. I'm still an active entertainer, but I pick my spots. In 1975, I played the Catskill Mountain resort areas around New York, the Poconos, and the Florida theater and club circuit. In

"I'm sixty-nine years old now. I'm still an active entertainer, but I pick my spots."

Chicago, I played two weeks at the Hyatt Regency, and for two months last summer I had a ball traveling with Ray McKinley and a revival band in a show called *Sounds of the Forties*. We did one-nighters all up and down the West Coast, from San Diego to Vancouver; then we came East and played Columbus, Ohio, Pittsburgh, and a few other cities.

I had to think twice about that McKinley tour. I hadn't done one-nighters like that in years, and Ray and the band planned to travel by bus. Finally I agreed to make the gig, but only if Ray would give me a flat fee with my travel money included and allow me to make my own travel arrangements. So while those guys hustled around in buses the way I used to do in the early thirties, I flew and stayed in the best hotels. It was still damned hard work, but it was worth it. We had a ball, and the crowds loved it. It's funny about the music of the big band period. It was such strong, clear material and so well-played that it jars people's memories immediately and they get right into it. The audiences remembered all the old tunes, and, of course, I had them rocking in the palm of my hand with "Minnie" and the hi-de-ho.

A lot of the work now is for Lael. Last October, Lael and I had a one-week gig in Florida. We stayed in Ft. Lauderdale and played about a dozen or so small theaters in the Florida condominiums. We left New York in the middle of that fantastic Indian summer and all I could think about was that this was the last week of the racing at Belmont Park. And I was missing it to run around Florida singing at little theaters. But it was to help Lael. That made it worthwhile.

Those are the kinds of gigs I'm doing now. I'll never retire. Nuffie swears that when I go, it will be on the stage. But I'm resting a lot more these days and picking the things that I do very carefully.

There's one more thing I want to get straight before I wind this up. I am not Duke Ellington. People are always confusing me with Duke. Even though he's been dead for two years now, people at dates and at the track still come up and call me Duke.

Richard Nixon, for example. I was invited to attend a big birthday party that President Nixon gave for Duke Ellington on Duke's seventy-second birthday in 1971. I was going down the reception line; the president and Mrs. Nixon were there, and the shah of Iran and a lot of other dignitaries. I got to President Nixon and he took my hand and shook it and smiled a big, wide smile, and of course I smiled back. Then he reached over and grasped my hand in both of his, and his grin widened more. I smiled back. It seemed that he was spending more time greeting

me than most of the other people on the reception line and I was beginning to feel pretty important. I figured, hell, even the president takes the
time to recognize the great Cab Calloway with a special welcome.

Then President Nixon said to me, "Ah, Mr. Ellington, it's so good
you're here. Happy, happy birthday. Pat and I just love your music."

Whoosh. There went my ego. But the last thing that I wanted was to
embarrass the president, so I just smiled and thanked him and kept on
stepping.

Later on I came to dislike Nixon and the things he was doing to the
country, but at the time I figured he was a man like any other, and men
make mistakes.

I was at the White House several other times, all during the Johnson
administration. Once, Lyndon invited Pearl Bailey and me to a party at
the White House while we were in Washington in *Dolly*. The president
and Ladybird had come to the theater to see *Dolly* and Pearl had called
them right up onto the stage. She would bring anybody out onto the
stage, she's got so much gumption. Well, after that they invited us to
visit them in return. I sang a special version of "Hello, Dolly!" that
went "Hello, Lyndon; Oh, hello, Lyndon; We're all so happy that
you're here with us. . . ." He got a big kick out of it.

I've known a lot of famous people besides presidents—people like
Bob Hope, Bing Crosby, Rudy Vallee, and many more. I've performed
with them and partied with them, but mostly my friends are just ordinary people: my pals at the track, a few guys who I've met in and out of
show business, and half a dozen fellows, members of a Negro philan-
throphic and social club in Westchester County, who I play poker with.
I love to play poker with them because they can never quite figure me
out. Sometimes when I have a sure winner, I'll play it hard, man, play
it hard and run everybody right out of the play. Other times when I've
got a winner in the hole, I'll play it quietly and suck the guys in for $50
or $60, then pop it on them. It drives them wild, and we stay up all
night at it.

Who are these guys? Nobody you've ever heard of, just ordinary
working professional men. They're all Negroes, all have a little money,
but not a lot. They're just sweet, middle-class guys who like to try their
best to beat this old-timer in a few hands of poker. What they sometimes forget, though, is that I learned poker from professionals, on the
road in the days of the big band. I know all the tricks, all the odds, and
it doesn't take me long to figure out where a player is coming from.

Another friend you've probably never heard of is Ned Williams, my public relations man during the days when Irving Mills and I were partners. Ned was a fantastic publicist. Man, he could sell blue cheese off the face of the moon. Ned was instrumental in putting together all the jive dictionaries and the Swingformation Bureau pamphlets, but he didn't like to travel very much. The only time Ned traveled with the band was that first trip through the deep South that Mrs. Knowles arranged. Maybe that business scared traveling out of him. I don't know, but he was strictly a New York City man.

Ned got me a whole lot of good publicity, but he also got me one piece of publicity that has haunted me ever since. In the early forties he put out a story that the Cab Calloway band had been banned from the radio because one night we jazzed up "The Star-Spangled Banner." All across the country people have asked me about that incident. Well, the truth of the matter is that it never happened. We never even played "The Star-Spangled Banner" on the air. Publicists in those days were very powerful guys. Newspapers and radio announcers didn't have the kinds of personal interviews that they do now or the large staffs. Columnists would print almost anything a publicist sent in, so when Ned sent in this juicy item they ate it up.

When it hit the papers I told Ned, "Man, I love the publicity but see if you can't get me exposure on stuff that's not so damned controversial." We laughed about it.

These have been my friends. It hasn't mattered to me whether their names were Lena Horne, Pearl (God bless her ornery soul) Bailey, Dizzy Gillespie, or Duke Ellington, or whether their names were unknown to the public. If they were straight with me, honest, and loved life, that's all I asked.

Yessir, I have been all over the lot in this life. I have lived this mother. I don't want to leave anyone with the impression that I haven't been that Sportin' Life or that King of the Hi-de-ho, but I want folks to see that it's not been only that.

During the forties they used to say that I had forty suits and forty pairs of shoes. It ain't true. I had fifty suits and fifty pairs of shoes and fifty pairs of pearl-gray gloves too. They used to say that I got arrested twice a month for speeding on the New Jersey Turnpike. That's a lie. Brother, I owned the New Jersey Turnpike, and I used to run that big old Lincoln through the Holland Tunnel and over the Jersey meadow-

"I love to play poker with them because they can never quite figure me out."

lands like there was no tomorrow. They used to say I was ornery and mean and always getting into fights. Hell, man, when I was young I used to think there wasn't anybody in the world who could take me in a street fight, and if they did they'd better watch out for my buddies in the mob. They used to say that I had a beautiful woman in every city and town in the country. Shoot, I had two, one for rainy days and one for sunny days.

They say I've had and lost millions of dollars. Buddy, they haven't stopped counting yet. Women, horses, cars, clothes. I did it all. And do you know what that's called, ladies and gentlemen. It's called living.

Minnie the Moocher, that low-down hoochy coocher, knows all about living. And she knows what I enjoy most out of life. It's making people happy, making them feel the fullness of life as I feel it and as I've lived it. Put me in the spotlight, give me two or three thousand people and a decent group of men behind me with instruments, and you can't give me more. Let me feel the vibrations of an audience that's really with me, that's clapping and stamping their feet and singing. Let me hear them cheer and holler. Let me know that I have reached the people with my energy and my joy of life. Let me feel that the people out there have for just a moment understood that it is possible to follow your dreams and to live the way you want to live and to be free with your emotions and to express what you feel deeply. Let the people know that there ain't no need to be afraid to catch ahold of life and to live it to the hilt. But it only happens when you live what's in your soul and sing your friggin' heart out—like Minnie the Moocher and me.

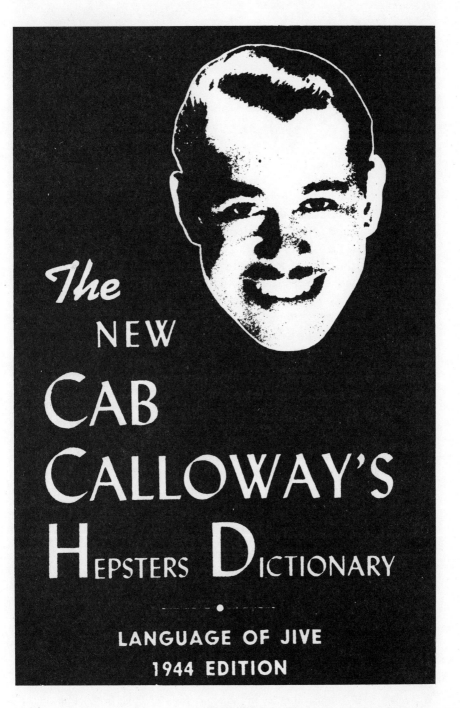

The
NEW
CAB
CALLOWAY'S
HEPSTERS DICTIONARY

LANGUAGE OF JIVE
1944 EDITION

FOREWORD

Some six years ago I compiled the first glossary of words, expressions, and the general patois employed by musicians and entertainers in New York's teeming Harlem. It seemed to me then, as it does now, that this colorful language should be called to the attention of as many people as possible. That the general public agreed with me is amply evidenced by the fact that the present issue is the sixth edition since 1938 and is the official jive language reference book of the New York Public Library.

"Jive talk" is now an everyday part of the English language. Its usage is now accepted in the movies, on the stage, and in the song products of Tin Pan Alley. It is reasonable to assume that jive will find new avenues in such hitherto remote places as Australia, the South Pacific, North Africa, China, Italy, France, Sicily, and inevitably Germany and wherever our Armed Forces will serve.

I don't want to lend the impression here that the many words contained in this edition are the figments of my imagination. They were gathered from every conceivable source. Many first saw the light of printer's ink in Billy Rowe's widely read column "The Notebook," in the Pittsburgh *Courier*.

To the many persons who have contributed to this and the other editions, this volume is respectfully and gratefully dedicated.

—Cab Calloway

A

A HUMMER (n.): exceptionally good. Ex., "Man, that boy is a hummer."
AIN'T COMING ON THAT TAB (v.): won't accept the proposition. Usually abbr. to "I ain't coming."
ALLIGATOR (n.): jitterbug.
APPLE (n.): the big town, the main stem, Harlem.
ARMSTRONGS (n.): musical notes in the upper register, high trumpet notes.

B

BARBECUE (n.): the girl friend, a beauty.
BARRELHOUSE (adj.): free and easy.
BATTLE (n.): a very homely girl, a crone.
BEAT (adj.): (1) tired, exhausted. Ex., "You look beat" or "I feel beat." (2) lacking anything. Ex., "I am beat for my cash"; "I am beat to my socks" (lacking everything).
BEAT IT OUT (v.): play it hot, emphasize the rhythm.
BEAT UP (adj.): sad, uncomplimentary, tired.
BEAT UP THE CHOPS (or the gums) (v.): to talk, converse, be loquacious.
BEEF (v.): to say, to state. Ex., "He beefed to me that, etc."
BIBLE (n.): the gospel truth. Ex., "It's the bible!"
BLACK (n.): night.
BLACK AND TAN (n.): dark and light colored folks. Not colored and white folks as erroneously assumed.
BLEW THEIR WIGS (adj.): excited with enthusiasm, gone crazy.
BLIP (n.): something very good. Ex., "That's a blip"; "She's a blip."
BLOW THE TOP (v.): to be overcome with emotion (delight). Ex., "You'll blow your top when you hear this one."
BOOGIE-WOOGIE (n.): harmony with accented bass.
BOOT (v.): to give. Ex., "Boot me that glove."
BREAK IT UP (v.): to win applause, to stop the show.
BREE (n.): girl.
BRIGHT (n.): day.
BRIGHTNIN' (n.): daybreak.
BRING DOWN: (1) (n.), something depressing. Ex., "That's a bring down." (2) (v.). Ex., "That brings me down."
BUDDY GHEE (n.): fellow.
BUST YOUR CONK (v.): apply yourself diligently, break your neck.

C

CANARY (n.): girl vocalist.
CAPPED (v.): outdone, surpassed.
CAT (n.): musician in swing band.
CHICK (n.): girl.
CHIME (n.): hour. Ex., "I got in at six chimes."
CLAMBAKE (n.): ad lib session, every man for himself, a jam session not in the groove.

CHIRP (n.): female singer.

COGS (n.): sun glasses.

COLLAR (v.): to get, to obtain, to comprehend. Ex., "I gotta collar me some food"; "Do you collar this jive?"

COME AGAIN (v.): try it over, do better than you are doing, I don't understand you.

COMES ON LIKE GANGBUSTERS (or like test pilot) (v.): plays, sings, or dances in a terrific manner, par excellence in any department. Sometimes abbr. to "That singer really comes on!"

COP (v.): to get, to obtain (see collar; knock).

CORNY (adj.): old-fashioned, stale.

CREEPS OUT LIKE THE SHADOW (v.): "comes on," but in smooth, suave, sophisticated manner.

CRUMB CRUSHERS (n.): teeth.

CUBBY (n.): room, flat, home.

CUPS (n.): sleep. Ex., "I gotta catch some cups."

CUT OUT (v.): to leave, to depart. Ex., "It's time to cut out"; "I cut out from the joint in the early bright."

CUT RATE (n.): a low, cheap person. Ex., "Don't play me cut rate, Jack!"

D

DICTY (adj.): high-class, nifty, smart.

DIG (v.): (1) meet. Ex., "I'll plant you now and dig you later." (2) look, see. Ex., "Dig the chick on your left duke." (3) comprehend, understand. Ex., "Do you dig this jive?"

DIM (n.): evening.

DIME NOTE (n.): ten-dollar bill.

DOGHOUSE (n.): bass fiddle.

DOMI (n.): ordinary place to live in. Ex., "I live in a righteous domi."

DOSS (n.): sleep. Ex., "I'm a little beat for my doss."

DOWN WITH IT (adj.): through with it.

DRAPE (n.): suit of clothes, dress, costume.

DREAMERS (n.): bed covers, blankets.

DRY-GOODS (n.): same as drape.

DUKE (n.): hand, mitt.

DUTCHESS (n.): girl.

E

EARLY BLACK (n.): evening.
EARLY BRIGHT (n.): morning.
EVIL (adj.): in ill humor, in a nasty temper.

F

FALL OUT (v.): to be overcome with emotion. Ex., "The cats fell out when he took that solo."
FEWS AND TWO (n.): money or cash in small quantity.
FINAL (v.): to leave, to go home. Ex., "I finaled to my pad" (went to bed); "We copped a final" (went home).
FINE DINNER (n.): a good-looking girl.
FOCUS (v.): to look, to see.
FOXY (v.): shrewd.
FRAME (n.): the body.
FRAUGHTY ISSUE (n.): a very sad message, a deplorable state of affairs.
FREEBY (n.): no charge, gratis. Ex., "The meal was a freeby."
FRISKING THE WHISKERS (v.): what the cats do when they are warming up for a swing session.
FROLIC PAD (n.): place of entertainment, theater, nightclub.
FROMPY (adj.): a frompy queen is a battle or faust.
FRONT (n.): a suit of clothes.
FRUITING (v.): fickle, fooling around with no particular object.
FRY (v.): to go to get hair straightened.

G

GABRIELS (n.): trumpet players.
GAMMIN' (adj.): showing off, flirtatious.
GASSER (n., adj.): sensational. Ex., "When it comes to dancing, she's a gasser."
GATE (n.): a male person (a salutation), abbr. for "gate-mouth."
GET IN THERE (an exclamation): go to work, get busy, make it hot, give all you've got.
GIMME SOME SKIN (v.): shake hands.

Glims (n.): the eyes.

Got your boots on: you know what it is all about, you are a hep cat, you are wise.

Got your glasses on: you are ritzy or snooty, you fail to recognize your friends, you are up-stage.

Gravy (n.): profits.

Grease (v.): to eat.

Groovy (adj.): fine. Ex., "I feel groovy."

Ground grippers (n.): new shoes.

Growl (n.): vibrant notes from a trumpet.

Gut-bucket (adj.): low-down music.

Guzzlin' foam (v.): drinking beer.

H

Hard (adj.): fine, good. Ex., "That's a hard tie your're wearing."

Hard spiel (n.): interesting line of talk.

Have a ball (v.): to enjoy yourself, stage a celebration. Ex., "I had myself a ball last night."

Hep cat (n.): a guy who knows all the answers, understands jive.

Hide-beater (n.): a drummer (see skin-beater).

Hincty (adj.): conceited, snooty.

Hip (adj.): wise, sophisticated, anyone with boots on. Ex., "She's a hip chick."

Home-cooking (n.): something very nice (see fine dinner).

Hot (adj.): musically torrid; before swing, tunes were hot or bands were hot.

Hype (n., v.): build up for a loan, wooing a girl, persuasive talk.

I

Icky (n.): one who is not hip, a stupid person, can't collar the jive.

Igg (v.): to ignore someone. Ex., "Don't igg me!"

In the groove (adj.): perfect, no deviation, down the alley.

J

Jack (n.): name for all male friends (see gate; pops).

Jam: (1) (n.): improvised swing music. Ex., "That's swell jam." (2) (v.): to play such music. Ex., "That cat surely can jam."

JEFF (n.): a pest, a bore, an icky.
JELLY (n.): anything free, on the house.
JITTERBUG (n.): a swing fan.
JIVE (n.): Harlemese speech.
JOINT IS JUMPING: the place is lively, the club is leaping with fun.
JUMPED IN PORT (v.): arrived in town.

K

KICK (n.): a pocket. Ex., "I've got five bucks in my kick."
KILL ME (v.): show me a good time, send me.
KILLER-DILLER (n.): a great thrill.
KNOCK (v.): give. Ex., "Knock me a kiss."
KOPASETIC (adj.): absolutely okay, the tops.

L

LAMP (v.): to see, to look at.
LAND O'DARKNESS (n.): Harlem.
LANE (n.): a male, usually a nonprofessional.
LATCH ON (v.): grab, take hold, get wise to.
LAY SOME IRON (v.): to tap dance. Ex., "Jack, you really laid some iron that last show!"
LAY YOUR RACKET (v.): to jive, to sell an idea, to promote a proposition.
LEAD SHEET (n.): a topcoat.
LEFT RAISE (n.): left side. Ex., "Dig the chick on your left raise."
LICKING THE CHOPS (v.): see frisking the whiskers.
LICKS (n.): hot musical phrases.
LILY WHITES (n.): bed sheets.
LINE (n.): cost, price, money. Ex., "What is the line on this drape" (how much does this suit cost)? "Have you got the line in the mouse" (do you have the cash in your pocket)? (Also, in replying, all figures are doubled. Ex., "This drape is line forty" (this suit costs twenty dollars).
LOCK UP: to acquire something exclusively. Ex., "He's got that chick locked up"; "I'm gonna lock up that deal."

M

MAIN KICK (n.): the stage.
MAIN ON THE HITCH (n.): husband.

Main queen (n.): favorite girl friend, sweetheart.
Man in gray (n.): the postman.
Mash me a fin (command): Give me $5.
Mellow (adj.): all right, fine. Ex., "That's mellow, Jack."
Melted out (adj.): broke.
Mess (n.): something good. Ex., "That last drink was a mess."
Meter (n.): quarter, twenty-five cents.
Mezz (n.): anything supreme, genuine. Ex., "This is really the mezz."
Mitt pounding (n.): applause.
Moo juice (n.): milk.
Mouse (n.): pocket. Ex., "I've got a meter in the mouse."
Muggin' (v.): making 'em laugh, putting on the jive. "Muggin' lightly," light staccato swing; "muggin' heavy," heavy staccato swing.
Murder (n.): something excellent or terrific. Ex., "That's solid murder, gate!"

N

Neigho, pops: Nothing doing, pal.
Nicklette (n.): automatic phonograph, music box.
Nickel note (n.): five-dollar bill.
Nix out (v.): to eliminate, get rid of. Ex., "I nixed that chick out last week"; "I nixed my garments" (undressed).
Nod (n.): sleep. Ex., "I think I'll cop a nod."

O

Ofay (n.): white person.
Off the cob (adj.): corny, out of date.
Off-time jive (n.): a sorry excuse, saying the wrong thing.
Orchestration (n.): an overcoat.
Out of the world (adj.): perfect rendition. Ex., "That sax chorus was out of the world."
Ow! an exclamation with varied meaning. When a beautiful chick passes by, it's "Ow!"; and when someone pulls an awful pun, it also is "Ow!"

P

Pad (n.): bed.
Pecking (n.): a dance introduced at the Cotton Club in 1937.

Peola (n.): a light person, almost white.
Pigeon (n.): a young girl.
Pops (n.): salutation for all males (see gate; Jack).
Pounders (n.): policemen.

Q

Queen (n.): a beautiful girl.

R

Rank (v.): to lower.
Ready (adj.): 100 per cent in every way. Ex., "That fried chicken was ready."
Ride (v.): to swing, to keep perfect tempo in playing or singing.
Riff (n.): hot lick, musical phrase.
Righteous (adj.): splendid, okay. Ex., "That was a righteous queen I dug you with last black."
Rock me (v.): send me, kill me, move me with rhythm.
Ruff (n.): quarter, twenty-five cents.
Rug cutter (n.): a very good dancer, an active jitterbug.

S

Sad (adj.): very bad. Ex., "That was the saddest meal I ever collared."
Sadder than a map (adj.): terrible. Ex., "That man is sadder than a map."
Salty (adj.): angry, ill-tempered.
Sam got you: you've been drafted into the army.
Send (v.): to arouse the emotions. (joyful). Ex., "That sends me!"
Set of seven brights (n.): one week.
Sharp (adj.): neat, smart, tricky. Ex., "That hat is sharp as a tack."
Signify (v.): to declare yourself, to brag, to boast.
Skins (n.): drums.
Skinn-beater (n.): drummer (see hide-beater).
Sky piece (n.): hat.
Slave (v.): to work, whether arduous labor or not.
Slide your jib (v.): to talk freely.
Snatcher (n.): detective.
So help me: it's the truth, that's a fact.
Solid (adj.): great, swell, okay.

Sounded off (v.): began a program or conversation.
Spoutin' (v.): talking too much.
Square (n.): an unhep person (see icky; Jeff).
Stache (v.): to file, to hide away, to secrete.
Stand one up (v.): to play one cheap, to assume one is a cut-rate.
To be stashed (v.): to stand or remain.
Susie-Q (n.): a dance introduced at the Cotton Club in 1936.

T

Take it slow (v.): be careful.
Take off (v.): play a solo.
The man (n.): the law.
Threads (n.): suit, dress or costume (see drape; dry-goods).
Tick (n.): minute, moment. Ex., "I'll dig you in a few ticks." Also, ticks are doubled in accounting time, just as money is doubled in giving "line." Ex., "I finaled to the pad this early bright at tick twenty" (I got to bed this morning at ten o'clock).
Timber (n.): toothpick.
To dribble (v.): to stutter. Ex., "He talked in dribbles."
Togged to the bricks : dressed to kill, from head to toe.
Too much (adj.): term of highest praise. Ex., "You are too much!"
Trickeration (n.): struttin' your stuff, muggin' lightly and politely.
Trilly (v.): to leave, to depart. Ex., "Well, I guess I'll trilly."
Truck (v.): to go somewhere. Ex., "I think I'll truck on down to the ginmill (bar)."
Trucking (n.): a dance introduced at the Cotton Club in 1933.
Twister to the slammer (n.): the key to the door.
Two cents (n.): two dollars.

U

Unhep (adj.): not wise to the jive, said of an icky, a Jeff, a square.

V

Vine (n.): a suit of clothes.
V-8 (n.): a chick who spurns company, is independent, is not amenable.

W

WHAT'S YOUR STORY? What do you want? What have you got to say for your-self? How are tricks? What excuse can you offer? Ex., "I don't know what his story is."

WHIPPED UP (adj.): worn out, exhausted, beat for your everything.

WREN (n.): a chick, a queen.

WRONG RIFF : the wrong thing said or done. Ex., "You're coming up on the wrong riff."

Y

YARDDOG (n.): uncouth, badly attired, unattractive male or female.

YEAH, MAN: an exclamation of assent.

Z

ZOOT (adj.): overexaggerated as applied to clothes.

ZOOT SUIT (n.): overexaggerated clothes.

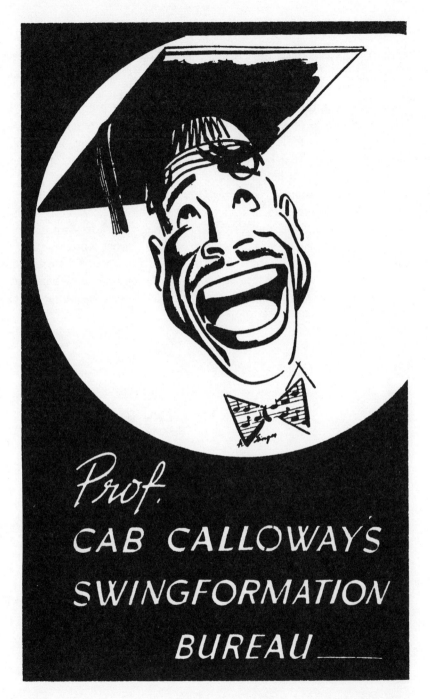

Prof.
CAB CALLOWAY'S
SWINGFORMATION
BUREAU

Jive has passed from the vocabulary stage to the next step, that of actual application to our everyday language. It is a fact that the American language has absorbed many of the quaint expressions that have had their origin in the Harlem section of New York City. It is not very uncommon to hear people in all walks of life say that a band sounds corny, or they do not feel in the groove. It is gratifying to know that we musicians have contributed something to posterity in the form of colorful expressions that help liven the tongue of a great people.

Last year I issued a *Hepster's Dictionary* which found favor with the public and the press because it was the first attempt to record for history the language of the musician. The picturesque terms and adjectives showed the musician to be a happy-go-lucky artist who gave his entire life to his music. This new hero in public life appealed to millions of Americans who wanted to know more about the way he lived and spoke, and what interested him. To this end *Swingformation Bureau* is dedicated.

—Cab Calloway

SWINGFORMATION BUREAU

In the daily life of American musicians, they discuss swing bands, musicians, songs, and singers in their colorful jargon. Many people have expressed a desire to know these subjects more thoroughly so that they can comprehend their arguments and join in the interesting discussions about contemporary music. This is the second in a series of booklets designed to stimulate that interest and act in a fashion of a textbook in question form on that lively topic of swing.

CONTENTS

ARE YOU HEP TO THE INSTRUMENTS?

Musicians have added to the jive language pet names for their instruments. Every hepster must know these tags, so take a chance and see if you can dig the following riffs. Each represents a different instrument.

1. A git-box or belly fiddle is a _____.
2. A horn is a _____ or _____.
3. A squeak-box is a _____.
4. A suitcase, hides, or skins are a set of _____.
5. A woodpile is a _____.
6. The ironsworks are a set of _____.
7. A tram or slush pump is a _____.
8. A stick or gob stick is a _____.
9. Plumbing or reeds are _____.
10. A squeeze-box or groan-box is an _____.
11. The doghouse is the _____.
12. The storehouse or ivories is the _____.
13. The fog horn is the _____.
14. A spark-jiver is an _____.

FOR CORRECT ANSWERS SEE PAGE 272.

ARE YOU HEP TO THE TAGS (NICKNAMES) OF THE GATES?

Just imagine yourself listening to a conversation between a pair of hepsters, who know all the famous musicians by their pet names. How many of these cats could you dig?

1. Father
2. Dumpy
3. Chu
4. Bojangles
5. Cabbage
6. Satchmo
7. Cozy
8. The rabbit
9. Tram
10. Bix

FOR CORRECT ANSWERS SEE PAGE 272.

ARE YOU HEP TO THE ETIQUETTE?

Cab Calloway, M.J. (master of jive), stresses the fact that no matter what language you speak, it is necessary to maintain a high standard of manners and customs. There are a number of situations that arise and require satisfactory replies—all, of course, in our new language of jive. Instructor Calloway has taken a series of situations and solutions. Before you turn to the answer page, try your hand at deciphering them, and then compare your results to the correct ones.

1. If you meet a fellow hepster at a bar, what is the proper greeting?
2. What is the proper way to ask a young lady to go to the movies with you?
3. If you are invited to someone's home for a visit, what is the proper manner in which to accept?
4. How would you compliment a young lady on her new and pretty dress?
5. What is the best way to ask a friend for some money?
6. How can you tell someone to stop annoying the young lady you are escorting?
7. If someone offers you a proposition you do not like, what is the proper way to refuse him?
8. How should you invite some one to a chicken dinner at a respectable restaurant in Harlem?

FOR CORRECT ANSWERS SEE PAGE 272.

ARE YOU HEP TO THE KILLER-DILLERS?

Every band has a favorite killer-diller, which is sure to be included on almost every program they broadcast. The following is a list of these numbers, which you are to identify with a bandleader.

1. "Begin the Beguine"
2. "One O'Clock Jump"
3. "Shoot the Meat Balls to Me, Dominick"
4. "Marie"
5. "The Jumpin' Jive"
6. "The Gal from Joe's"
7. "Wrappin' It Up"
8. "South Rampart Street Parade"
9. "Smoke Rings"
10. "Jazznocracy"

FOR CORRECT ANSWERS SEE PAGE 272.

ARE YOU HEP TO THE EVENTS IN THE WORLD OF JIVE?

This is an important year in current events, with many changes being made in our world of swing. There are movements trying to change the name of our government to "bounce," "jump," "groove," and other foreign-isms, but we must protect the good name of swing. The best way to do this is to know your subject thoroughly and defend it at every turn. The following questions are general ones designed to stimulate the mind.

1. Who created the name "jitterbug"?
2. What song was chosen as the representative swing song for Grace Moore's Columbia picture *When You're in Love*?
3. Who is Benny Carter, and what instruments does he play?
4. Did Artie Shaw ever have a band featuring violins?
5. Did Bobby Hackett play cornet regularly when he was with Joe Marsala at the Hickory House in 1937?
6. Did Bix Beiderbecke ever play any other instrument professionally besides the cornet?
7. Name the three songs that use the following phrases: a. "Hi-de-ho"; b. "Frrr-eeyadasacki"; c. "Hep! Hep!"
8. Name eight dances first introduced at the famous New York Cotton Club.
9. Name the bands using these themes: a. "Jazznocracy"; b. "East St. Louis Toodleloo"; c. "Alexander's Swingin'."
10. What was the first jazz song composed with the word "swing" in the title?

FOR CORRECT ANSWERS SEE PAGE 272.

ARE YOU HEP TO THE ALL-AMERICAN SWING CATS?

Cab Calloway has taken a consensus of the polls of the various All-American Swing Bands chosen by various publications in the past year, mixed it with a little of his personal observations, and out comes his own All-American Cats. Cab wants you to select the men you think belong on this great band and compare it with his.

RHYTHM SECTION

Guitar _____   Drums _____
Piano _____   Bass _____

TRUMPETS

Hot Man _____   Third Choice _____
Second Choice _____   Fourth Choice _____

TROMBONES

Hot Man _____   Third Man _____
Melody _____

SAXOPHONES

Tenor First _____   Alto Second _____
Tenor Second _____   Baritone _____
Alto First _____   Clarinet _____

SPECIALTY

Accordion _____   Girl Vocalist _____
Vibraphone _____   Male Vocalist _____
Xylophone _____

CAB CALLOWAY'S SELECTIONS ARE ON PAGE 273.

SWING MAGAZINES IN AMERICA
(IN 1939)

While daily newspapers and national magazines give a great deal of space to matters pertaining to modern music and musicians, still it is not enough to satisfy the dyed-in-the-wool devotees; they need their own magazines, and there are enough of them to support five different ones. Most of the news in the general publications is mild and tame compared to the blasts and pannings from the outspoken trade publications. Woe to the bandleader who mistreats his musicians, or who does not dish out a pure brand of swing. These boys lash out with both fists and tell off the biggest names in the business. There is never a dull moment when scanning any of the following monthly publications.

DOWN BEAT MAGAZINE
Chicago, Illinois

EDITORS: Carl Cons,
Glen Burrs, and Dave Dexter

TEMPO MAGAZINE
Los Angeles, California

EDITOR: Charles Emge

SWING MAGAZINE
New York City

EDITOR: Howard Richmond

METRONOME New York City	EDITORS: Richard Gilbert and George Simon
ORCHESTRA WORLD New York City	EDITOR: Sid Berman
SONG HITS New York City	*Reprints authorized lyrics and* *stories on swing personal-* *ities* EDITOR: Lyle K. Engel

SWING MAGAZINES THROUGHOUT THE WORLD (IN 1939)

Swing is no longer localized to any one section of the country nor is it restricted to just this country. Throughout the entire world, youth has responded to the calls of this thrilling and exciting music known as swing. To satisfy the desire for news about their idols, magazines devoted to this new jazz have sprung up in countries throughout the world. Names like Cab Calloway, Duke Ellington, Bobby Hackett, and Benny Carter are as well known to the "hepsters" in the far corners of the world as the names of Joe Di Maggio and Carl Hubbell to the baseball fans of America. These men are international heroes and you can pick up any of the following magazines to read about the local favorites you are so fortunate to have perform on your very doorstep. What these fans would give to hear a solo by a Chu Berry, or a Johnny Hodges, in person. Harry Lim, president of the Swing Club of Batavia, in far-off Java, to get firsthand information for *Swing,* the official magazine for jitterbugs in Java, about 10,000 miles away, traveled all the way to New York to hear his favorites.

England: *Melody Maker* (weekly), *Rhythm* (monthly). **Holland:** *Jazzwereld* (monthly). **Belgium:** *Music.* **Java:** *Swing.* **Finland:** *Rytmi.* **Australia:** *Australian Music Maker; Tempo.* **Argentina:** *Pauta* (monthly). **France:** *Hot Jazz* (monthly). **Switzerland:** *Jazz.* **Sweden:** *Estrada; Orkester Jornalen.*

ANSWERS

"Are You Hep to the Instruments?"

1. guitar. 2. trumpet or cornet. 3. violin. 4. drums. 5. xylophone. 6. vibraphones. 7. trombone. 8. clarinet. 9. saxophones. 10. accordion. 11. bass. 12. piano. 13. tuba. 14. electric organ.

"Are You Hep to the Tags (Nicknames) of the Gates?"

1. Earl Hines. 2. Duke Ellington. 3. Chu Berry. 4. Bill Robinson. 5. Cab Calloway. 6. Louis Armstrong. 7. Cozy Cole. 8. Johnny Hodges. 9. Frankie Trumbauer. 10. Bix Beiderbecke.

"Are You Hep to the Etiquette?"

1. "Greetings, gate, let's dissipate." 2. "Wouldst like to con a glimmer with me this early black?" 3. "Solid, Jack, I'll dig you in your den gradually." 4. "My solid pigeon, that drape is a killer-diller, an E-flat Dillinger, a bit of a fly thing all on one page." 5. "Closest to my ticker, could you send a little cabbage my way until my garden starts growing a little." 6. "Take it slow, loud and wrong, you come on like Gangbusters but you're going out like Wayne King. That chick is locked up in this direction, so just cut out while your conk is all in one portion." 7. "I ain't comin' on that tab." 8. "Would you like to collar some ready chicken at a dicty hash house in the land o' darkness?"

"Are You Hep to the Killer-dillers?"

1. Artie Shaw. 2. Count Basie. 3. Jimmy Dorsey. 4. Tommy Dorsey. 5. Cab Calloway. 6. Duke Ellington. 7. Benny Goodman. 8. Bob Crosby. 9. Glen Gray. 10. Jimmie Lunceford.

"Are You Hep to the Events in the World of Jive?"

1. Cab Calloway and Irving Mills wrote "Jitterbug," a popular song, in 1934, which was the first time the term was used. Jitterbug clubs were formed throughout the country with Cab Calloway the national president. 2. "Min-

nie the Moocher.'' 3. Benny Carter is a famous colored arranger who now has his own band. Besides arranging, Carter plays the trumpet, clarinet, and alto saxophone. 4. In 1937, Artie Shaw had a swing band featuring violins. 5. Bobby Hackett worked with Joe Marsala as a guitarist and only on rare occasions did he ever play the cornet. 6. Bix Beiderbecke played piano on the record he made of ''In a Mist.'' 7. a. ''Minnie the Moocher''; b. ''Hold Tight''; c. ''The Jumpin' Jive.'' 8. Truckin', Peckin', Scrontch, Boogie Woogie, Suzie-Q, Harlem Bolero, Shakin' the African, and The Floogie Walk. 9. a. Jimmie Lunceford; b. Duke Ellington; c. Van Alexander. 10. ''It Don't Mean a Thing If It Don't Have That Swing'' by Duke Ellington and Irving Mills in 1929.

CAB CALLOWAY'S ALL-AMERICAN SWING CATS

Cab Calloway has chosen the men for his All-American Cats not on what they did ten years ago or are supposed to be able to do. His selections are based on their performances during the past year. While many selections may be a surprise, the reasons for their choice may be found in listening to the latest recordings or hearing these stars in person.

RHYTHM SECTION

Guitar: Eddie Condon
Piano: Billy Kyle

Drums: Cozy Cole
Bass: Milton Hinton

TRUMPETS

Hot Man: Harry James
Second Choice: Roy Eldridge

Third Choice: Bunny Berigan
Fourth Choice: Yank Lawson

TROMBONES

Hot Man: J. C. Higginbotham
Melody: Tommy Dorsey

Third Man: Jack Teagarden

SAXOPHONES

Tenor: Chu Berry
Tenor: Tex Beneke
Alto: Johnny Hodges
Alto: Benny Carter

Baritone: Harry Carney
Clarinet: Benny Goodman
and Artie Shaw

SPECIALTY

Vibraphone: Lionel Hampton
Xylophone: Red Norvo

Girl Vocalist: Ella Fitzgerald
Male Vocalist: Jack Leonard

FINAL EXAMINATION

Now that you have completed our course in jive you are ready for the supreme test. If you studied diligently and can attain a high rating you can be considered an interheptual and can mingle with the intelligamsia. As a graduate of Cab Calloway's Swingformation Bureau, you are entitled to your catskin hiploma.

1. What is the automatic phonograph called in jive?
2. Give the jive names for the instruments in the rhythm section.
3. What famous musicians have the following nicknames: Bunny, Lucky, and The Hawk?
4. What musician became famous as a comedian with his expression "Greetings, gate"?
5. Who originated "scat" singing?
6. What musician had the song "Ride, Red, Ride" dedicated to him?
7. What city is known as the birthplace of jazz?
8. Name three famous orchestras that were jazz favorites between 1920 and 1925.
9. Give your definition of swing music in not more than twenty-five words.
10. Write a letter in jive of not more than fifty words describing an evening spent in Harlem dining and listening to swing bands.

The Works of Cab Calloway

Composition	Year	Composers and Lyricists	Publisher
Minnie the Moocher	1931	Cab Calloway and Irving Mills	Mills Music
Scat Song	1932	Frank Perkins, Cab Calloway, and Mitchell Parrish	Mills Music
Lady with the Fan	1933	Cab Calloway, Jeanne Burhs, and Al Brackman	Mills Music
Zaz Zu Zaz	1934	Cab Calloway and Harry White	Mills Music
Jitterbug	1934	Cab Calloway, Irving Mills, and Ed Swayzee	Mills Music
Weakness	1934	Cab Calloway, Irving Mills, and Ed Swayzee	Mills Music
Chinese Rhythm	1935	Cab Calloway, Harry White, and Irving Mills	Mills Music
Good Sauce from the Gravy Bowl	1935	Cab Calloway, Ed Swayzee, and Irving Mills	Mills Music
Get That Hi-de-ho in Your Soul	1935	Cab Calloway, Irving Mills, and H. White	Mills Music
Echoes	1935	Cab Calloway, Irving Mills, and Benny Payne	Mills Music

Are You in Love with Me Again?	1937	Cab Calloway	Mills Music
Big-Mouth Minnie	1938	Walter Thomas, Joe Davis, Cab Calloway, and Andy Razaf	Mayfair Music Corp.
That Man's Here Again	1938	Cab Calloway, Edgar Sampson, and Roy Collins	Mills Music
Peek-A-Doodle-Do	1938	Cab Calloway, Irving Mills, Esvan Mosby, and Claude Jones	Mills Music
A-Minor Breakdown	1938	Ralph Yaw and Cab Calloway	Mills Music
I Like Music	1938	Cab Calloway	Mills Music
Rustle of Swing	1938	Ralph Yaw and Cab Calloway	Mills Music
Three Swings and Out	1938	Ralph Yaw and Cab Calloway	Mills Music
Rhapsody in Rhumba	1938	Cab Calloway and Buster Harding	Mills Music
I Like Music Played with a Swing Like This	1938	Ralph Yaw and Cab Calloway	Mills Music
Jive	1938	Chu Berry, Benny Payne, and Cab Calloway	Mills Music
The Jumpin' Jive	1939	Cab Calloway, Frank Froeba, and Jack Palmer	Marks Music

We're Breaking Up a Lovely Affair	1939	Ralph Yaw, Irving Mills, and Cab Calloway	Mills Music
For the Last Time I Cried Over You	1939	Cab Calloway, Frank Froeba, and Jack Palmer	Mills Music
I Ain't Gettin' Nowhere Fast	1939	Cab Calloway, Porter Grainger, and Chappie Willet	Lewis Music Pub. Co.
Chop, Chop, Charlie Chan	1940	Cab Calloway, Buck Ram, and Jack Palmer	Robbins Music Corp.
Are You Hep to the Jive?	1940	Cab Calloway and Buck Ram	Advanced Music Corp.
Boogit	1940	Cab Calloway, Buck Ram, and Jack Palmer	Jewel Music Pub. Co.
Come On with the Come-On	1940	Cab Calloway and Andy Gibson	Mills Music
Do I Care? No, No	1940	Cab Calloway, Dan Shapiro, Jerry See-len, and Lester Lee	Marks Music
Silly Old Moon	1940	Lee Ricks, Cab Calloway, Andy Gibson, and Danny Barker	Mills Music
Sunset	1940	Lee Ricks, Cab Calloway, Danny Barker, and Buster Harding	Mills Music

Topsy Turvey	1940	Cab Calloway, Milt Noel, and Edgar Battle	Advanced Music Corp.
Are You All Reet?	1941	Cab Calloway, Allan Clark, and Jack Palmer	Mills Music
The Workers' Train (The Eight-Fifteen)	1941	Cab Calloway, Sonny Skyler, and Artie Shaftel	Mills Music
Hot Air	1941	Cab Calloway and Gene Novello	Mills Music
Virginia, Georgia, and Carolina	1941	George A. Little, Larry Shay, and Cab Calloway	Mills Music
Levee Lullaby	1942	Cab Calloway, Edgar Battle, and F. Shuman	Mills Music
Nein, Nein	1942	Buck Ram and Cab Calloway	Gleam Music
Cy from Chi	1942	Jack Palmer and Cab Calloway	Mills Music
Geechy Joe	1942	Jack Palmer, Cab Calloway, and Andy Gibson	Mills Music
Ogeachee River Lullaby	1942	Jack Palmer, Cab Calloway, and Guy Wood	Rytvoc
Let's Go, Joe	1942	Cab Calloway, Jack Palmer, and Willie "The Lion" Smith	Rytvoc

Pitchin' Up a Boogie	1942	Cab Calloway, Nat King Cole, and Buster Harding	Mills Music
Special Delivery	1942	Cab Calloway and Andy Gibson	Mills Music
The Jive's Been Here and Gone	1943	Cab Calloway, Buster Harding, and Jack Palmer	Crescendo Music Corp.
The Great Lie	1943	Cab Calloway and Andy Gibson	Jewel Music Pub. Co.
Jonah Joins the Cab	1943	Cab Calloway	Mills Music
We the Cats Shall Hep Ya	1944	Cab Calloway, Buster Harding, and Jack Palmer	Crescendo Music Corp.
Foo A Little Bally Hoo	1944	Cab Calloway, Buster Harding, and Jack Palmer	Crescendo Music Corp.
My Lovin' Baby and Me	1944	Duke Ellington, Don George, and Cab Calloway	Robbins Music Corp.
Frantic in the Atlantic	1944	Cab Calloway	Robbins Music Corp.
Glider	1944	Cab Calloway	Robbins Music Corp.
On Account of Love	1945	Cab Calloway and Mercer Ellington	Crescendo Music Corp.
If This Isn't Love	1945	Cab Calloway and Helen Dewitt Jacobs	Crescendo Music Corp.
Zanzi	1945	Elton Hill and Cab Calloway	Crescendo Music Corp.

My Lament for V-Day	1945	Gerald Wilson and Cab Calloway	Crescendo Music Corp.
Rackin' 'em Back	1945	Cab Calloway and Buster Harding	Crescendo Music Corp.
Trumpetology	1945	Elton Hill and Cab Calloway	Crescendo Music Corp.
Cruisin' with Cab	1945	Gerald Wilson and Cab Calloway	Crescendo Music Corp.
I Got a Gal Named Nettie	1946	Cab Calloway and Elton Hill	Crescendo Music Corp.
Hey Now, Hey Now	1946	Cab Calloway and Elton Hill	Crescendo Music Corp.
How Big Can You Be	1946	Cab Calloway and Buck Ram	Crescendo Music Corp.
I Loves You, Honest I Does	1946	Cab Calloway and Elton Hill	Crescendo Music Corp.
Going Where I Can Do Some Good	1946	Cab Calloway and Elton Hill	Crescendo Music Corp.
Let's Call It Quits	1946	William Tennyson, Cliff White, and Cab Calloway	Crescendo Music Corp.
Maybe It's Dinah	1946	Cab Calloway	Crescendo Music Corp.
Old Man Bounce	1946	Cab Calloway	Crescendo Music Corp.
Get Back on the Road	1946	Juan Tizol, Cab Calloway, and Jack Palmer	Crescendo Music Corp.

Hi-de-ho Man, That's Me	1947	Cab Calloway, Buster Harding, and Jack Palmer	Crescendo Music Corp.
Don't Falter at the Altar	1947	Cab Calloway, Hal Seeger, and Buster Harding	Crescendo Music Corp.
Minnie Grew Up Overnight	1947	Cab Calloway, Hal Seeger, and Buster Harding	Crescendo Music Corp.
Fiesta in Brass	1947	Cab Calloway	Crescendo Music Corp.
Ole Hops	1947	Cab Calloway and Milton Hinton	Crescendo Music Corp.
Calloway Boogy	1947	Cab Calloway and Alfred Gibson	Crescendo Music Corp.
Bop Blues	1949	Gerald Wilson and Cab Calloway	Crescendo Music Corp.
Rhythm Cocktail	1949	Buster Harding, Cab Calloway, and Illinois Jacquet	Crescendo Music Corp.